Film, Comedy, and Disability

Comedy and humour have frequently played a key role in disabled people's lives, for better or for worse. Comedy has also played a crucial part in constructing cultural representations of disability and impairments, contributing to the formation and maintenance of cultural attitudes towards disabled people, and potentially shaping disabled people's images of themselves. As a complex and often polysemic form of communication, there is a need for greater understanding of the way we make meanings from comedy.

This is the first book which explores the specific role of comedic film genres in representations of disability and impairment. Wilde argues that there is a need to explore different ways to synthesise Critical/Disability Studies with Film Studies approaches, and that a better understanding of genre conventions is necessary if we are to understand the conditions of possibility for new representational forms and challenges to ableism.

After a discussion of the possibilities of a 'fusion' between Disability Studies and Film Studies, and a consideration of the relationships of comedy to disability, Wilde undertakes analysis of contemporary films from the romantic comedy, satire, and gross-out genres. Analysis is focused upon the place of disabled and non-disabled people in particular films, considering visual, audio, and narrative dimensions of representation and the ways they might shape the expectations of film audiences.

This book is of particular value to those in Film and Media Studies, and Critical/Disability Studies, especially for those who are investigating more inclusive practices in cultural representation.

Alison Wilde is Senior Lecturer at Leeds Beckett University. Alison has written mainly on topics of screen media, disability, gender, and audiences, in addition to researching and publishing on disability and educational inclusion, parenting, gender, social care, and health care. She co-founded the MeCCSA Disability Studies Network, and the BSA's Disability Studies group.

Interdisciplinary Disability Studies

Series editors

Mark Sherry, The University of Toledo, USA

Disability studies has made great strides in exploring power and the body. This series extends the interdisciplinary dialogue between disability studies and other fields by asking how disability studies can influence a particular field. It will show how a deep engagement with disability studies changes our understanding of the following fields: sociology, literary studies, gender studies, bioethics, social work, law, education, or history. This ground-breaking series identifies both the practical and theoretical implications of such an interdisciplinary dialogue and challenges people in disability studies as well as other disciplinary fields to critically reflect on their professional praxis in terms of theory, practice, and methods.

A Feminist Ethnography of Secure Wards for Women with Learning Disabilities
Locked Away
Rebecca Fish

International Perspectives on Teaching with Disability
Overcoming Obstacles and Enriching Lives
Edited by Michael S. Jeffress

Disability, Gender and Violence over the Life Course
Global Perspectives and Human Rights Approaches
Edited by Sonali Shah and Caroline Bradbury-Jones

Film, Comedy and Disability
Understanding Humour and Genre in Cinematic Constructions of Impairment and Disability
Alison Wilde

Disability and Music Peformance
Alejandro Alberto Téllez Vargas

For a full list of titles in this series, please visit www.routledge.com/series/ASHSER1401

Film, Comedy, and Disability
Understanding Humour and Genre in Cinematic Constructions of Impairment and Disability

Alison Wilde

LONDON AND NEW YORK

First published 2018
by Routledge
2 Park Square, Milton Park, Abingdon, Oxon OX14 4RN

and by Routledge
52 Vanderbilt Avenue, New York, NY 10017

First issued in paperback 2020

Routledge is an imprint of the Taylor & Francis Group, an informa business

© 2019 Alison Wilde

The right of Alison Wilde to be identified as the author of this work has been asserted by her in accordance with sections 77 and 78 of the Copyright, Designs and Patents Act 1988.

All rights reserved. No part of this book may be reprinted or reproduced or utilised in any form or by any electronic, mechanical, or other means, now known or hereafter invented, including photocopying and recording, or in any information storage or retrieval system, without permission in writing from the publishers.

Trademark notice: Product or corporate names may be trademarks or registered trademarks, and are used only for identification and explanation without intent to infringe.

British Library Cataloguing in Publication Data
A catalogue record for this book is available from the British Library

Library of Congress Cataloging in Publication Data
Names: Wilde, Alison, 1959- author.
Title: Film, comedy and disability : understanding humour and genre in cinematic constructions of impairment and disability / Alison Wilde.
Description: 1st Edition. | New York : Routledge, 2018. |
Series: Interdisciplinary disability studies | Includes bibliographical references and index.
Identifiers: LCCN 2018014401| ISBN 9781472455451 (hardback) | ISBN 9781315582368 (ebook)
Subjects: LCSH: Disability studies. | Disabilities in motion pictures. | Comedy. | People with disabilities--Social conditions. | Sociology of disability.
Classification: LCC HV1568.2 .W55 2018 | DDC 791.43/6527--dc23
LC record available at https://lccn.loc.gov/2018014401

ISBN 13: 978-0-36-758768-0 (pbk)
ISBN 13: 978-1-4724-5545-1 (hbk)

Typeset in Times New Roman
by Taylor & Francis Books

For Mum, Sarah, and Debbie.

Contents

	Acknowledgements	viii
1	Introduction	1
2	Comedy and disability	25
3	Contemporary comedy: subjectivity, genre, and impairment	50
4	Romantic comedy and disability	63
5	Romantic comedy meets satire: Yorgos Lanthimos' *The Lobster*	101
6	The gross-out genre, the Farrelly Brothers, and disability: mapping representational change	118
7	Conclusion, or when is an ending not an ending?	151
	Bibliography	161
	Index	191

Acknowledgements

I would like to dedicate this book to disabled people who the world has lost while I was busy writing this book, two people in particular. My sister Sarah, without ever speaking a word, was the person who founded my curiosity in cultural attitudes towards disabled people, and remains central to my thoughts. I miss the multitude of discussions I had with Debbie Jolly, about disability, art and many other things; she was a unique and dynamic activist and intellectual force for good and I count myself as very fortunate that she was my friend.

I am grateful to the publishers, especially for their support and patience. Mark Sherry's support has been invaluable at every stage of writing the book, not least in restoring my faith and stamina to carry on when times were hard. My work on the book has benefitted a great deal from talking and listening to a number of people, including academic colleagues, friends, and people within the disabled people's community, especially disability arts (not mutually exclusive!). I am especially appreciative of the conversations I have had with Kathryn Smith, Lee Spracklen, Alison Sheldon, Nick Watson, Yinka Olusoga, Dot Moss, Bev Keen, Carol Potter, James McGrath, Chrissie Rogers, Alison Allam, Victoria Browning, Gwilym Siôn ap Gruffudd, Tara Brabazon, Shan Ashton, Jessica Clapham, Catherine Long, Dolly Sen, Colin Hambrook, Saffron Walking, Deborah Williams, Barbara Lisicki, and Gill Crawshaw. I also want to express big thanks to those who provided crucial comradeship when I needed it most – including Sara Ryan, Dan Goodley, Rebecca Lawthom, Jo Ferrie, and Nick Whitworth.

I have seen some truly dreadful films over the past ten years (part of the pleasure) but remain in awe of the wonder of cinema. Indeed, my thanks are also due to City Screen cinema in York, where many of my ideas evolved. Film has provided me with many laughs, but the most joy has come from those close to me, so my final thanks are to Matilda Rose, Indigo Wilde, Minnie Rose, Naomi Slater (the loves of my life) and Steve Millett. This book would not have been completed without Steve's criticality, editing skills, patience, generosity, friendship, superb culinary skills, and healing hands.

1 Introduction

The fusion of Film Studies and Disability Studies – why and how?

This book has been written in an effort to discern some of the limits to representation for portrayals of disability in media, focussing on what is attributable to cinema as a specific medium.[1] I will show that there is much understanding to be gained from a synthesis of Disability Studies (and Critical Disability Studies) with Film Studies, not least in understanding how images of disability are constructed in ways which are specific to the practices and processes of cinema, and also in exploring the ways in which audiences make meanings from them, shaping, and being shaped by, individual attitudes and wider cultural outlooks.[2] Most obviously, insights gained from deeper analysis of cinematic representations of disability might be used to improve representations in film and wider media.

Analysis of disability in film and wider media is a relatively new area of study, predominantly stemming from disabled activists and Disability Studies scholars in the late 1980s and 1990s. However, echoing a call for deeper and more 'objective' understandings of cinematic representations of disability by Safran in 1998, and questioning the political bias of earlier work, Hoeksema and Smit (2001) argued that there was a need for a more scholarly approach to the analysis of cinematic representations. They called for a fusion of film theory with Disability Studies, as a synthesis deemed necessary in order to understand the complexity of cultural images and the myriad ways that people make meanings from them. Since then, there has been a burgeoning of studies on cinema, from a range of theorists straddling several disciplines (see Chivers and Markotić, 2010; Fraser, 2016; Markotić, 2016; Brylla and Hughes, 2017) as well as Disability Studies, but little further discussion on how the study of cinema and disability should proceed, and why. There are many reasons why Hoeksema and Smit's recommendation was an important one. It is crucial to revisit questions of theory and methodology in the analysis of disability and media, and cinema in particular, if we are to tackle the dilemmas of representation, and find new ways of addressing the gaping inequalities in cinematic content, and the marginalisation of disabled people at all levels of the film industry.[3] Early work on disability and media demonstrated how a very limited range of stereotypes of impairments (as individual accredited deviations from medical norms), were pervasive across all media, and portrayals of disability (as social oppression) were not. However, later critics (e.g. Shakespeare, 1999a; Mitchell and Snyder, 2000; Wilde, 2004a; Mallett, 2010) have shown how the explanatory power of such categorical approaches, or indeed the content/frequency analyses of work on disability and media, had rarely gone beyond value-driven assertions about 'good' and 'bad' portrayals of disability (e.g. Barnes, 1992; Cumberbatch and Negrine, 1992; Gartner and Joe, 1987; Klobas, 1988; Pointon and Davies, 1997). As much as these responses to such limited and limiting forms of imagery are understandable (given the misrecognition of disabled people's lives and the pervasiveness of pathologising images of impairment – see Gilbey [2016] for more recent examples), it has been demonstrated that the use of such criticism often resulted in mechanistic solutions such as those seen in journalism guidelines and broadcasting manifestos in the early late 1990s and early 2000s. Thus, we often saw the 'problem' of disability representation reduced to recipes for avoiding particular stereotypes (Ellis and Goggin, 2015, 28; and Wilde, 2004b).

Smit and Enns (2001) explained how academic work on disability and cinema has followed a similar trajectory to 'feminist film criticism', especially in the capacity to set analysis within a paradigm which is founded on 'exposing and reversing the discriminatory ideology underlying most portrayals of disability in film' (2001, x). A central goal of changing, or removing, an objectifying 'non-disabled gaze' on disabled people can be seen as the equivalent of Laura Mulvey's psychoanalytically informed exposition of the 'male gaze' in 'Visual Pleasure and Narrative Cinema' (1975). Thus, it can be argued that Disability Studies, analyses of cinematic images have often replaced women with disabled people as carriers of 'to-be-looked-at-ness' (1975, 12), and placed non-disabled people as the owner of the 'gaze'. In films featuring disability, this perspective would mean that it is the non-disabled person, rather than Mulvey's male, who is conceptualised to be positioned as the 'bearer of the look of the spectator' who 'controls the film phantasy' (ibid., 13). Further, like later feminist film scholars' critiques of Mulvey's theory of the gaze (e.g. Ettinger, 2006), critics of disability in cinema such as Smit and Enns suggest that these early positions taken towards disability representations tended to be crude and essentialist.[4] While by this time there was already a recognition of the polyphonic character of cinema texts – Shakespeare (1999a), for example, had explored potential differences in interpretation from a disability-informed point of view, in the films *Shine* (1996) and *Breaking the Waves* (1996) – the shaping of the contradictory, sometimes oppositional, readings which are extrapolated by people holding ostensibly similar politics and subject positions (e.g. disabled activists) remain unexplored. Acknowledgement of the processes of interpretation at play may well reveal the implications of particular representational strategies for both niche and wider audience understandings.

Smit and Enns (2001) compared feminist film theory and Disability Studies histories to conclude that scholars of disability and film must re-examine their basic assumptions. Although they did not elucidate any further on the similarities of feminist and Disability Studies film criticism, they suggest that the logic of Disability Studies scholars' early work on cultural representation was flawed in similar ways. Primarily, their argument centred on comparisons with criticisms of gender essentialism and the mapping to gendered subjectivities, found in early theorisations of 'the gaze', which, it is suggested, are replicated according to presumed biosocial differences. Thereby, viewing positions are likely to be theorised as corresponding too neatly to fixed ideas of subjectivities shaped by impairment experiences and disabled identities, or too-equally rigid notions of non-disabled identities, promulgating simplistic ideas of a 'non-disabled gaze'. They argued that first-wave studies of disability representations were characterised by 'political correctness' (2001, x) and that the goal of promoting positive change was put in a central position, as an answer to what earlier scholars believed to be the inherent prejudice of cultural representations of disability, premised on what might be viewed as this (monolithic) 'non-disabled gaze'. It is these types of aims and assumptions which were seen as crude, leading Smit and Enns (ibid.) to argue that such approaches are inadequate for acknowledging 'contradiction in the text' or the subjectivities of viewers, contending that they neglect 'resistance' in the interpretations of an active audience (Smit and Enns, 2001, xi).

In the same edited collection on 'Screening Disability', and in the spirit of contributing to a more nuanced analytical framework, Hoeksema and Smit (2001) developed these themes further, making some initial recommendations for change. Their central proposition was the need for a greater fusion of Disability Studies with Film Studies. Here, they provided a provocative and necessary start to such a project, calling for a move beyond 'a posture of disability activism' towards 'stylistic, analytical or structural' methods which position film as 'cinematic expression' (ibid., 34). However, they did not elaborate on the 'missing insights' (ibid., 33) that Disability Studies theorisations have failed to generate, or show exactly *how* Film Studies may help us to understand the interactions and relationships between 'cultural beliefs' (ibid., 35) and cinema. Nonetheless, their call to recognise the 'art' of film and pay closer attention to cinematic aspects of film is essential if we are to take the theorisation of disability imagery as seriously as other aspects of representation. Accordingly, this troubled relationship between 'art' and 'politics' will be explored a little further as a precursor to examining some of the ways that analysis of cinematic representations of disability might be best embedded in Film Studies; this latter concern will be the primary focus of the remainder of the Introduction as a rationale, and template for the remainder of the book.

Disability politics and film theory

In working out how to conduct sophisticated analyses of cinematic representations of disability, we are immediately faced with a problem inherent within Film Studies itself – that of providing more holistic forms of investigation which contextualise micro levels of study within macro analysis, and vice versa. At the heart of the perceived difficulties of a fusion of Disability and Film Studies there seems to be an unacknowledged need to find ways to meld methodologies and to seek forms of criticism which interrogate the internal worlds created by cinema, in conjunction with the external forces influencing and shaping individual films, including the political and economic decisions and vested interests of film-makers. All of these factors are likely to be inherent within the stories films tell us, evident in the decisions made at the top about what audiences want to see, low levels of participation of disabled people in the film industry, and content which is deemed inadequate or discriminatory by critics.

However, Hoeksema and Smit's (2001) critique rather reduces Film Studies' strengths to its capacity for exploring the minutiae and artistic intent of film. Although they also illustrate the importance of wider considerations in the form of a suggestion to explore dimensions of auteurship in their call to comprehend the 'particular purpose a filmmaker is trying to accomplish' (ibid., 36), they tend to compare the art of film quite starkly with a Disability Studies macro- focus on society and its disabling dynamics, as conventionally (perceived to be) placed at the centre of the social model of disability. Hoeksema and Smit (2001) suggest that this is a trait of later theories, which might be associated with Critical Disability Studies. There is a degree of academic snobbery to be found here, including a common tendency to deny the theoretical character of politically motivated work on disability, relegating it to 'advocacy' or positioning it as an extension of the aims of the disabled people's movement (Evans, 1999; Smit and Enns, 2001; Hoeksema and Smit, 2001). Effectively, this can maintain perceptions of a chasm between activism, creative practice, and the academy, and the hierarchies and inequalities inscribed within each of these sectors, e.g. working to perpetuate divisions between 'creatives' and critics whilst inflating the importance of those at the top of such hierarchies (e.g. film directors and professors), simultaneously marginalising the efforts and ideas of those who struggle to be heard. It also raises crucial questions about the purposes of our investigations, the objectives of allegiances made, and the potential impact of research (see Blomley, 1994, and Greyser and Weiss, 2012, for example), especially in relation to links between academic endeavours, creative practices, the film industry, and wider cultural outlooks. Criticisms which do not seek synthesis and balance across disability politics/studies and Film Studies are thus likely to widen the gap between theory and practice, minimising possibilities for collaborations between academics and creative practitioners, and thwarting strategies aimed at representational diversity and change.

So, although Hoeksema and Smit have indicated that there are a range of important aspects of film which need to be synthesised with Disability Studies, including an appreciation of art and cinematic strategies, I am proposing that any fusion with Disability Studies should engage with political agency, and an understanding of the multiple ways in which viewers experience, and make meanings from, film. Like Hoeksema and Smit, and Smit and Enns, I will show the importance of a fusion between disability and film theory, but will do this by exploring some of the *potential* ways forward and showing how both disciplines will benefit from interdisciplinary dialogues, ongoing reflection on political goals, and attention to communicative structures.

Moreover, many of those who have worked on feminist, queer, and critical race critiques of film have demonstrated that a core reason for doing such work should be to interrogate the ideological foundations and implications of contemporary cinema (e.g. Mulvey, 1975; and Dyer, 1990, and 1997). More recently, such objectives have become central to those who are working on themes within representations of transgender people (Smith, 2017). The Oscars awards of 2016, and the boycotts of the award ceremony itself (see Smith, 2016), illuminated the growing dissatisfaction about the lack of 'diverse' portrayals in film, specifically the exclusion of Black people. These increasing calls for greater diversity, common to feminist, anti-racist, queer, and trans criticisms of film, call our attention to the narrowness of cinematic storytelling. A cursory examination of film theory and philosophy might also reveal that principles of 'normalcy' are embedded within the narrative and visual/audio aspects of the film, the intent of the director/writers and cinematographers, the agendas and the commissioning/distribution and employment practices of the film industry, and in conceptualisations of wider film audiences and the way they are addressed, demonstrating that politics is always present in cinema.

It is important to recognise, then, that although we can detect an excess of politically driven argument in early Disability Studies work on media, which overlooks crucial aspects of cinema, especially in the identification of stereotypes and quantitative surveys on content (e.g. Barnes, 1992; Klobas, 1988), this fusion of both 'sides' of academic analysis (disability and film theory/studies) also needs to address the under-theorisation and depoliticisation of disabled bodies and disablement within cinema and the wider mediascape. It is also clear that the audience's relationship to representations should be reconceptualised. First, this is important if we are to move beyond assumptions that there is a simple cause and effect between portrayals deemed to be 'negative/positive' or 'bad/good', and the suppositions about stereotypes, media effects and cultural attitudes. Second, it is crucial that insights from both disciplines are synthesised if we are to move beyond individualistic, shallow assumptions of disability, which tend to view 'disability' as impairment in ways which spurn, marginalise, or even ignore the social causes of disablement, rendering the film viewer as an 'outsider' to the world of disabled characters.

Two good examples of individualistic analysis can be found in Evans and Hall's collection on *Visual Culture* (1999). Evans' chapter counterposed individualist explanations of disability with social model views where, despite the provision of valuable insights into the exclusion of disabled people from culture (deployed as ciphers by charities), the social model is relegated to the status of political activism rather than theory. This is a dualism which clearly cannot be sustained given Evans' (political) choice to position herself within a form of analysis which, whilst critical of a medical model of disability, anchors itself within an individualist paradigm. There is quite an explicit appeal to the 'we' of the audience, implicitly positioned as non-disabled witnesses of the charitable spectacle, as judges of the meanings attributed to people with specific impairments, suggesting disability should be measured in impairment terms. The questions posed seem to be whether these images are an accurate account of impairment, i.e. 'the reality of the image' (Evans, 1999, 283), and what feelings they are likely to evoke in the viewer. Whilst matters of audience affect are crucial to any analysis which attempts to consider the 'rights and wrongs' of disability imagery and its effects within society and culture, the marginalisation of the social model in Evans' exposition means that disabled people are presented as rather misguided activists, and as passive figures used to sell charitable messages. Overall, they are defined predominantly by their impairments, not as fully-fledged people with their own stories to tell.

In a more extreme manner, Fenichel's chapter (1999), within this collection, illustrates the dangers of a politically uninformed theoretical approach to disability and impairment (or other) representations. Published in 1954, before the disabled people's movement was formed, with none of the insights provided by the social model, he offered a psychoanalytic appeal to relationships between fetishism, masturbation, and visual impairment. Although Fenichel argues that 'there is no reason to suppose that every case of myopia is psychogenic' (ibid., 338), he suggested that there is common agreement that blindness is associated with shame (ibid., 337) and begins his analysis by stating that,

> we regard it as a matter of course that the eye is a phallic symbol and that, accordingly, to be blinded signifies to be castrated (especially as a punishment for some transgression promoted by the scoptophilic impulse).
> (ibid., 333)

Given what might be called the 'ableist' (Campbell, 2009) assumptions of the author (rather than the 'non-disabled gaze, given that this idea centres and reifies the idea of a straightforwardly non-disabled psyche or subject position), such analysis is an exemplar of how 'theory' can perpetuate common discriminatory stereotypes and cultural attitudes towards the (deviant) sexualities of people with visual impairments.[5] However, following Vehmas and Watson's (2014) recommendations for a 'critical theory of disability', neither Evans' nor Fenichel's accounts of disability as difference deconstruct representations (as cultural goods) or attitudes in ways which are 'ethically or politically ... helpful' or 'offer guidance on how to solve moral dilemmas and on how to distribute goods in society fairly' (ibid., 649).

Although cultural representations of disability and the needs and desires of audiences are likely to be seen by some as residing outside the distributive sphere, cultural portrayals of impairment and disability can be seen as fundamental to informing ideas of disabled people as different, as a mechanism for the transformation of prejudicial attitudes which discriminate and perpetuate cultural, social, and economic inequalities. As such, these ethical and political questions, and matters of social justice, must surely have a central role to play in Disability Studies approaches to culture and media. Moreover, Film and Media Studies approaches which neglect the development of theory and research on disability, as a social phenomenon, seem destined to default to the theorisation of disability and impairment as 'otherness', and to the narrow confines of an individualistic model which implicitly frames the viewer and the theorist as non-disabled, or the 'normal subject' of Film Studies.

Understandably, Hoeksema and Smit's (2001) agenda does not ask for a return to the individualistic methods of film and cultural analysis which predominate in such analyses from cultural studies/visual culture scholars, but this concealment of the political bias of individualistic approaches to disability within Media and Film Studies, was not addressed directly in their call for a fusion of Disability and Film Studies. Moreover, they glossed over the heterogeneity of Film Studies itself. One example of this can be found in their appeal to consider the director's intentions as 'vital' (2001, 36), suggesting that auteur theory, as a type of formalist film theory, is a central mode of analysis in Film Studies. Although this is a crucial analytical approach in many cases, and is taken into account in the films discussed in the later chapters, Hoeksema and Smit's emphasis obscures the contestation in this area of Film Studies. There are important critiques of the auteur approach (see Emerson, 2012 for a discussion of these debates over time), but perhaps most significantly, an auterist emphasis obscures the creative input of those who have often played a large part 'behind the scenes'. This means that there is a neglect of the role of writers and cinematographers, obscuring many who are pioneers of cinema. Challenging the domination of film-making by white men, Hawkins (2014) and O'Hara (2016) have uncovered some of the groundbreaking roles that women have played in all areas of cinema, from writing to acting, directing, costume, cinematographic and technological contributions, noting their continuing lack of recognition by the film industry. The invisibility of contributions from many other people who are marginalised by the film industry is apparent, discernible in the content and characterisations of films, the employment hierarchies within the industry, and recent criticisms of industry practices. The latter of these include denunciations of the homogeneity of Hollywood cinema, including disapproval of disability representations and casting decisions which overwhelmingly favour non-disabled actors in 'disabled roles' (e.g. Birrell, 2016), widespread complaints about the sexism (Day et al., 2015), and racism (Lorenzo, 2016) of the industry, and the lack of Black people and women as protagonists (Lorenzo, 2016; Lang, 2015; Lauzen, 2015).[6] The predominance of white males as directors (Smith et al., 2018) can be seen to perpetuate the lack of diversity in the film industry, simultaneously feeding notions of cinematic genius being reliant on a single and singular man, rather than a wider creative team.

Returning to Film Studies, Hoeksema and Smit's emphasis on auterism, as formalism, tends to veil the importance of ideological formalism on the other 'side' of Film Studies, e.g. feminist, anti-racist, and queer approaches. Clearly, Disability Studies critiques could be seen to fall into this latter category, as a form of analysis which positions social, economic, and political forces as central influences on styles and categories of film, e.g. Hollywood, independent, new wave, and 'smart film' (see Wilde, 2018b for analysis of counter-ideological practices and mental illness in smart films). Hoeksema and Smit (2001) also expressed concern at the potential lack of an 'abled-bodied' critique (2001, 42) in Disability Studies critiques of cinema, which they considered as vital to understanding the 'cultural power' of representations of disability in films.[7] The call for this critique is somewhat ambiguous, as they did not provide reasons for this. Paradoxically, the acknowledgement and inclusion of 'social model' approaches *fused* within all forms of media criticism may help to explicate what Hoeksema and Smit (2001) have termed as an 'able-bodied' critique of cinema. For example, the challenging of non-disabled, often termed 'able-bodied' (or, alternatively, ableist), normativities would be a welcome development for cinematic analysis, contributing to reflexivity within Film Studies. Not least, this might illuminate the 'contours of ableism' (Campbell, 2009) contributing to theorisations of 'normative' bodies within cinematic practices and film critique, helping to pave the ways forward for envisaging representational change. It might also work to contest wider discourses of normativity, such as lifestyle, cultural aspirations, 'pure relationships', and (often therapeutically based) trajectories of the self (Giddens, 1991).[8]

Indeed, following scholars such as Linton (1998, 4), analysis which shows 'how knowledge about disability is socially produced to uphold existing practices', I am suggesting that the non-disabled core of cinematic practices, and most Film Studies approaches, need to be challenged, encouraging academics to move beyond the type of individualistic theorisations outlined earlier. Linton argued that the academy's resistance to variants of the social model results in a 'paltry and lopsided vision of disability' which 'compromises the knowledge base' (ibid., 7). Nowhere is this truer than in academic analysis of cinema. Further, in a wider critique of cinema's cultural power, focussed on an analysis of James Cameron's *Avatar* (2009), Wetherbee (2015, 56) used a Foucauldian framework to show how cinema should be seen as an 'institution capable of real political violence', with considerable, if slow (insidious), ideological power. His call for rhetorical criticism as a tool to debunk 'reified beliefs and assumptions' (ibid.) is crucial to a fusion of Film Studies and Disability Studies, acknowledging the inherently political character of concepts of disability and impairment, simultaneously capturing the workings of cinematic processes and investigating their potential purposes and effects.[9]

In addition to the analysis of film texts, this could include analysis of the industry and its audiences, examining the ways people produce, or re-make/ articulate, meaning in, and from, cinematic symbols, narratives and modes, and genres, and the interactions of the industry with its audience, and its perceptions of the model viewer.[10] Such a fusion should also deploy tools from any relevant disciplines. Indeed, such trans-disciplinary approaches are inherent within the broad scope of Film Studies itself. As I will argue in the rest of this chapter, Film Studies encompasses a wide range of approaches and theoretical tools for analysis, and cannot be reduced to a singular theoretical or methodological approach. As such, the ethical and political dimensions of cinematic analysis will be central throughout the book, as I explore a range of Film Studies tools, chosen for their suitability for the task. There is a need to challenge the social and cultural dimensions of disablement, without this being contingent upon a particular version of the social model, or one particular Film Studies approach. My analysis of cinema is thus informed by disabled people's politics and contributions to Disability Studies across a range of views, fused with a variety of tools from Film Studies.[11] My aim is to use such strategies to demonstrate some of the ways in which both disciplines can be synthesised to valuable effect, whilst providing deeper analysis of 'disability films' than might otherwise be the case.

In defence of such an eclectic approach, I am in agreement with Vehmas and Watson about the political or ethical need to retain a disabled/non-disabled binary, when identifying disabled characters and disabling discourses in the films chosen. Despite acknowledgement that the boundaries between the two are difficult to sustain, and the impossibilities of defining viewers', or directors', subject positions as categorially disabled or non-disabled, the continuing oppression of disabled people, within a culture and society which is founded on a perpetual reinforcement of these forms of difference, means there is both a political and cultural imperative to examine how disabled people, and their experiences of the world (however heterogeneous they may be) continue to be subjugated or absent knowledge. However, work which interrogates and questions these binaries and the way they are deployed is also considered as essential to the task of interrogating how and why cinema devalues or values people with impairments; analysis of how dualisms between disabled and non-disabled identities are constructed will be used primarily in ways which seek to understand how we can work towards 'relational justice' (Vehmas and Watson, 2014, 249).

Narrowing the topic further to allow deeper forms of analysis and investigation of the important role genre plays in the creation of meaning, comedy films and their sub-genres have been chosen as the central focus for such analysis, explained further in the first chapter, and addressed in a number of its cinematic forms throughout the rest of the book. Before outlining the book's content, I will first consider the strengths of a number of Film Studies approaches to film to review some of the contributions already made, before outlining the following chapters on comedy and disability, and analysis of films within a range of comedy sub-genres.

Exploring ways forward for the fusion of Disability and Film Studies

A cursory examination of academic literature on cinema and disability reveals that a number of Film Studies methodologies have already been used to inform the work of Disability Studies scholars' work on cinema, including narrative forms of analysis and genre theories, both approaches being crucial in Film Studies. A number of these scholars have also explored the visual aesthetics of film, including Darke (1998; 2010) and Shakespeare (1999a). Nonetheless, there is a sense that the projects of Disability Studies and Film Studies, or Film Theory, remain separate, or even that Disability Studies is ill-equipped for the task of cinematic analysis.

However, there is little consensus within Film Studies on which film theory is the most useful for the analysis of any film. In a rather scathing criticism of the idea of 'film Theory', Carroll suggested that the idea of film Theory has been successfully utilised as an ideological and economic argument to sell Film Studies to the world of academia, as an authentic form of intellectual endeavour, easily distinguishable from other disciplines (Carroll, 1996, 40). He proposed, rather, that Film Studies 'should be piecemeal', 'multidisciplinary' and 'interdisciplinary', and that:

> It should be pursued without the expectation of discovering a unified theory, cinematic or otherwise. That is, it should be catholic about the methodological frameworks it explores.
>
> (ibid.)

In their introduction to a collection of contributions discussing the need for a 'unified theory', Bordwell and Carroll argue that the 'Theory' promoted from the 1980s (especially psychoanalytic) is better replaced by recognising the multiplicity of 'theor*ies*' (their emphasis), 'and the activity of theorizing' (1996, xiv). Claiming a central role for middle-range research and theorising, and for an acceptance of the 'constraints of theorising' (1996, xv), they stated:

> A theory of film defines a problem within the domain of cinema (defined nondogmatically) and sets out to solve it through logical reflection, empirical research, or a combination of both. Theorizing is a commitment to using the best canons of inference and evidence available to answer the question posed.
>
> (Bordwell and Carroll, 1996, xiv)

This call for a primary commitment to intellectual endeavour and robustness of analysis has much to offer to a fusion of Disability and Film Studies, and is potentially mutually beneficial, mitigating the potential constraints of both fields of study in their current forms. However, Hoeksema and Smit's call for closer attention to a consideration of the audio/visual aspects of the ways film impacts on our experiences of viewing is a compelling reason to analyse visual aesthetics more closely, not least because these elements of film play a large role in the production of affect and meaning-making in viewers (Presence, 2012). So, the beginning of my investigation starts there, taking the need to comprehend cinema as a visual medium which takes a unique form.

Within the work by Darke (1998) and Mitchell and Snyder (2000) on genre and narrative, there is an emphasis placed on visual strategies and the language of cinema (such as camera shots and techniques). Recognising the importance of such areas, and bringing us closer to a greater synthesis of Film and Disability Studies, Chivers and Markotić (2010), in their edited collection on disability in cinema, have also emphasised the study of narrative and mise en scène, placing it at the centre of analysis of 'the problem body' – if we consider mise en scène as the collective result of everyone involved in the design and elements of each shot (including location, lighting, set design, use of space, costume/make up, type of film, aspect ratio, camera angles and movement, and acting and performance style). A good example of this can be seen in Barnard's chapter on close ups and the representation of the disabled body in Hollywood (Barnard, 2010).

So, what might a useful multiplicity of theories include in the analysis of disability films? Following Bordwell and Carroll (1996), I believe this fusion of theories and methodologies will be best informed by the task in each case. In turn, each case may reveal valuable insights into the cinematic construction of disability and impairment. I will explain why my starting point is the comedy film mode in the second chapter, drawing out key areas for analysis; the term 'mode' is being used in an adjectival sense here to denote a 'manner of presentation' (King, 2002, 2), which could apply to all genres.[12] My analysis of comedy films will involve the discussion of film theories, visual aesthetics and institutional/directorial context, whilst also drawing on elements which have predominated in Disability Studies literature – the semiotics of impairment, analysis of dialogue, and narrative analysis.

Like Richardson's (2016) study of cultural representations of 'transgressive bodies' in film and popular culture, my approach to the book is one which will not take a formalist approach towards individual films, but will attempt to meld Film Studies and Disability Studies perspectives together in a more holistic fashion, to place an exploration of the meanings embedded within texts at centre stage, within the context of audience concerns, viewer positioning, and wider 'assemblages' (Deleuze and Guatarri, 2003). Appadurai provides a succinct explanation of the concept of assemblage as

> temporary arrangements of many kinds of monads, actants, molecules, and other dynamic "dividuals" in an endless, nonhierarchical array of shifting associations of varying degrees of durability.
> (Appadurai, 2015, 221)

Such an analysis might begin anywhere, and my choice is to begin this exploration with a preliminary investigation of common criticisms of media portrayals of disability and an outline of previous theorisations of disability in film, alongside discussion of potentially fruitful approaches from Film Studies. To these ends, the remainder of my introductory discussion will focus on visual aesthetics and film 'Theory', exploring some ways forward.

Theory, visual aesthetics and beyond – some tentative explorations of cinematic representations of disability within a 'multiplicity of film theories'

Norden's theorisation of disability stereotypes is a good example of work which has synthesised visual analysis and other Film Studies approaches to undertake the tracing of a history of disability stereotypes in cinema, using similar psychoanalytic strategies as Mulvey used in 1975. Although film theory has developed a great deal since Mulvey's seminal essay on visual pleasure, and the idea of psychoanalysis as the primary, or necessary, ingredient in film 'Theory' should be challenged, as Bordwell and Carroll (1996) suggest, psychoanalytic theory can still be a valuable tool in Film Studies, not least in exploring subtexts of images, and forms of narrative and characterisations which render disabled people as 'other' and disablement as an 'adventitious happening' (Giddens, 1991). It can also be used to examine links to the unconscious and the so-called 'unconscious bias' of film-makers (see Baughan, 2016, for example) and their audiences, e.g. viewers' experiences and subjectivities and the interpretation of what is seen and heard on screen. As perhaps the world's most eminent psychanalytic analyst of cinema, Slavoj Žižek has said, 'Cinema is the ultimate pervert art. It doesn't give you what you desire – it tells you how to desire' (2006, 37–44s).

Although this may suggest a considerable lack of agency in cinema viewers, the possibility that films might seduce us into desires which instruct us into the disavowal of disabled people's lives (Shakespeare, 2004) is of clear importance to understanding disabling imagery and its effects. Indeed, notwithstanding the dangers outlined earlier of a crude, individualistic, psychoanalytic approach – without any consideration of the politics of disability – authors such as Inahara have appropriated Irigarayan psychoanalytic approaches to theorise the 'multiplicity' (ibid. 47) of disabled subjectivities whilst retaining a commitment to challenging ableism and disablism, not least by challenging notions of ideal bodies, invulnerability, and the binaries on which they depend (ibid.), problematising 'an able-bodied symbolic, in which the able-bodied takes itself as normal' (ibid., 47).

It is clear that Mulvey's essay provided much stimuli for those who went on to develop more sophisticated analyses of spectatorship (including her own later work), as Smit and Enns point out (2001). The use of psychoanalytic approaches has been put to valuable use in a range of studies of subjectivity, from the variety of sexualised, gendered, racialised, colonialised, and generally 'othered' subjectivities discussed by Mansfield (2000), to Branney's exploration of psychodiscursive approaches (combined with discourse analysis) in order to theorise individual subjectivities within social contexts (2008). Goodley (2012) has also advocated psychoanalytic approaches for the study of ableism and the 'influence of culture on subjectivities and "resistance"', arguing that an early, influential article about stigma, written by Paul Hunt (a pioneer of Disability Studies), bore 'the marks of a piece of critical psychoanalytic analysis' (ibid., 179).

So, despite the rejection of Mulvey's theorising of spectatorship as a totalising approach, psychoanalytic (especially Lacanian) and poststructuralist film theory are used to inform a wide range of contemporary film scholarship. Recent examples of the use of Lacanian theory can be found in Žižek's work and in Deleuzian perspectives on film (see Jagodzinski, 2012, for examples of the value of such approaches). Although some might see the schizoanalysis of Deleuze and Lacanian, and other psychoanalytic theories, as incompatible, a synthesis of these theories in a study of David Lynch's films was put forward by Beckman (2012) as a way of understanding how the

> machinery of a truly audiovisual cinema can be employed to activate the number of linkages that can be made beyond representational demands on narrative continuity and synchronisation
>
> (2012, 86)

I am suggesting that such a synthesis of differing, and occasionally opposing and ostensibly contradictory, approaches produces useful ways of comprehending cinematic representations of disability, audience affect, and their potential impacts on cultural outlooks.

The important role which philosophy has always played in film theory/studies is also apparent in the development of phenomenological analyses of film, especially in exploring the 'fusion of horizons' between cinematic worlds and the 'the world of the viewers' (Yates, 2006). Such tools are of great value to a disability-centred critique, bringing together questions of spectatorship and artistic practices, to investigate further themes of affect and ideological context, applicable to individual films as well as genres. Chamarette conceptualises subjectivity in film-viewing as a 'chiasmic in-betweenness' (2012) emanating from the 'contact between viewer and the viewed' (ibid., 3), an idea which aids us in understanding the complex interactions between film viewers (both disabled and non-disabled) and cinematic representations. Far from the simplicity of conceptualising the 'gaze' as founded upon biosocial categories such as sex, gender, and impairment status, she conceptualises subjectivities as slippery and plural (ibid., 6), emerging from 'gaps in language' (ibid., 69), having particular relationships to temporality, embodiment, sensory knowledge, presence, and issues of representation (ibid., 20). Such a view of subjectivity is more likely to position and understand disabled, and non-disabled, bodies and experiences as a facet of cinematic representation, production/direction, and viewer embodiment, whilst avoiding essentialism. In turn, this enables us to avoid mapping a reductive, unitary and/or categorical psyche onto either disabled or non-disabled film viewers and their interpretations of, and interactions with, representations of disability in cinema. Further, whilst simultaneously retaining the value of a Disability Studies–informed approach, phenomenological analysis can also allow us to challenge this binary of disabled and non-disabled subjectivities, which does little justice to understanding the emotional attachments and engagements made with films, or to explain the lack of consensus on what a 'good' or 'positive' cinematic representation of disability is deemed to be (Shakespeare, 1999a). An obvious example of a slippery and plural subjectivity would also be the 'mixed feelings' likely to be experienced by a viewer with an impairment acquired later in life, and the multiple, and possibly contradictory, subjectivities they may embody. Using such tools might allow us a more thoughtful, less dogmatic, approach to our analysis of films which tell suicide stories, a common narrative for those who acquire impairments, including *Me Before You* (2016), and *The Sea Inside* (2004), perhaps allowing insights into how cinema tells, or can tell, a more polyphonic story, which does not privilege one view over the other.

Embodiment, affect, space and positioning

Williams' work on film and genre (1991) is also valuable in its propensity to explore how viewers' experiences and perceptions relate to viewers' embodiment and affect, especially in showing how presumed audiences make emotional engagements and personal investments in particular modes and genres. Focussing particularly on horror, pornography, and melodrama, she shows how these particular genres all signify excess, exhibit 'sensational bodies' (ibid., 4), and are inextricably linked to violence, sex and emotion (respectively). Drawing on Film Studies tools, such as the coding of aural, visual, and narrative 'excesses', she examines features of temporality where key moments are 'too early', 'on time' and 'too late' and explains that our experiences of these 'genres' are characterised by our expectations of time, a lack of 'esthetic distance', and a 'sense of over-involvement in sensation and emotion' (ibid., 5). She characterises horror as a 'fear jerker' and melodrama as a 'tear jerker', both of which could easily be imputed to the kind of manipulations found in the majority of disability films, particularly those which may be recognised as 'normality genres' (Darke, 1998), or through depictions which are commonly used to elicit pity, fear, and sorrow.

This indicates that there seems to be much more work to be done in analysing just how (or whether) the micro-world of films shapes the whole story as 'normality genre', disabling themes within the film (e.g. objectification, dependency, character traits embedded in biosocial difference), or how it reaffirms and perpetuates ideas of disabled people as flaws in a social fabric which is in need of repair (Mitchell and Snyder, 2000). Areas which will be fruitful include analysis of the often overlooked use of temporal strategies, and the use of space within films (examined in some depth in Darke's work [1999]), both of which are fundamental aspects of our perceptions of movement in film. The documentary *Hitchcock/Truffaut* (2016) underlines these fundamentally important aspects of cinema; in the film, Olivier Assayas states that it is Hitchcock's excellence in being a 'theoretician of space' which marks him out as one of the most celebrated film directors. He shows how the meanings we take from the film are shaped by very deliberate use of space, proximity of the camera, and the manipulation of movement (e.g. expansion and contraction of time), contributing significantly to our understanding of character, and our closeness to the experiences of the characters within the scene. In turn, it is argued that these features shape our understanding of what characters are feeling, and the depth and type of our emotional engagements.

These aspects of film seem to offer significant fields of enquiry for further investigation, especially when the correspondences with Disability Studies concerns are investigated. The spatial and temporal dimensions of film resonate with writing by disability theorists who focus on the geographies of impairment and disability, e.g. Freund (2001), signalling the importance of the use of space, time, and movement in disabled people's lives, and the 'temporal/spatial fluidity of (disabled people's) identities' (Imrie and Edwards, 2007, 26). These are dimensions of life which need to be recognised in our understanding of disability representations and also in our conceptualisations of disabled spectators (who are rarely considered, especially in relation to film).[13] Imrie and Edwards also speak of the wider 'need to develop understanding of time contrasts and continuities in the lives of disabled people' (24). Drawing on the work of phenomenologists such as Chamarette, psychoanalytic/semiotic theorists such as Žižek, and work on embodiment and genre such as that of Williams, may mean that we can undertake explorations of how spectators are positioned by film texts, and the ways in which identifications and emotional engagements are likely to be made.

Investigating such cinematic strategies in relation to the construction of impairment and disability may offer us many insights into how images can be deconstructed and reconstructed to minimise unnecessary constructions of disabled people's 'difference' from non-disabled people. Further, it is in the interests of storytelling to draw our attention to the ways in which we ourselves participate in such processes of meaning making, e.g. how and why cinema is using physical features and the camera to construct particular expectations of character and impairment, and how this could be done differently to thwart expectations of disability tropes.

Reality, accuracy, subjectivity, and cultural recognition – common complaints from audiences

Both phenomenological and psychoanalytic perspectives add weight to the arguments made against an insistence on accuracy in disability portrayals. Following arguments that ideas of truth and reality are ideological, and something of a fiction, e.g. presented as 'staged fakes' (Žižek 2002, 385), recent developments in film theory have usefully demonstrated that the imperative to present 'accuracy' is futile. Apart from anything else, something that is an accurate depiction of disabled reality to one will be inaccurate to another, and there has been a recognition of this since the 1980s; this includes Kent's (1987) criticism of Kriegel's characterisation of Laura Wingfield (*The Glass Menagerie*) as a 'Realistic Cripple' (1987) as a reading based on gendered assumptions of women. Žižek, using a Lacanian approach, offers a framework which may be helpful in repositioning questions about the accuracy of disability imagery, particularly as ideas of 'the real' of disabled people's experiences of both impairment and disablement are often at the core of criticisms of disability imagery. Put simply, how and why do cultural representations fail to depict images which correspond with this 'reality', and how can the vast range of realities at stake be represented?

He explains three modalities of 'the Real': the 'symbolic Real', 'the real Real' and, the 'imaginary Real'. The Real is conceptualised, as that

> which escapes inscription, (the Real of the sexual relation, for example); but at the same time, the Real is the writing itself as opposed to the signifier.
> (Žižek, 2008, 193, cited in Willis, 2016)

As Willis points out, the Real is 'coded' and 'behind the symbolic universe'; as such it 'escapes signification' (ibid. 70). Žižek's theorisation of these modalities is perhaps most easily understood in showing how he conceives of Jesus Christ as the 'imaginary Real', 'a mediating figure between the "real Real" of the God-Father-Thing and the "symbolic Real" of the Holy Spirit' (Žižek 2001, 82–83, cited in Piggford, 2016).

Many criticisms of disability representation can be seen to indicate the frustrations which may be attached to the impossibility of representing the real Real of disabled people's lives, but a brief examination of critiques of impairment and disability imagery reveals that most criticisms operate on the level of the second and third of these modalities, with many analyses showing how portrayals of disability are formulaic, especially in constructions of narrative. Darke (1999) and Shakespeare's (1994) work, for example, has been instructive on the way disabled characters tend to be used in terms of the symbolic and imaginary real. In terms of the symbolic real, Darke and Shakespeare have demonstrated that impairment, illness, and disability are often used as signals or symbols which reinforce cultural attitudes and social positions, e.g. where disabled people are usually used as metaphors for abnormality. Ideas of the 'imaginary Real' can be seen in the analysis of disabled people as 'ciphers' for 'abhorrent feelings' (Shakespeare, 1994). The imaginary real is valuable in conveying emotions such as fear, horror, or pity, the experiences we are 'buying' as Žižek would say.

Elsewhere, Žižek (2009) speaks of 'semantic over investments' (ibid., 2) in 'cultural capitalism'. He explains how consumerism and anti-consumerism are often intertwined in our lives, in the form of products sold with charitable acts embedded in their appeal to the consumer. He says that the product we buy 'already includes the price for its opposite' (ibid). One of the examples given is the buying of a Starbucks coffee which 'supports' a fair-trade initiative, where comfortable furniture for its customers is costed into the price so 'your redemption from being only a consumerist' (ibid.) (continuing to cause a more limited form of harm and monocultural farming practices) can be enjoyed in comfort, with the doing of a good deed having heightened the experience. In much the same way, we can see this operates in cinema, often with the sorrow and adversity of the disabled person woven into the fabric of pleasure afforded to the audience, promoting pity and a Nietzschean 'practical nihilism' and negative values associated with disabled people (Hughes, 2012, 72). Just as problematic is the possibility that the audience believe that their awareness has been raised and that their new understandings will help to make things better, a disposition which might explain the dominance of Oscar-winning tales of disability (Rodgers, 2012). Treating depictions such as these as 'imaginary real', emotionally-oriented constructions of disabled people, and utilising the idea of the semantic over investments we are sold as part of this package, also offers promising ways to interrogate portrayals of disability, e.g. in exploring how the audience read, or 'buy into', them.

Žižek's 'real Real' refers to the 'actual' properties of an object, but has also been theorised by Žižek (in later work) as 'nothing but a grimace of reality' (2002). For him, none of these positions can be equated with reality itself (seen by him an impossible quest), being inextricable from our perceptions of it. Yet, this is something which is often demanded of disability representation, in appeals to everyday, and ordinary, or accurate representation. The concern with reality (and the marginalisation of disabled actors with the industry) is also a good example of this (an issue I will return to briefly in later chapters).[14] Simon Startin, speaking of the transmission of knowledge and empathy of impairment and disability, has argued that neither disabled or non-disabled actors should be aligned with their embodied identities in their casting for roles. Speaking first of the casting of character with unspecified forms of embodiment (usually presumed non-disabled), he said:

> A disabled actor has just as good a chance of transmitting all this knowledge and empathy as an enabled actor. There is nothing intrinsic to the non-disabled experience that aids that process of transmission. And crucially, there is nothing in the disabled experience that prevents this transmission.
>
> (Startin 2017)[15]

This impossibility of presenting reality is an important point which might also suggest that discourses of (non-disabled) normality are taken, uncritically, as resonant with the lives of real non-disabled people, which are often assumed to possess greater verisimilitude than representations of disabled people. This too should be questioned. As Darke's work begins to reveal, spurious ideas of non-disabled normality are core to the ideas of reality being portrayed, and the places disabled people occupy within them. A more valuable approach might be to explore how far films demonstrate the fictional nature of truth and reality (Žižek, 2001), and persuade us to accept or challenge them.

At the heart of the complaints from disabled people, and from Disability Studies scholars who have advocated for better and more realistic or accurate portrayals of disability and impairment, lies disabled people's thwarted need

18 *Introduction*

for cultural recognition (Fraser, 2000). The lack of portrayals of disabled people as people with agency seems to deny recognition of disability in several interconnecting ways; complaints from disabled people often emphasise how such portrayals fail to address the 'real' conditions of disabled people's lives, especially the inequalities and barriers imposed on the many facets of their everyday existence, simultaneously denying them a subject position as spectators, leaving them feeling that they are portrayed as the object of a non-disabled person's 'gaze' (Wilde, 2004a; Wilde, 2009a). Indeed Bolt (2004) has demonstrated how pivotal these forms of enunciation are to the politics of representation; drawing on Heidegger, she elaborates on his ideas on representation (2004, 13) saying, 'representation or representationalism is a relationship where, whatever *is*, is figured as an object for man-as-subject' (sic).[16]

Clearly, empirical research in the area of audience attitudes to cultural representations speaks loudly of representations of impairment and disability in which disabled people seldom recognise themselves; they tend to feel uncomfortable, devalued, or used as 'inspiration porn' when they do (Cumberbatch and Negrine, 1992; Sancho, 2003; Wilde, 2004a, 2004b, 2010). This highlights a high degree of fixity in disability imagery, in that disabled people consistently express that these images are 'not for them' (Wilde, 2009a). Following Deleuze's appeal to 'experiment' with the 'limits' of representation in order to move beyond them, Bolt (speaking more broadly) suggests a strategy of 'handleability', in order to 'disrupt the fixity of representation' (Bolt, 2004, 13). Put simply, she regards this as an artistic practice which is embedded within a practice-based 'relation of care and concernful dealings' (Bolt, 2006, 4) which moves beyond 'the fixity of representation' (Bolt, 2004, 14), towards a 'creative arts pedagogy' where the creator of art allows art 'to emerge', 'producing a crucial moment of understanding or circumspection' (Bolt, 2006, 6). Although new, and arguably better, images of disability may not necessarily entail disabled actors and film-makers, it is clear that this need for circumspection, in relation to disability imagery, is contingent on a much more comprehensive knowledge of, and empathy for, disability and impairment. This is especially true the transmission of recognisable experiences, commensurate with more elements of the lived experiences, or 'world-slices', of disabled people's lives are to gain greater verisimilitude (as impossible as this task may be).

Down the rabbit hole – stereotypes, archetypes, and the meanings of disability

Mallett has argued that analysis of 'disability stereotypes' can 'be seen to foreclose its own theoretical and political reach' (2009, 4), especially where this might be seen to be tied too closely to the censure of depictions deemed to be 'negative', perhaps leading to a representational impasse. Like Mallett, I believe that stereotypes need to be seen in their 'social and political contexts' (Mallett, 2010). As suggested, I will argue that such 'critical analysis' needs to go further in interrogating notions of realism and the 'real', paying close attention to personal/phenomenological, embodied, and cultural contexts of viewing. So, far from spurning 'stereotypical images', stereotypes will be seen to carry important truths about societal discourses on disability, often related to significant cultural narratives of impairment and disability.

Frank's (1995) typology of illness narratives shows, for example, how closely people's health subjectivities are related to cultural expectations of illness and our attitudes to a limited range of narratives and associated stereotypes. Here, following Thomas (2007), I am approaching illness and disability as phenomena which are treated as 'social deviance' by society. Disability stereotypes designated as 'negative', such as those presenting the disabled person as pitiable, bitter, and violent (see, for example, Barnes, 1992, Kriegel, 1987, and Norden, 1994) can easily be mapped into Frank's category of illness as 'chaos' narrative in their characteristics of disorder, 'vulnerability, futility, and impotence' (Frank 1995, 97), just as those deemed 'positive' often correspond to Frank's illness as 'quest' narrative, 'accepting' and 'using' (ibid.,115) illness/impairment to render them as survivors whilst fuelling the 'trajectory of the self' (Giddens, 1991).[17] Stereotypes buying into archetypes of suffering, self-sacrifice, and courage, within the quest narrative, might include Norden's idea of the Saintly Sage (1994, 131), Kriegel's Survivor Cripple (1987), or Barnes' 'disabled person as normal' (1992, 18). Although the latter narratives and stereotypes can be seen as more favourable, they have all been seen as problematic for fixing people's identities and expectations, not least in the promotion of 'inspiration porn' (Young, 2014). Conversely, such narratives are impossible to avoid in the processes of storytelling, and 'inspiration porn' itself can be seen to resonate with some of the empowering or affirmative ideas of the disabled people's movement (Grue, 2016).

Indeed, stereotypes and archetypes seem to be essential ingredients in cinema, and the links between changing stereotypes and archetypes can be seen to be a significant dimension of shifts in disability representation, just as they contribute to the evolution of genre and mode (as illustrated in the following chapters). But these are not restricted to disabled people – they apply to all as part of our strategies for understanding and speaking of the world. In his study of Japanese film, Barrett defined archetypes as 'changing personified representations of constant motifs', listing motifs such as the 'inevitable human condition' of 'initiation', 'suffering and death', 'moral problems', such as 'guilt and forgiveness', and ideals such as 'loyalty', 'courage' and 'purity' (Barrett, 1989, 19). Perhaps most importantly, Barrett indicates that 'motifs don't change but sentiments about them do, as expressed through their representations' (ibid., 19).

Representations of archetypes often take the form of stereotypes, usually used as the template for characterisations, but, in contrast to Barrett's explanation of archetypes, the term stereotype indicates a fixed, one-dimensional, clichéd characterisation, with recognisable traits. Significantly, such stereotypes are more likely to be found in supporting roles, and are frequently used to further the more nuanced, fluid, and comparatively complex roles of the

20 *Introduction*

central protagonist. As Darke's theorisation of the normality genre demonstrates (1998), these supporting roles are where many disabled characters are to be found, perhaps most obviously as villains in James Bond films, who often have impairments, facial scars, or other 'extraordinary' features (such as steel capped teeth in the character of Jaws, played by Richard Kiel in *The Spy Who Loved Me* [1977] and *Moonraker* [1979]). These are also invariably linked to mental illness and/or evil. Darke illustrates how these archetypes and stereotypes are often captured in a form of storytelling which renders disabled characters as overused tropes which align disability with abnormality.

Similarly, my aim is to explore comedy films in such a relational manner, focussing on how disability films (defined here as telling a story which puts a person with an impairment, or themes of disability, closer to the centre) are informed by, and interpellate, the stereotypic (or possibly pre-ideological) expectations of viewers. Given the constitution and evolution of genres in relation to the film industry's conception of the audience, a focus on specific genres will afford a deeper investigation of processes of meaning-making within specific contexts.[18] As Gavin has demonstrated, analysis of genre and its interpretative possibilities is a valuable 'hermeneutic tool' to undertake examinations of the ways in which some meanings are 'opened-up' and others 'closed off' (Gavin, 2001, 91), not least in the 'didactic exhortations' encoded within them (ibid., 92).

Why comedy?

Haller (2003, para 6), writing on disability and 'humor', said it 'flies in the face of centuries of sentimentality and tragic portrayals. That is why it deserves scholarly attention.' It is clear from disabled people's histories and criticisms of cultural representation that comedy and humour have played a major part in forming cultural attitudes towards disabled people, shaping disabled people's images of themselves (Sutherland, 1981; Stronach and Allan, 1999; Shakespeare, 1999b; Clark, 2003). As such, analysis will be grounded in Film Studies and the sociology of humour in the quest to understand comedic constructions of disability and impairment and to engage fully with the complexity and polysemy of humour. Such an enterprise is essential if we are to avoid one-dimensional (e.g. right or wrong) or overly optimistic explanations of the transgressive possibilities of comedy, e.g. diagnoses of negative (Barnes, 1992), 'dodgy' (Montgomerie, 2015) or 'ironic' forms which may be dependent solely on the unacknowledged position of the analyst's reading. In keeping with these aims, opportunities, and risks, I will explore some of the dangers of comedy representations whilst engaging with the conditions of possibility they present for new representational forms and challenges to normalcy. The remainder of this book analyses representations of disability in comedy films, arguing that meanings of disability and impairment drawn from cinema need to be grounded in an understanding of cinematic practices and processes. I will demonstrate that a valuable framework for so doing involves recognising the importance of mode and genre in the production of cinematic texts and also in shaping the expectations of the audience. I argue that an understanding of mode and genre, and of processes of audience interpellation and viewing positions, is crucial to such enterprises, alongside other key cinematic issues discussed on the previous pages, e.g. narrative analysis, cinematography, sound, and mise en scène.

Despite the epistemological, methodological, and ontological disagreements outlined in this introduction, it is also clear that there is a high degree of agreement across both Disability Studies and Critical Disability Studies that there is a need to understand how disabled people are re-presented, and why particular tropes are dominant; this would include those likely to elicit feelings such as pity, disgust, and inspiration, or stories which re-iterate the need for relationships based on dependency, acceptance, and courage; like Hoeksema and Smit (2001), and Smit and Enns (2001), I have suggested that we need to take the fusion of Disability Studies and Film Studies seriously and have offered some potential starting points for analysis.

Contending that there is much to be gained from a synthesis of elements from Critical/Disability Studies with Film Studies, my exploration begins by recognising the importance of genre in the production and reception of cinematic texts, especially in shaping the expectations of the audience. This is undertaken through close examination of a small number of contemporary films, from three genres: the romantic comedy genre; a satirical film which also fits 'black comedy'/romantic genres; and a charting of the evolution of disability representations in the gross-out genre. The films discussed have all been chosen for their significance to recent debates on disability representation.

My discussion commences with a fuller discussion of genre, mode, and comedy in the next chapter. Chapter Two positions the study of comedy and popular culture within wider academic disciplines, showing some of the reasons why the use of comedy and humour should be taken 'seriously' in discourses of disablement, as significant forms of social interaction, entertainment, and ways of knowing the world. Positioning ideas of funniness within a discussion of embodied cultural capital and taste hierarchies, the discussion moves on to consider the role of humour in disabled people's lives and the range of approaches which have been used to theorise humour. I outline my own aesthetic/theoretical preferences in an examination of the major arguments on comedy by writers aligned with Critical/Disability Studies, and key topics within these debates; exploring ideas of tragedy, taboo, notions of the abject, political correctness, and transgression. Before a brief analysis of politically incorrect comedy, there is also a discussion of 'punching' up and down, television comedy, and the idea of 'tolerant subject'; this is explained to be a 'fragile' position by McRuer who views it as 'a dutiful (and flexible) tolerance toward the minority groups' (2006, 18).

Before a discussion of specific comedy modes and genres, Chapter Three continues to explore contemporary debates in humour, comedy, and disability, continuing the discussion on the tolerant subject with a brief examination of different forms of comedy in popular television genres, before moving on to a consideration of impairment representations and the importance of genre.

An exploration of disability, impairment, disabled people, and the Romantic Comedy film genre is undertaken in Chapter Four – a genre choice made in part to examine disabled people as romantic agents; complaints that disabled people are not treated equally in terms of sexuality in cultural representations are common (Shakespeare, 1996; Wilde, 2004b). One film is discussed at length, relating it to wider issues of diversity, scholarship on the romantic comedy genre, and other relevant films in the genre. Thea Sharrock's *Me Before You*, has been chosen as a very close fit to conventional definitions of the romantic comedy, but also because it was opposed by disabled people across the world on the basis of its romanticisation of suicide narratives for disabled people (see Jessen, 2016, for example). Rather than focusing on this narrative of suicide as the single determining feature of the film, the discussion explores how cinematic elements are used (such as colour, and use of camera), exploring how the film works to position the leading romantic protagonists very differently. It also explores how both characters are used, relationally, to uphold moral discourses of social and economic value, Randian ideals, tropes of gender (disabled and non-disabled), and taste hierarchies (rather a paradoxical message, given the romantic comedy's status as low culture). As a film adapted from a novel, this chapter also raises questions about the ways popular cinema can reshape, and diminish, the polyphonic attributes of the books they are based on.

In contrast, in Chapter Five, Lanthimos' *The Lobster* is explored as a satirical and surreal (Kermode, 2016) black comedy. This was chosen in part because it can also be defined as a romantic comedy, and could be seen as the antithesis to *Me Before You*, as a less mainstream film. This chapter develops earlier questions about the role of communicative structures, and the positioning of viewers within them. As a film which is designed to demand that the audience engage with difficult (perhaps unanswerable) questions, the discussion is focussed on the queering of boundaries between bodies, and the degree to which the film is a satire of contemporary romantic relationships (in sharp contrast to *Me Before You*)

Chapter Six examines disability in the gross-out comedy. The genre has been chosen in order to confront another problematic area in cultural representations, the idea of the disabled body as abject (Hughes, 2009). A different approach is taken in this chapter in that the discussion charts the evolution of disability representations in the work of the Farrelly Brothers. Arguably the introduction of anti-discrimination legislation in the 1990s (especially the 1990 *Americans with Disabilities Act* in the United States) set new cultural opportunities for shifts in representation, the period in which their work emerged. Drawing some parallels with television portrayals, the chapter takes questions about the positioning of the audience forward, investigating the increasing use of mimetic strategies, and the limits of the film industry in accepting or promoting politicised images of disability.

Chapter Six concludes the book by revisiting topics of communicative structure, the role of disabled people, characters, and themes within comedy and wider forms of cinematic storytelling. Demonstrating just a few of the multiplicity of factors which work towards the monologic tendencies of disability representations within contemporary film, I ask questions about the 'tolerant subject', perceptions of comedic risk, and the inclusion of those deemed as 'other', highlighting some of the ways these continue to shape the stories that are allowed to be told.

Notes

1 Following the terminology of the British social model of disability, throughout this book the terms *impairment* and *disability* will be used to refer to two distinctively different phenomena. Impairment is designated as 'variations in the structure, function and workings of bodies which, in Western culture, are medically defined as significant abnormalities or pathologies' (Thomas, 1999, 8). Conversely, disability is used, in a general sense, to denote the social oppression of people with impairments. Explanation of varying models based on these ideas can be found in Thomas (1999), Meekosha and Shuttleworth (2009), and Goodley (2011).
2 Both of these fields of study are explained in Meekosha and Shuttleworth (2009).
3 For example, an early Diamond report found only 6.5 per cent of their sample of on-screen employees from UK television companies were disabled, and 5.5 per cent off-screen (Creative Diversity Network, 2017).
4 Bracha Ettinger (2006) argues for a matrixial gaze (of trans-subjectivity) in publications such as 'Matrixial trans-subjectivity'.
5 Despite her acknowledgement of the concepts 'limited definitional or conceptual specificity' (Campbell, 2009, 5, cited in Campbell, 2017b, 9), Campbell explained, 'Ableism is not just a matter of ignorance or negative attitudes towards disabled people; it is a trajectory of perfection, a deep way of thinking about bodies, wholeness and permeability. Bluntly, ableism functions to "inaugurat[e] the norm"' (ibid.), cited in Campbell (2017b, 8).

However, she went on to offer this revised approach, of ableism as a

> system of causal relations about the order of life that produces processes and systems of entitlement and exclusion. This causality fosters conditions of microaggression, internalised ableism and, in their jostling, notions of (un) encumbrance. A system of dividing practices, ableism institutes the reification and classification of populations. Ableist systems involve the differentiation, ranking, negation, notification and prioritisation of sentient life.
> (Campbell, 2017a: 287–288, cited in Campbell, 2017b)

Elsewhere, reflecting the emphasis he believed should be placed on the analysis of disability in neoliberal societies, Goodley refers to ableism as,

> a space fit for normative citizens; encourages a bias towards autonomous, independent bodies; and lends support to economic and material dependence on neoliberal and hyper-capitalist forms of production.
> (Goodley, 2014, 21)

Bearing these theoretical ideas in mind (notwithstanding a) my doubts about the utility of the concept of microaggression – a concept with even less clarity and specificity, and b) whether and how ableism might manifest itself outside neoliberal societies) my use of the term ableism adopts a similar approach. However, it will be used in much the same way that cis-centredness, or whiteness, is used in critiques of racism and transphobia. Conversely disablism is conceptualised as a core principle of social model and Disability Studies approaches, as social relational, as a

> form of social oppression involving the social imposition of restrictions on activity on people with impairments and the socially engendered undermining of their psycho-emotional well-being.
>
> (Thomas, 2007, 73)

6 This is, of course, reliant on the statistics available on the identification of the actor's impairments. It is possible that some actors identifying as disabled may be cast in roles where impairment/disablement is not present or evident in any way in the narrative or visual images. One such example is Kiera Knightley, who has played leading roles in many films. For a discussion of her dyslexia see Child (2012).
7 The idea of a nondisabled or disabled subjectivity, or approach towards film or anything else is, of course, problematic as there are certainly dangers of essentialism lurking in research and theory which is based on the simple mapping of ontological status according to impairment and disability status.
8 See endnote 5.
9 There has been increasing work on both the social construction and politics of impairment, including early work by Abberley (1987) and later work such as that by Sherry (2016) and Coleman-Fountain and McLaughlin (2013).
10 See King (2002) for a discussion of the differences between mode and genre.
11 Much of the work I use will be from those who have worked on the more cultural aspects of disability, due to their obvious relevancy. However, I will draw on scholarship from work which may be best described as Disability Studies (ascribing to the social model, as defined by Oliver, 1990, for example) to more recent work which extends, and is critical of the binarism of earlier work (e.g. Corker, 1999 (Marian Hill Scott), and Goodley, 2011).
12 It is often used as a noun by the film industry to refer to a comedy genre. As King indicates, Altman has argued that such instances should 'commandeer entire texts and demonstrate a clear ability to pilot them independently' (Altman, 1999, 51, also cited in King, 2002, 3).
13 Exceptions to this include, apart from my own studies, Darke's unpublished study of disabled people's opinions on niche disability programming (1995) and Sancho's study (2003).
14 One example of this is the *The Ruderman Report*, which found that disabled actors were significantly under-represented on television, with 95 per cent of disabled characters being played by non-disabled people (Woodburn and Kopić, 2016, 1). See Birrell (2016) for a similar analysis of disabled actors in cinema.
15 In personal communications – permission gained.
16 Bolt is not discussing disability or impairment within her work – her discussion is more general.
17 It is perhaps significant that these attributes are most often assigned to men – see Wilde (2004c).
18 On some occasions, for example, it is possible (if improbable) that a film may present a new impairment which might be located outside our previous understandings.

2 Comedy and disability

Comedy as/and art

Comedy is rarely seen in terms of art. Commonly, it is associated with lower forms of culture, alternatively referred to as a part of 'mass culture' (Irwin and Gracia, 2007, 42–43) or 'popular culture', and often positioned on the bottom rung of taste hierarchies (Kuipers, 2006). In some ways, then, the study of popular film comedy in this book can be seen to be at odds with the types of film theory discussed so far. It might easily be assumed to be peripheral, trivial, or even external to studies of cinema (Medhurst, 2007, 16), particularly in relation to the more serious concerns of ideology, art, and philosophy in 'disability films'. The approaches informed by philosophical scholars such as Deleuze, Chamarette, and Žižek are more commonly applied to cinema which is associated with experimental and art films, and audiences which might be seen to be associated with higher degrees of cultural capital; typical examples might include a Deleuzian analysis of Tarkovsky's cinema or Dreyer's *The Passion of Joan of Arc*.[1] The same can be seen to be true of Bakhtin's work (see, for example, Luzzi's study of the aesthetics of Italian art film, 2016).[2] However, these approaches are just as valuable in their application to 'lower' forms of culture; Bakhtin's concept of the 'carnivalesque' has been used widely in studies of comedy and humour (see White, 1993) and can be seen to have particular resonance with portrayals of impairment and disability, due to the emphasis placed on embodiment (Mihailovic, 1997). Basic bodily needs, senses/sensuality, and bodily performance (especially transgressive forms) are theorised as central aspects of carnival (see Gilliard and Higgs, 2014, 13). However, as Irwin has argued, the application of philosophy to 'popular culture' often seems to be thought of as a case of 'pairing the perishable with the perennial' (Irwin and Gracia, 2007, 4), despite the important place it has within philosophical thinking (Nikulin, 2014). It is also my contention that the study of comedy warrants a key position within discussions of the cultural representation of disability and impairment, not least as a neglected area of study.

Sociological, cultural studies, and academic disciplines generally have 'ignored comedy', despite the promise that studies of comedy and humour show for understanding significant forms of cultural 'currency' and production, and for analysing taste and social stratification (Friedman, 2014, 11). Further, Watson (2015, 2) has argued that academics often neglect the 'unique opportunities' provided by humour for social analysis, while simultaneously demonstrating how humour is often used within academia for representational purposes, even as an unacknowledged analytical tool, shaping and perpetuating boundaries, barriers, inequalities, and hierarchies of knowledge within academic life.[3] Andy Medhurst, speaking to *Guardian* journalist Chris Arnot, noted that 'Snobbery against people who write about comedy is alive and well' (2007, para 13); elsewhere, in his analysis of English cultural identities and comedy, he writes of the whole education system as a 'key arena' for shaping and containing humour, by drawing strict boundaries around seriousness, and avoiding the 'contamination' of 'low discourses' of play and humour (as subversive) (Medhurst, 2007, 16). He draws on the work of Allon White (1993) to emphasise the education system's complicity in perpetuating such hierarchies of taste. Arguing that seriousness is shaped more by power than content, White stated that,

> the authority to denigrate what is to be taken seriously (and the authority to enforce reverential solemnity in certain contexts) is a way of creating and maintaining power.
>
> (White, 1993,128)

This power dynamic is exacerbated by the seriousness of academia, even the need to maintain 'respectability' in Media Studies and especially Film Studies, as Medhurst points out (2007, 16–17). Dominant concepts of seriousness serve to create a binary between the trivial baseness of comedy and the important/significant, cultured, and respectable world/sophisticated sphere of formal knowledge and the approved 'gravity' of 'high' topics and discourses. Medhurst argues that higher ideas are seen to operate in law, medicine, and the military, even theatrical tragedy, and that comparatively trivial/insignificant, subversive, plebeian, and crude thinking is more closely aligned to the domain of humour/pleasure and other forms of play. These dualities tend to reinforce notions that the concerns deemed 'serious' are more 'real', suggesting a limited value for comedy, pleasure, and play as a means to understand significant human and social experiences.

Despite its lowly and 'non-serious' status, it is unsurprising then to find that even a cursory examination of literature on comedy demonstrates that, contrary to its marginalisation in academic hierarchies of knowledge, comedy *has* received scholarly attention in philosophy and literature/theatre, gaining the attention of philosophers going back to Plato and Aristotle (Frye, 2002; Nikulin, 2014). Further, Watson, has shown that the neglect, and even 'rejection', of humour as a legitimate area of study has a long history, from Plato onwards, on the grounds of its 'irresponsible' threat to 'rationality and self-control' (Watson, 2015, 1). She suggests that the 'irresponsibility' of humour was also seen as a discouragement or distraction from action (ibid., 2), possibly due to Plato's perception of comedy as an off-putting synthesis of opposing feelings, as an 'unwelcome mixture of pain (*lypē*) and pleasure (*hēdonē*), or of fear and love' (Nikulin, 2014, 6, *his emphasis*). These ambivalent attitudes towards comedy, over such a long period, perhaps explain some of the contemporary reluctance to treating it as a serious social and cultural concern.

But, as both Watson, Nikulin, and many others cited here, have demonstrated, the study of humour and comedy can be seen as indispensable to understanding many facets of the human experience, and crucial to the analysis of vast range of social phenomena. Nikulin goes as far as saying that comedy 'shows itself as philosophy in action' and claims it to be a

> paradigm of interaction as acting together towards the realisation of a good ending, which is never final but always comes as a liberating statement of human goodness found in a shared wellbeing and the renewal of life.
> (2014, 135)

It is in this spirit of endeavour that we begin to examine comedy in representations of disability and impairment.

Comedy and disability in popular culture

One of the main reasons comedy has been chosen as a discrete area of study for this book is that it has the potential to illuminate 'interpretative diversity' (Friedman, 2014, 2) more than any other form of media communication, most obviously in how and why some people find particular forms of humour funny and others do not. It also has potential to show how our choices in the consumption of arts and media, and our investments in it, are closely linked to 'cultural capital' (Bourdieu, 1986), and significant aspects of our social position and social and cultural identities. Further, work such as Friedman's has shown how cultural tastes in comedy have increasingly been used to mark social distinctions, particularly those drawn along class lines. He explains how cultural producers have found larger markets and how there have been shifts in consumption which have been seen as moves towards greater 'cultural diversity', away from 'snobbism' (Bennett et al. 2009, 186). However, despite some evidence of cultural omnivorousness (Bennett et al., 2009) and shifts towards 'disruption to symbolic hierarchies' (Friedman, 2014, 39), Friedman makes a strong case against arguing for qualities of 'universal funniness' (ibid., 174), showing how an apparent 'indifference' to 'aesthetic hierarchies' masks more entrenched cultural hierarchies perpetuated in the consumption of cultural products. Friedman shows that this is especially so in the 'way they are consumed and the aims pursued in doing so' (ibid., 39). He also argues that contemporary forms of privileged cultural capital are 'embodied' rather than 'objectified' in comedy, most often appealing to 'rarefied and "disinterested" forms of cultural capital' (ibid., 4). Challenging the idea of the omnivorous consumer, he argues that this is an identity which pertains to a cultural elite, who are free to 'borrow expression' from all cultural fields and to 'culturally empower forms of popular art' (ibid., 41).

His ideas on embodied cultural capital and taste hierarchies have great relevance here to an analysis of comedy and its audiences, and also to understanding the forms of class and impairment status brought to viewing experiences of disability films in the comedy genre. For example, we might question how far any democratising tendencies in comedy extend to the portrayal of disabled people as objects, the extent to which they are depicted as subjects within comedy, and treated as subjects by the audience. The presumption of an ableist position, for the telling and receiving of a joke, can be seen as a 'form of long-lasting dispositions of the mind and body' (Bourdieu, 1986, 47). We might ask how far comedy films have moved in traversing conventional aesthetic hierarchies, e.g. where disabled people have often been the target. Even though it may appear that the tendency to put disabled people and specific impairments at the centre of comedies, often as the 'butt of the joke' (Barnes, 1992, 14), has become less acceptable (especially after the disability discrimination laws of the 1990s in the UK and USA), novel forms of comedy have arisen which might be characterised by their stance of post-political correctness, often with disability and impairment as their object of ridicule.

Although Allan and Burridge show that one of the first uses of the term 'political correctness' was in 1793, as part of a legal decision in the US Supreme Court, it is perhaps of some significance to note that this term began to be used more regularly by the American New Left in the 1960s, gaining more common use in the 1980s and 1990s, with popularity of the term 'peaking' between 1991 to 1995 (Allan and Burridge, 2006, 91), partly as a response to recognition of the need to repair discriminatory employment practices, and improve curricula and 'speech codes' (ibid.). Often aligned with left-wing views, alternative comedy tends to be associated with political correctness (Littlewood and Pickering, 1998), and is often seen in terms of its inclusion of marginal groups and its challenge to the 'status quo' (Williams, 1998, 146). Despite the resurgence of political correctness at the end of the twentieth century and the increase in the popularity of alternative comedy from the late 1980s in the UK, US, and elsewhere, forms of 'alternative comedy' did exist before this period, in a number forms, not least in the films and stand-up comedy of Mel Brooks and Woody Allen (Davis, 2003). Similarly, explicitly disablist comedians such as Roy Chubby Brown, Jim Davidson, and Bernard Manning (comedians who 'punched down' at those with less social power and privilege as themselves), rose to prominence in the comedy landscape of the 1970s (in the UK) but such humour is not new, with a long history of disabling comedy before this (Lockyer, 2015).

Nonetheless, we can see a questioning of, and some opposition to, what seems to have been seen as a new sensibility (Davis, 2003) in comedy in the late 1990s. This was there in Farrelly Brother films, released in the 1990s, discussed in Chapter Six, and later television programming such as *The Office* (UK, 2001–2003). Post-political, or anti-politically correct humour (henceforth anti-PC), tends to use the central characters' ignorance of the need to reconsider discriminatory attitudes to comic effect, seen perhaps as 'ironic bigotry' (Logan, 2017), invariably serving to encourage attachments with non-disabled characters and their pain through recognition of their dilemmas. David Brent, for example, is a white middle-class man who struggles to understand others as a 'tolerant subject' (Mallett, 2010) of a changing world of (uncertain) social expectations. Whilst he is an agent of oppression towards those around him, he remains central.

As suggested in Chapter One, Haller (2003) recommends that Disability Studies scholars' attention should be given to humour, precisely because it can be seen as being opposed to the portrayals which have dominated in cultural representations of disabled people, particularly those which emphasise sentimentality and tragedy. Although comedy and tragedy/sentimentality can often be found together, it is usually the more serious side of media which preoccupies disability (and cultural/media) scholars' analysis of cultural representations of impairment and disability. Commonly, studies concern themselves with 'pathological' and normalising representations, particularly those found in realist forms of drama, and more 'serious' matters. These include recent discussions of body genres and the roles and interpretations of the audience as 'panopticon voyeurs' (Chivers and Markotić, 2010, 3–19), a welcome development in acknowledging interpretive diversity, the 'active audience', and the multiple readings which may be wrought from a single portrayal. Themes such as pathological representations, voyeurism, body genres, and the positioning of audiences are key themes in the work of Darke (1998, 1999, and later), Mitchell and Snyder (2000, 2006), and Chivers and Markotić's collection *The Problem Body* (2010), all seen as central texts in cultural analyses of disability. However, as indispensable as these have been in demonstrating the narrow range of disability portrayals, the impairment and 'normality' tropes within them, and the limited conditions of possibility for understanding disabled people on other terms, the examination of comedy and humour is a marginal area of analysis within this work.

As such, the capacity which humour and comedy have for portraying disability remains under-theorised, and our understanding of how meanings are attributed to disabled people, in the media and in cultural attitudes, remain underdeveloped, despite the unique worth they both have for illuminating the 'irrationality' of conventional/serious discourses. The value of comedy for undermining and 'revealing the precarious absurdities on which rationality rests' (as Watson suggests [2015, 1]) puts it in a favourable position for questioning notions of normality, abnormality, ideas of difference, and so on. This gives humour a crucial place in the deconstruction of ableism and disablism, across both comedy and drama genres, shedding light on (idealised) non-disabled normalities, a crucial type of absurdity central to the workings of rationality, ableism, and disablism (Goodley, 2014). It is also possible that an examination of the catharsis or 'purification' effected in audiences (Nikulin, 2014, 7), e.g. the moving 'through the interaction of opposites' (ibid., 83), might illuminate some of the ways in which comedy *has been, is*, and *can be* used to understand popular attitudes to disability and impairment. The catharsis, or purification, afforded by comedy has been theorised to allow 'a well-conceived resolution of the conflict and a dramatic – though not speculative – reconciliation of opposites' (ibid.), thus allowing the audience to gain pleasurable engagement in 'solving problems' (ibid., 85), in this case the truth of the cultural meanings attributed to impairment and disability. This will extend the analyses of body genres and spectatorial shaping, or positioning, found in Chivers and Markotić (following Williams, 1991).

The links between humour and oppression

It is clear from the analysis of disabled people's histories and criticisms of cultural representation that comedy and humour have played a major part in forming cultural attitudes towards them, in the mockery, humiliation, and cruelty visited on them/us. Barnes, for example, has written of the common use of people with impairments for amusement and ridicule in ancient Rome, particularly people of restricted growth or small/little people, and those with visual impairments. He showed that this was also true for entertainment purposes in England during the Middle Ages and the Tudor and Stuart periods, where a greater number of disabled people were used to extend the opportunities for amusement further, hence 'every impairment from idiocy to insanity to diabetes and bad breath was a welcome source of amusement' (Thomas, 1977, 80–81, cited in Barnes, 1997, 18). Invariably, the dominance of such attitudes in society shapes disabled people's images of themselves (Sutherland, 1981; Stronach and Allan, 1999; Shakespeare, 1999b; Clark, 2003).

Perhaps the seriousness of humour in all of our lives is exemplified in the way it is often imbricated within bullying, humiliation, intimidation, and even 'hate crimes'. A particularly horrific example of this was the use of mocking and laughter in the killing of Brendan Mason, a young man with learning difficulties, in 2016, for which two men were subsequently given life prison sentences (Mills, 2017). Similarly, Margaret Carlson (2017, para 8) has written about hate crime and the taunting forms of humour in the life of her disabled brother, providing further evidence of the 'epidemic' in the everyday use of 'taunting' as an accepted form of torture and threat ('epidemic' and 'taunting' were her own words). This was also evident in the diary testimonies of incidents against Fiona Pilkington, a woman who made the decision to kill herself and her daughter Frankie (who had learning difficulties) after police had failed to take remedial action against the taunting and abuse from local young people (Walker, 2011). Indeed, the classifying of such bullying as 'low-priority anti-social behaviour' is indicative of attitudes to people with learning difficulties and the trivialisation of hate speech which is deemed to pass as humour. The words 'mock' and 'taunt' are both on Koller's (1988) list of synonyms for humour, as verbs; their status as a verb seems significant, especially as all these examples of human action have been seen to have fed, directly, or indirectly, into the misery and/or deaths of those involved.

My own memories of the abuse of people with learning difficulties in a large residential hospital, in the early 1980s, are replete with the use of humour to support such bullying and abuse. The laughter of other nurses was a daily occurrence as they witnessed the barbaric treatment of residents, actions which were usually initiated as jokes to break the tedium of institutionalised routines (wake, clean, 'toilet', feed, medicate, send to OT/play therapy, feed, 'toilet', clean, put to bed). Far from being merely a form of amusement, pleasure, release, or entertainment, comedy and humour can clearly be seen to be also an instrument of violence and oppression. As Medhurst points out, comedy often 'supports inequalities' whilst 'cloaking them in an aura of inevitability' which often veils cruelty in the real world of disabled people's lives, as a means of 'selling us bigotry in the name of entertainment' in the commercial world (2007, 19). Supporting Medhurst's relational view, and echoing King's (2002) argument that comedy within cinema is a mode rather than a genre, Moran has explained that humour can be seen (amongst other things) as a 'cognitive style', in terms of 'stimuli' such as jokes, 'responses' to a range of social phenomena, and also as 'an ability to generate a response, produce a response, or detect/observe the two' (Moran, 2003, cited in Coogan and Mallett, 2013, 248). As these scholars, and the philosophers discussed earlier, argued, humour and comedy have a key role to play in understanding power relationships, and in this case, the ways in which specific forms of power operate in ableism and disablism, in the minutiae of everyday life, and in wider cultural trends.

It is also clear that similar elements of popular media influence the everyday treatment of disabled people, including debate about how the character of Derek Noakes (from Ricky Gervais's TV show *Derek*, 2012–2014) can be seen as an encouragement to mock disabled people in everyday life. Christopher Stevens' (2014) expression of these concerns in the right-wing press, who usually take an anti-political correctness stance, seems to indicate that there is widespread concern that such programmes encourage the ridicule of disabled people, also seen in comments made on, and debates involving, Gervais and his regular broadcasting team, on twitter and other online sites.[4]

Theories of humour

Attitudes to humour and comedy are complicated even further by their relationships to a vast range of related concepts; Koller, on his partial inventory, identified 114 words which are synonyms for humour (1988, 5), a list which is likely to be far longer now, thirty years later. He also argued that concepts which have so many words identified with them signify how important they are within given cultures, e.g. Inuit and Yupik cultures are reputed to use fifty words for snow (Robson, 2013).

Overall then, comedy and humour have clear associations with words such as wit, laughter, joking, and so on, but clearly mean a diverse range of things to many people, meanings which can perhaps be most clearly mapped onto class and other social and cultural positions. Disagreements on what is funny, and why, continue to rage in contemporary culture (as above), suggesting that comedy has an undeniable prominence in society. Adding to this lack of consensus are the diverse ways in which intellectuals have theorised humour and comedy. These include well-known theories such as the 'relief' explanations of Sigmund Freud and Herbert Spencer, ideas which emphasise 'physiological, psychological or social restrictions' (Koller, 1988, 8), and the superiority theories of philosophers such as Plato, Aristotle, Thomas Hobbes, and Henri Bergson (see following paragraphs).

Other prominent theories are those which discuss humour in terms of 'ambivalence' and 'incongruity', the former emphasising the play of 'opposing emotions and feeling states' (ibid., 8), with incongruity approaches exposing the juxtaposition between 'two or more conceptualisations which do not fit together'. Incongruity theories are espoused by scholars such as Arthur Schopenhauer and Arthur Koestler (ibid., 7). Whilst these, and a number of other theories, have been proposed, and many correspondences can be found between them (e.g. relief theories and ambivalence), there has been no agreement on which is the most useful approach. But all of them are, as Koller suggested, valuable 'baselines' for exploring humour. As such, they warn us against prescriptive arguments which tend to neglect other explanations and significant aspects of humour. Clearly, superiority theory lends itself well to understanding humour used in the service of the torment, or condemnation, of others (ostensibly applicable to all political perspectives, to raise one point of view over others, for example). Likewise, relief theory can help us understand how overtly political humour might be used as a means to cope with the trials of an oppressive political regime – as Koller suggests, this is a perspective which stresses liberation (ibid., 8). Both of these approaches have clear relevance to understanding the place of disability and impairment in comedy and humour, in understanding the adverse effects of comedic 'taunts', an as well as more liberatory forms, such as counter-hegemonic humour. The same can be said of incongruity theory, not least in challenging the rationality of common-sense discourses of normality and disability. Indeed, it should be borne in mind, by myself and the reader (not least for transparency and critique), that in my continual search for strategies which might lead to a greater 'cultural recognition' (Fraser, 2000) of, and for, disabled people, I tend to lean towards a preference for incongruity-based explanations, in the belief that we need to illuminate how people have been misrecognised, as a prerequisite for representational change.[5] At the same time, the desire for better portrayals of disabled people could also lead me to overlook the ways in which my aesthetic preferences neglect to acknowledge how superiority is embedded within humour which I perceive to work for, rather than against, disabled people. In turn, my penchant for one explanation of a joke, or an image, over another may lead me to neglect some of the potential effects on the audience for those with different interpretations of a story or image, or varying viewpoints on what is funny, and why. Thus, presumption of a fixed or preferred reading (Hall, 1980) could disregard the consequences for different people, especially in underestimating the perceived threats which jokes may arouse and the ways in which spectators build their defences against them. As such, a recognition of these, and other theories, has been used as a guide for my analysis throughout the book, as a heuristic framework to check biases within my own analysis. With this in mind, I will now turn to explore some of the main themes which have dominated in Disability Studies discussions on comedy.

Comedy and Disability Studies – tragedy, comedy, and 'aesthetic nervousness'

The links between abuse, agency, and disability in comedy has caused considerable debate. Much of this was initiated by Stronach and Allan (1999), who argued that there is a common taboo against laughing at the 'comic' in 'joking with disability'. Like later work by scholars such as Coogan and Mallett (Mallett, 2009; Mallett, 2010; Coogan and Mallett, 2013), they expressed concern at the concept of political correctness, and the potential censure of comedy. Their dialogue on joking and disability, focussing on two disabled people's actions in particular situations, raised some significant points about agency, the positioning of the disabled person in the creation of comedy, and performances of the disabled self. It was argued that the 'self-work' undertaken by the two disabled people discussed in the article would 'enable them to continue in the conspiracy of "normality"' (Stronach and Allan, 1999, 36). Stronach and Allan also highlighted the 'interleaving – the braiding – of the discourses of the tragic, the heroic and the comic in relation to notions of disability (and ultimately) equity' (ibid.). Specifically, invoking superiority theory, they argued that what Bergson has termed the 'latent comic effect' (Bergson, 1911, 44, cited in Stronach and Allan, 1999, 37) is evident in situations where disabled people are present, contending that 'the comic is never quite absent from the discourse of tragedy, distasteful though we must find that contamination' (ibid., 39). Significantly, they used this sample of two disabled people to argue that this 'comic element', i.e. laughing at disabled people, is culturally forbidden (ibid., 37). Here we can see that positioning disabled people as the perceived inferiors within the comedic theory of superiority can easily lead to the belief that selfwork, as opposition against this hierarchy, is a brave, or 'heroic', decision for a disabled person to take (ibid., 35). Conversely, many Disability Studies scholars have opposed such ideas, often seen as central to ideas of 'good crips' or 'super crips', creating categories which maintain concepts of disabled people's difference, whilst perpetuating ideas of good and bad impairment/disability identities (a brief summary of this work can be found in Sandell et al., 2010, 107).

As Robillard (1999) and others (below) have suggested, Stronach and Allan raised significant questions about comedy and disability, which deserve far greater investigation, not least in exploring how these cultural expectations may differ according to who is saying what to who, and at what level; valuable explorations might include micro-interactions such as these, examinations of who speaks about disability, to who, on a world stage of comedy, and the roles of disabled people or non-disabled people as the agents of, or audiences for, comedy. But a number of scholars have raised objections to their argument. Indeed, Robillard questions Stronach and Allan for their functionalist interpretation of the material used, particularly the implication that 'humour produced by disabled people about themselves serves to ease the alienation they would otherwise experience' (Robillard, 1999, 62). He suggests that, as well as being a restricted sample of disabled people using humour, the article is framed in a very individualistic way, which does not contextualise the material within the multiple contingencies of life, not least within broader social interactions and 'naturally-occurring communication' (Robillard, 1999, 64). Indeed, the presence of disabling social, cultural, discursive, environmental, and carnal pressures is likely to lead to a limited number of responses from disabled people, as seen in Stronach and Allan's examples. Hughes and Paterson's analysis of interactions in a lift, for example, showed how the embodiment of a 'subtle interplay of micro- and macro-relations of power' and the practices, processes, and geographies of everyday life, mitigate against communication and the satisfaction of carnal needs (1999, 606). As Paterson argues,

> micro- and macro-relations of everyday 'codes of conduct' (which favour the corporeal status of non-disabled people over my own) are in complicity with the oppression of disabled people.[6]

This form of interaction seems particularly evident in Stronach and Allan's analysis of the disabled person's 'failure' leading to their selfwork responsibilities, whereupon disabled people's actions/reactions to their own weaknesses, mistakes, and vulnerabilities are argued to work in 'reclaiming the event for farce, rather than tragedy', 'switching the register' to help in 'attracting the laughter of others' (Stronach and Allan, 1999, 32). Thus, deemed as outsiders, disabled people's resistance buys back into the hierarchy of superiority. This suggests a dichotomy, and a dependency on the accommodations made by non-disabled people, whereby disabled people are perhaps complicit in the cultural misrecognition of themselves as failed 'others', by acting to remove the symbolic barriers created by ableist culture, and re-create the conditions for a joint community. This can be seen to offer what Medhurst might refer to as offering 'an invitation to belong' (2007, 19) to non-disabled people.

Comedy and disability   35

This move relates to points made forcefully by Corker, who shows that 'narratives of "disability"' are 'happening twice' in their account, with difference conceived of as a 'negatively generative boundary' and the 'implicit and unreflexive marginalisation of a collective view of disability' (Corker, 1999, 77). Indeed, Stronach and Allan's examples counter much of the work authored by members of the Disability Arts community, especially those whose efforts are focused on building solidarity forged on belonging to a community *of* disabled people and sharing cultural meanings of themselves (Wilde, 2014).[7] Corker also challenged their theorisation of the heroic, and the relationship of the tragic to the comic presented by their argument, as 'interpretative discourses' chosen by the authors, reflective of their implicit, though explicitly acknowledged, positioning as non-disabled academics. Additionally, as Stronach and Allan's work is centred on the humour of two disabled people located within their own everyday lives, it does not provide evidence of how disability as comedy is taboo in non-disabled people's humorous exchanges or wider society. This is a theme which is of utmost importance in understanding the place of humorous dispositions towards disabled people in society and culture, and one I will return to, and emphasise, especially as non-disabled people have continued to dominate in mainstream 'disability comedy', often leading the challenge to perceived taboos and pushing the limits of comedy disability.

Going back to a major point in their analysis of humour and disability, Stronach and Allan use Bergson's and Freud's arguments to say that 'such a taboo is almost inviolable in relation to serious subjects, evoking, pity, horror, etc.' (1999, 37), thereby assuming that tragedy is inherent in disabled people's lives. Thus, disabled people can be seen as a more 'serious subject' than non-disabled people, conflating Bergson's and Freud's theorisation of the comic and 'the serious' with the presumption of the tragedy of disabled people's lives, as Corker suggested. These assumptions reflect the dominance of ideas of tragedy in wider discourses of disability and impairment, and notions of invulnerability in those who are non-disabled, both of which have been theorised and challenged by scholars aligned with Disability Studies, especially in work on cultural representations of disabled people (see Gartner and Joe, 1987; Kriegel, 1987; Longmore, 1987; Barnes, 1992; Norden, 1994; Shakespeare, 1994; Mitchell and Snyder, 2000; Wilde, 2004b; and Quayson, 2007). Again, on this topic of the centring of tragedy, Corker was critical of the *dys* appearance of disabled bodies in their work. She explained that '*dys*'-appears means that the disabled body only 'appears' as a body which is in a dysfunctional state (*her emphasis*), a point which is echoed in various studies by Disability Studies scholars (as above), particularly Hughes and Paterson (1999). This *dys* appearance works to centre tragic discourses of disability. She wrote that Stronach and Allan had,

> made the dys-embodied disabled body central to both their text and counter-text, without problematizing the association between impairment

and materiality, and are thus unable to separate the disabled body and its subjectivity from the 'conspiracy of normality'. Because the dys-embodied disabled body is itself an enactment of naming 'tragedy' – a euphemism for individual impairment and 'lack' – disability in the collective sense disappears.

(Corker, 1999, 77)

Given the predominance of ideas which link comedy and tragedy in the cultural imaginary, a wide range of contemporary media, and much scholarly work on comedy and humour, it is clear that the relationship between the comic and the tragic is crucial to understanding the place of humour and comedy in society and culture and that it will play a big part in comprehending how comedy in general, and comedy film in particular, works to produce interpretations of impairment and disability. This can be seen to be an especially crucial area of analysis when considering how the 'tragedy model' of disability continues to dominate in a wide range of media, from newspapers (Briant et al., 2011) to Oscar winning films (Rodgers, 2012).

Quayson's extended analysis of what he terms 'aesthetic nervousness' is useful to a discussion of the relationship between tragedy and disability here. He defined aesthetic nervousness as 'when the dominant protocols of representation within the literary text are short-circuited in relation to disability' (Quayson, 2007, 15). This is evident, in character interactions, plot, narrative, 'symbols and motifs', text and reader and so on, all working together towards the 'construction of a universe of apparent corporeal normativity'

Further, Bolt has explained that Quayson's work on aesthetic nervousness' focuses on the 'extreme anxiety' (Quayson, 2007, 17, cited in Bolt, 2013, 7) non-disabled people have in encountering disabled people, and says that Quayson

> recognizes corporeal difference as part of a structure of power that is based on the normate's unmarked regularities, but it is stressed that the impulse to categorize during interpersonal encounters is part of an assumed ideal of order.
>
> (Bolt, 2013, 7)

However, Quayson's analysis of Samuel Beckett's work on disability and impairment shows how Beckett resisted such anxiety, and it can therefore be seen to avoid the inevitability of the troubled relationship between comedy and tragedy posited by Stronach and Allen's argument. Quayson demonstrated how Beckett's work invariably included, and is often centred around, tragedy, comedy, and impairments, but that 'the absence of a structure of interlocution for addressing pain', 'allows' Beckett's drama to 'reside uneasily between tragedy and comedy' (Quayson, 2007, 83). Discussing the character of Molloy in the novel *Molloy*, he says 'His physical disabilities (*sic*) are not determinant factors of his identity and can be thus be set aside quickly once they are mentioned', arguing that impairments are seen here as 'ciphers of the frailty of the human condition and not to be read as markers of any real disability as such' (ibid.).[8] Similarly, speaking of *Molloy* as a whole (with no reference to the treatment of impairment), Parks (2014) has stated that there is 'something inexplicably recognisable about it all'. Thus, both Quayson and Parks have suggested a more universal appeal to all readers in Beckett's work, which contrasts sharply with Stronach and Allan's theorising of the co-presence of tragedy and impairment.

As suggested earlier, Stronach and Allan's argument for the existence of a taboo, and their analysis of disabled people's selfwork, offers a kind of permission to non-disabled people but also implies a self-policing, non-disabled audience, who have an 'aesthetic nervousness' about laughing at disability and 'impairment effects' (Thomas, 1999). The selfwork they propose is at its most obvious where the disabled people take responsibility for dealing with the consequences of impairment effects, e.g. when Laura, one of the two disabled people they analyse, rescues the situation of having accidentally poured water from a vase on her meal by laughing at herself. As Corker suggested (1999), Stronach and Allan's argument is dependent on the disabled person fitting themselves into normality, by making light of their own behaviour, where any humour is contingent on the disabled person's impairment, and/or impairment effects (Thomas, 1999). As some of the previous incidents of abuse from non-disabled people demonstrate, non-disabled people frequently laugh without 'permission' even in the face of considerable opposition.

Following Stronach and Allan's theorisation of tragedy and impairment, it might also be expected that narratives in theatre, television, and film must follow a trajectory which ties tragedy and impairment together in limited and almost inevitable ways, where the route beyond stereotypic assumptions is a dead end. Conversely, Parks' comment on Beckett's *Molloy* suggests that the novel challenges readers' prior assumptions and his own 'sense of what can be done with literature' (Parks, 2014, para 4). Also, given Quayson's reading of Beckett's work and the 'absence of a structure of interlocution for addressing pain', Beckett can be seen to extend what is possible in the comedic representation of impairment and disability, throwing any previous assumptions about the inevitability of particular kinds of portrayal (including links between impairment, disability, and comedy) into doubt. It might be argued, of course, that Samuel Beckett's work should be seen as an exceptional example of how to write impairment and disability differently in relation to comedy. However, as suggested, work such as Beckett's contests the specific idea that tragedy and comedy are inevitably intertwined, in particular and immutable ways, when it comes to disabled people. Indeed, examining the strategies used by writers who go beyond conventional tropes, as Beckett does, is far more likely to take us closer to understanding the transgressive possibilities of textual equity, or equality. This is a crucial aim for the reimagining of disabled people's lives, and for changing the ways in which media portrayals impact on the cultural recognition of disabled people, a goal which undoubtedly initiated Stronach and Allan's work on the tragic and the comic in the first place (Stronach and Allan, 1999, 31). Before the analysis of strategies which use or contest conventional tropes is conducted, in the next few chapters, it is first necessary to examine the seductive ideas of transgression, taboo, and political correctness in more depth, contextualising them in wider debates of comedic offence, especially to explore the relationship of authors to audience, and the potential injuries caused by punching 'up' or 'down'.

A closer look at political correctness, comedy, social hierarchies and the construction of 'offence' in recent television comedy

It is perhaps unsurprising, given the lack of evidence that the taboo theorised by Stronach and Allan exists, that a number of Deaf and disabled scholars have argued against the idea that there are taboos about laughing at disability and impairment, even if the debate on the desirability of 'political correctness' (PC) is far from resolved (see Mallett, 2009; Mallet, 2010; Coogan and Mallett, 2013). Shakespeare (1999b) has argued against the existence of such a taboo, suggesting that if some people feel joking about disabled people is wrong, then this is more to do with the *discomfort* they may feel about the harm it does to disabled people than a concern not to offend, or a taboo against making such jokes. Further, this belief that the comic is forbidden in discourses of disability is likely to feed into the idea that political correctness reigns and should therefore be opposed, ideas which are discussed in the work of scholars such as Mallett (2009; 2010). This belief is likely to be exacerbated by our knowledge of the public service broadcasting responsibilities of broadcasters. Mills, for example, has written of the 'public utility' element expected of comedy on British TV, and how this should fulfil purposes of meeting 'taste and standards' (Mills, 2011, 213), 'minimising offence while upholding ideas of free speech' (ibid., 224), simultaneously catering to audiences with very different perspectives and diverse ideas on what is and is not 'acceptable' (ibid.). As Mills demonstrates, through a case study of racist and disablist discourse on *Top Gear* (a TV programme about cars which promotes blustering forms of macho masculinity), there has been a continuing strain between the tendency to afford comedy a 'special freedom' (ibid., 212–216) and to regulate against those who are deemed to have gone too far, potentially to 'destabilise the social order' (ibid., 216).

However, there has been an opposition to the perceived yoke of political correctness over the past two decades, something which can be seen to be a hallmark of 'disability comedy' which has been commissioned by UK broadcasters since the early 2000s, especially shows such as *Little Britain* and *The Office*, and even in *The Last Leg*. The challenge to 'political correctness' could also be seen to be present in cinema throughout the 1990s, most notably in the films of the Farrelly Brothers, and the genre of 'gross-out' comedy, which I discuss in Chapter Six, focussing specifically on the ways in which political correctness and the agency of disabled and non-disabled people are addressed in the gross-out cinema genre. Indeed, Littlewood and Pickering, writing on comedy, suggest that some forms of discrimination were mitigated by this challenge (Littlewood and Pickering, 1998), though they focus on sexism and racism, not disability.

The recent, and current, assaults on political correctness can be seen in the terms of a backlash. We have seen evidence of backlash against anti-racist trends and multiculturalism from the early 2000s which has been analysed in collections such as Vertovec and Wessendorf (2010). Faludi (1991) argued that there is a backlash against women whenever they are perceived to have gained more equal rights, and are seen to have more agency, and these socio-cultural dynamics which work to re-adjust shifts (or perceived shifts) of power are just as apparent in disability politics. This can be seen to be driven by the new media, in a similar way as Faludi theorised of the feminist backlash, evident for example in the report on disability in the print media (Briant et al., 2011) and the 'pejorative' ways in which disabled people are discussed and conceptualised, as 'scroungers', 'scivers', and 'cheats', in articles which position people with impairments as a 'burden' to economy and society (ibid., 5). Given the rise of such reporting, it is unsurprising that surveys in the UK demonstrated a decline in public attitudes towards disabled people in this period (Aiden and McCarthy, 2014).

Although some may believe such a backlash is good, and possibly progressive, welcoming new and liberating freedoms of speech into our lives,[9] even seen to encourage debate, (Nicholson, 2016), I question the basis for assuming there is a need to break these supposed taboos, even if the right-wing media might promote it for these very reasons, as Stewart Lee (2007) suggests. Given such media messages it is also probable that much of their popularity and success is based upon such suppositions. It is possible, even easy, to read *Little Britain, The Office, Extras, Derek, Life's Too Short, I'm Spazticus,* and *The Last Leg*, from a position which would reveal the intent to raise public awareness of prejudice and discrimination; for analysis of some of these television programmes, see Lockyer, 2010; Brabazon, 2005; Higgie, 2017; McKenna, 2015, and Heaney, 2016. *The Last Leg* in particular set out with such intentions from the beginning, aiming to combine 'self-deprecation' with 'inclusive language', to the point where journalist Gary Nunn asked if we were now 'at the point where political correctness has paid off' (2012, para 10) and therefore ready for 'humour in coverage of disabled people without it sounding patronising' (ibid., para 13).

However, discussing the work of non-disabled comedians such as Sasha Baron Cohen (*Borat*), David Walliams and Matt Lucas (*Little Britain*), and Ricky Gervais (*The Office* and *Extras*), Stewart Lee goes further in his comments (below) on how 'some sections of the viewing public' assume anti-PC sentiments and intent (Lee, 2007, para 3) in these particular shows. Like him, I believe there is a need to understand why some people 'insist on seeing attacks on PC' where there perhaps are none (ibid.) and whether this has shaped the dominance of anti-PC humour in contemporary comedy (regardless of its authors' intent), both in terms of the comedy content we expect and appreciate, and also in who is most likely to be presenting it, e.g. who gets their work commissioned and why.[10] Referring to both television and film, Lee discussed so-called anti-PC shows on his website in 2007, saying that they can be 'broadly lumped under a banner of the comedy of shock, bad taste and outrage', and he wrote that such television shows

> show no immediate signs of disappearing. But reading about these shows in print and on-line, they are often described in a way that makes me, for one, feel as if I have been watching different material to everyone else. For many viewers and critics, Borat, Little Britain and The Office and Extras represent blows against the monstrous, and perhaps largely imagined, regiment of politically correct thinkers, who impinge upon our basic freedoms on a daily basis. (2007, para 1)

Some of the answers to why these writers, and some of the audience imagine this 'regiment', can perhaps be traced to the history of political correctness which Allan and Burridge outlined. As they explained, the American New Left's appropriation of this term to mock their own political/ideological excesses, used as an ironic form of policing, was subsequently

> co-opted by conservatives, who stripped it of its ironical element and turned the meaning on its head, thereby creating a sneer (or snarl) phrase to rubbish left-wing activities such as affirmative action.
> (Allan and Burridge, 2006, 92)

In many ways then, political positioning is at the centre of these debates, discussions which tend to have been held mainly in the UK and the US in the last century, being representative of political disputes going back as far as Plato and Aristotle, the former with a more negative view of its 'subversive' traits and the diminishment of the authority of the elites, and the latter claiming its 'cathartic and educative' properties (Ritchie, 2010, 159–160). However, as Medhurst (2007) argued, comedy and humour are always contextual, and bound up with specific cultures and nationalities and frequently indexed closely to feelings of belonging and home. He stated, 'momentarily, comedy settles you and the place you feel settled is often the place you feel at home' (2007, 20). A corollary of this is that nothing, or perhaps, few things, can be universally funny, and that interpretation will differ according to social and subject positioning and psychological and emotional needs. So, even the project of defining political correctness and alternative comedy will differ according to context and perspective, even within a homogenous audience. But, untying this Gordian knot of what makes humour and comedy funny, and evaluating the rights and wrongs of these forms of pleasure, must surely demand analysis of politics and political positioning?[11] Taking such an approach to comedy and humour means that we go further in finding the means to 'unlock the mystery of meaning in language' (Evans, 2015), as fundamental to understanding communication in general, and, here, the meanings attributed to disability more specifically.

Punching up and down – political and social divisions, and perceptions of offence

One dimension of humour common to all audiences will be the recognition of the politics of different types of comedy in terms of 'punching up' or 'punching down' (or kicking up or down), unless, of course, we see the hierarchy of power differently.[12] The notion of kicking up or down has also been regularly discussed by journalists and comedians in the UK and US; for example, Green's article about Molly Ivins (an outspoken US columnist and author) finishes with this quote from Ivins:

> There are two kinds of humor, . . . One kind that makes us chuckle about our foibles and our shared humanity – like what Garrison Keillor does. The other kind holds people up to public contempt and ridicule – that's what I do. Satire is traditionally the weapon of the powerless against the powerful. I only aim at the powerful. When satire is aimed at the powerless, it is not only cruel – it's vulgar.
>
> (Green, 1991, Para 15)

Here Ivins is asserting both a political and moral agenda in the use of humour, also referencing matters of 'good' or 'vulgar' taste. This echoes the work of Friedman (2014), especially his call for us to take comedy and humour seriously as a form of cultural currency which plays a significant role in our understanding and judgements of taste, attitudes embodied in the processes and dynamics of social stratification. Humour could be seen to encourage unanticipated shifts in cultural taste and to perpetuate elitism and cultural snobbery. British comedian and writer Ivor Dembina, for example, sees alternative comedy as having played a role in the maintenance of social boundaries, in encouraging/dictating more bourgeois senses of 'taste'. Dembina is reported to have argued 'working-class people talking to a working-class audience' were replaced with middle-class comedians, a process which was driven both by 'hatred of the working class' and commercialisation (Chortle, 2016). Echoing these sentiments, Littlewood and Pickering have demonstrated the homogeneity of the alternative comedy trend (1998, 300–302) particularly in respect of the dominance of the alternative comedy scene by male, white heterosexual men (I would also add non-disabled). In particular, they question 'the relationship between the dominant teller and the "other-who-is-told", even if told afresh' (ibid., 302). It is also a notable omission that alternative comedy, as a new mode which was 'united by an experimental approach to comedy' which was 'overtly political' with the 'vilification of the bigotry attributed to the trad generation' who had come before (Friedman, 2014, 19; 20), did not lead to greater expectations of the need for 'permission' from disabled people to make jokes *about* them, or a recognition that disabled people should be making such jokes.

This also resonates strongly with contemporary debates in comedy about disability (alternative and 'anti-PC'), where non-disabled people, such as Ricky Gervais, as story-tellers seem to lead the field (especially as writers/directors), raising significant questions about the voice of disabled people, often implying that there was a period of political correctness in respect of disabled people. This is significant, especially when a considerable number of disabled comedians are working, but are largely excluded from the mainstream (see Cockburn, 2012) particularly where they proffer similar types of 'cynical' comedy as Gervais; Ted Shiress (2013, para 3) said that, after doing a pilot, a TV company declined to broadcast his show because 'my views are too much of a contrast to how they want to illustrate disability'. This lends weight to Dembina's argument, and suggests that it is not always the content of the stories told which determines contracts and careers, but who is telling them. And on the other side, there are audiences who are waiting to hear views which resonate with their own experiences and opinions; this is clear across a range of marginalised groups who tend to have to make identifications with a limited a number of restricted stereotypes, due to the centring of characters which relate most closely with the biosocial characteristics of the presumed white, male, non-disabled viewers (see Latif, and Latif, 2016, on race, for example).

Class and comedy

In the case of class, however, marginalisation is often reduced to a particular section of the working class, with right-wing attitudes towards the inclusion of oppressed groups. In an interview with Arnot (2007), Medhurst suggested that Roy Chubby Brown, a comedian who would be aligned with a working-class, 'offensive' (sexist, racist, homophobic, and disablist) tradition

> gives a voice to people who don't have one. He sticks up two fingers at the liberal-progressive consensus, and stands up for the white, predominantly northern working class that Tony Blair liked to pretend doesn't exist anymore. He says things that they've been told they can't say and, because of that, he's a hero to them.

As a white man who came from a precarious background (Brown, 2006), Chubby Brown's positioning and popularity with working-class audiences has clear analogies with the rise of Donald Trump and the symbolic value of Trump offering to make the so-called 'forgotten majority' feel that they matter (Capehart, 2017). This suggests the long-standing existence of an audience demographic who never went away, welcoming, or seeking, cultural outlets for resentment and discriminatory ideas which support feelings of superiority, as a means to enhanced self-worth (on the grounds of race, ethnicity, gender, and sexuality, if not so much on class), despite perceptions that comedy tastes have changed.

The evidence of different trends in comedy across time periods, with sexist, racist, and homophobic comedians dominating the 1970s, such as Bernard Manning, Jim Davidson, and Roy Chubby Brown (in the UK), is thus rather over-simplified. A cursory glimpse further back into the twentieth century suggests cycles of popularity, revealing that popular comedy before this time (and during the 1970s and 1980s) was dominated by a very middle-class range of (mainly white, male) comedians. Many previous comedians have been members of Oxbridge, e.g. the Cambridge Footlights; people such as Peter Cook, Dudley Moore, Jonathan Miller, David Frost, Michael Bentine (also an Eton schoolboy), and the members of the Monty Python Comedy Group. Moreover, 'higher' and 'lower' forms of comedy taste can also be found when examining the history of radio (Foster and Furst, 1996; Nesteroff, 2016) and music hall comedy (Kift, 1996).

It is also clear that internationally the comedy landscape invariably includes a mix of comedy types, with people such as Andrew Dice Clay becoming famous in the US in the alternative comedy climate of late 1980s and early 1990s, especially for his anti-PC offensiveness (see Zinoman, 2016, for example). Similarly, Joan Rivers' popularity grew in this period (Goldman, 2009), who was also considered 'offensive', first performing in the 1960s but becoming a major television celebrity from the 1980s, just before the ascendancy of the US alternative comedy scene Kharach (2006).

It is also clear to see that alternative comedy and non-PC comedy cannot be mapped onto social background so easily, and that there are many anomalies to these trends, not least that both Clay (Clay, 2014) and Rivers (Goldman, 2009) were not from poor backgrounds, even if Rivers' family had more precarious roots (Goldman, 2009). However, the few examples given on this and the previous page might suggest that working-class comedians and their audiences prefer comedy which is more likely to be anti-PC, favouring racist, sexist, xenophobic, homophobic, transphobic, and disablist humour, primarily because they give 'voice' to white working-class people who feel 'silenced', 'invalidated', and 'dismissed' (Capehart, 2017). But there are also many famous and well-loved comedians from, or associated with, more working-class backgrounds, who have tended not to 'punch down' at groups commonly discriminated against. This would include comedians such as Peter Kay, Victoria Wood and Billy Connolly, whose content would align them more with observational and music comedies.

Similarly, despite Friedman's finding that there were high degrees of social stratification in comedy tastes in British Society, the tastes of audience members he identified as having 'Low Cultural Capital' (LCC) were not found to be an exact fit with the anti-PC comedians. That is, although those from lower socio-economic groups tended to align themselves more closely with lowbrow comedy, where UK anti-PC comedians, such as Bernard Manning, Jim Davidson, Benny Hill and Roy 'Chubby' Brown, were to be found

(Friedman, 2014, 51), Friedman found less evidence of an 'aversion' to 'highbrow' comedy amongst them; their choices suggested, rather, a lack of awareness of their existence. The majority of 'alternative comedians' were located in the highbrow range (ibid.). However, significantly, the lowbrow status category includes others who could not be aligned with anti-PC sentiments, having become increasingly associated with Michael McIntyre over time. Friedman indicated that this is linked to his increased popularity, giving weight to the idea that 'popularity devalues' (ibid. 53), and rarity increases worth, especially for the 'culturally privileged', acting as sign of distinction, as a 'status marker' (ibid., 61).

It is of some significance, then, that Friedman found that those from LCC backgrounds often appreciated the skills or 'aesthetic superiority' (ibid., 84) of the comedians most associated with High Cultural Capital (HCC), but simultaneously demonstrated a reluctance to accept the 'moral values communicated through highbrow comedy' (2014, 84). In accordance with these tendencies, Friedman theorised a 'tension between defiance vs deference in LCC styles of appreciation' (ibid., Friedman's emphasis). Friedman contends that this is related to the need of people designated as possessing LCC to use moral worth and 'sub-cultural capital' as a means to 'preserve their dignity' (ibid., 85) as a so-called 'forgotten majority'. This, in turn might tell us something about the moral values of those with HCC and MCC (mixed cultural capital) status, and their relative cultural omnivorousness. It perhaps suggests an ease and feelings of greater freedom in moral positioning, which might emanate from the propensity of those on the higher social rungs to 'feel that they matter'. Somewhat ironically then, as Stewart Lee's own comedy has suggested, identification with alternative comedy such as his own is associated with HCC, in an aesthetic ranking which places him at the pinnacle, which can be seen to act as an expression of cultural taste and identity which works to 'identify and pathologise' those with less cultural capital and lower socioeconomic positions.[13] This can be seen to be exposing a 'stark form of cultural snobbery and render visible comedy's role in contemporary processes of symbolic violence' (ibid., 4). There are perhaps lessons to be learned here for those seeking to re-position the voice of disabled people within representations of disability, especially in relation to popularity, aesthetic value, symbolic violence, and the perceived risks of what is being said, who is saying it and who they are telling it to. On that note, we may ask . . .

When is an offensive joke not an offensive joke? And what does it tell us about comedy and the media industries? An analysis of an anti-pc joke told by Jerry Sadowitz

Simon Munnery has stated that there were 'three tenets' to alternative comedy in the UK; anti-racist, anti-sexist and 'do your own material' (Munnery, 2016, para 4). However, even the apolitical performers did not 'punch down', including two of the 'beyond genre' acts Munnery identifies – the ice-melting

Ice Man, and Jerry Sadowitz (Munnery, 2016). Sadowitz's comedy is of particular note in that he is claimed for alternative comedy (as above), and also as the 'godfather of a new breed of PC-baiting comics' such as Ricky Gervais (Kettle, 2011, para 4), with Sadowitz, claiming himself to be more offensive than Bernard Manning (Blackpool Gazette, 2011). However, as someone who began to 'say the unsayable', a quality often attributed to the PC-baiters, Kettle reports Sadowitz's regret that anti-PC comedians have 'hijacked' his material to give 'nasty people a good living' (ibid., para 4). As vitriolic as Sadowitz's comedy is (commonly referred to as 'black' 'sick' and 'irreverent'), he is a good, if complex, example of what Ivins was saying about satire, especially in his treatment of the powerful as targets of humour, and cruelty, with much of his comedy punching 'up'. An oft-quoted line of his came from the *Just for Laughs* comedy festival in Montreal, which has been cited in a number of media articles and reviews, almost always without reference to the wider point/context of the joke, understandably 'causing offence' to Canadians and others. Revolvy.com (2017, para 10), one of the very few sources to quote the whole joke, reported it thus:

> 'Hello moosefuckers! I tell you why I hate Canada, half of you speak French, and the other half let them.' . . . The rarely quoted follow up line, which Sadowitz claims is what actually led to him being attacked was 'Why don't you speak Indian? You might as well speak the language of the people you stole the country off of in the first place.'

So, the first part of the joke may encourage us to think that Sadowitz's humour is divisive of the local population, stirring up pre-existing tensions in an area he knows has French as its only official language. However, his greeting of 'Hello Moosefuckers!' clearly establishes him as an outsider from the start, an action which can be read as an insult to the local population, or as a way of including himself as a member of a wider community of nationalist bigots. It is also of some note that Scottish people are reputed (or stereotyped) as being rude (Scotney, 2010), whereas Canada is known for politeness (Cardona, 2017), so Sadowitz can be seen to be drawing on both of these stereotypes, ostensibly leaving no-one out in his drive to 'say the unsayable'. Nonetheless, the main aim of the part of the joke can be interpreted as an attack on French speakers which simultaneously positions those with a first language of English as superior; i.e. the word 'let' suggests an authoritative position which endows permission. However, the follow-up line is a direct reference to pre-existing language, the greater authenticity of native claims, and cultural robbery, which works to remove any such feelings of superiority, potentially equalising the colonialising pasts of both the British and the French, and bringing attention to their brutalities, whilst reminding us of the wider historical/geographical, and linguistic picture, before European settlers. This can be seen to disrupt both English and French discourses, reconfiguring his ostensible support for English speakers' claims, challenging the desirability of nationalistic discourses en masse (pun intended).

Thus, with the full joke, we can see the attack on Sadowitz by the audience member is most likely to have been caused by the 'punch-up' conclusion of the joke. Looking at 'offence' evoked by this joke which throws 'contempt and ridicule' at the powerful (in this case, predominantly white settlers), this can be seen as satire rather than cruelty (in Green's terms, 1991). It is possibly of some significance, then, that this joke has often been quoted to suggest that Sadowitz is 'punching down', perhaps lending some weight to those who 'hijack' his approach to claim that it is legitimate, or preferable, to be an 'equal opportunities offender'.

One of the things which seems key here is social context, as suggested in part by scholars such as Shakespeare and Corker. Put simply, is it actually possible to be an 'equal opportunities offender' in a society which has such gaping inequalities, and where the opportunity to speak of the social world seems to be largely premised on one's position within an increasingly unequal society where opportunities to contribute to public discourse are indexed closely to one's position in the social-economic hierarchy? Put in the context of what is produced in the cultural industries, this becomes a crucial point. Hall (2012, para 2) has reported on the importance of family ties, correct 'accents, hair, clothes and backgrounds' in gaining entry to the film and television industries, placing matters of class position, the possession of the right sorts of cultural capital, and particular forms of embodiment (racialised, gendered and so on) at the forefront of concerns.

Although we might expect comedy to lie outside the domain of cultural elitism, due to perceptions of its lowly cultural status, Friedman's ethnographic investigation of 'the strength and legitimacy of cultural capital' (2014, 125–161) shows this to be far from the case. In particular, he found an 'informal association between the aesthetic principles valued by comedy critics' (mainly journalistic reviewers) and comedy audience interviewees who were identified as having High Cultural Capital and suggested that they play 'an important role in the *mediation of cultural value*' (Friedman, 2014,142, his *emphasis*), even if this may not constitute a 'causal relationship' between critic and audiences. However, his analysis of comedy scouts, who he refers to as the 'hidden tastemakers', provides a much greater link between audience comedy tastes and the dominance of elites within the industry. He explained that comedy scouts are usually 'positioned in the sub-field of mass production' (2014, 147), including comedy agents of both 'high-profile' and 'emerging talent', comedy commissioners for television and radio broadcasters, owners of comedy clubs, comedy bookers, producers from production companies, and other comedy producers (ibid.). Despite using a theoretical sample of people, chosen to 'reflect' the 'contours in the wider field' (ibid.), he found that eight out of nine of these scouts came from 'privileged backgrounds'. This has clear implications for who gets seen and heard on the comedy landscape, not least for those comedians who cannot access the venues in which they might be 'discovered' (see Cockburn, 2012, for a brief exploration of inaccessibility for disabled comedians). It also has wider implications for whose voices are heard in film comedy, exacerbated by the tendency for the film industry to 'overuse familiar ties', weakening both quality and diversity (de Lange, 2011, 42–43).

There are, of course, other ways of looking at the issue of 'offensive humour'. Palmer explains that, apart from the issues of political viewpoints, and perceptions that a comedian, or writer, is punching down or up, offence is more likely to be taken when jokes fail to amuse. He said

> this is the grounds for failure that Freud mentions in passing: a joke at someone's expense is unlikely to succeed if the audience consists of that person's friends, just as a cynical joke is unlikely to appeal to those who believe in the value or institution in question.
>
> (Palmer, 1994, 164)

Palmer offered three main variables which determine whether the joke will be considered 'offensive' rather than funny:

1. the structure of the joke itself, considered as a representation of the world external to the joke;
2. the relationship between the joke-teller and the others involved in the enunciation – the butt and the audience;
3. the nature of the occasion on which the attempt at humour is made.

(ibid., 164)

This framework is of some help in discerning issues of comedy co-production between comedians and their audiences, and it is worth noting that all these dimensions were key aspects of Stronach and Allan's analysis. Indeed, it may also help us in understanding why Sadowitz was punched in Montreal and why it was then misrepresented by the media. It is perhaps informative also in understanding, and contextualising, the reaction of disabled scholars (including myself) to Stronach and Allan's ideas on disability and comedy.

Taking Sadowitz's joke as an example, even though we might ordinarily expect an audience member to identify themselves with the humour they have chosen to see, it is likely that Sadowitz, as someone who is commonly perceived and referred to as Scottish, though he was born in America, was seen by the attacker (and possibly other local audience members) as an outsider to the culture of Quebec. If we take the second part of the joke as the catalyst for offence, or as the final straw to the joke which references Québécois tensions on the primacy of the French language, we can see that the punchline (sic) actually punches up, in line with alternative comedy. However, the structure of the joke allows a double representation of Québécois culture and history, and the way it might be perceived as an outsider to Canada, as a culture divided by language (and a first comment which can be initially read as 'punching down', as suggested), with a doubly troubling past, mired in colonialism. Further, in relation to the second of Palmer's points, on the context and relations of enunciation, Sadowitz might easily be deemed as a guest who is expected to be respectful of the province which was hosting him – a principle which was clearly breached. Finally, this was an occasion which was celebrating Montreal as a host for comedy, providing another reason for offence. However, taking us back to all three variables, it is perhaps the subsequent circulation of this joke which is of greatest cultural significance, especially given the ambiguous position that Sadowitz occupies between alternative comedy and the more recent trend for anti-PC comedy. The main question I am raising here is why his offensiveness has been indexed to the former part of the joke in mainstream media, particularly as this is the part of the joke which can be seen to punch down, as discussed, enabling racists to claim Sadowitz as a taboo-busting renegade. The structure is completely changed in the re-telling, and the enunciative relationship I have explained is radically different to the re-presentation of Sadowitz as a xenophobe. Subsequent media coverage changes the butt of the joke from the entire audience and xenophobes in general to the Québécois members of the audience and their wider community. The editing of this joke for a much wider potential audience is also a very different occasion to the intimacy, and context-rich milieu, of its origin. Additionally, the reconfiguration of the joke, added to his reputation as a 'comedy genius', can be seen to play a significant role in representing the world external to the joke as one where anything goes and taboos are there to be broken. In sum, these changes could be seen as a misrepresentation of Sadowitz's comedy, and a re-purposing of his 'no taboos' approach for political ends. The highlighting of national tensions and the support of the media's status quo seems to be far from his original intentions whilst media coverage spares us the detail of the broader historical critique and his explicit exposition of its distinctly racist dimensions.

Bearing Palmer's variables, intentionality and social context, in mind, the following chapters will use tools and approaches from film studies and disability studies to examine such intersections of offensive and political humour in comedy films, exploring the ways in which humour and comedy has been used to re-present disability and impairment. Like the joke above, I will consider the complexity of humour, in order to explore who is speaking about who, for whom, and what the embedding of these positions in comedy might mean for different audiences.

Notes

1 See, for example, Deleuze (2013a), *Cinema 1*, pp. 119–21. This is discussed briefly by Vitale (2011b).
2 Indeed, Totoro (2000) argues that Deleuze's ideas, especially his 'noted shift from movement-image to time-image' are closely related to 'Tarkovsky's views on cinema as *sculpting in time*' (para 27, author's asterisks).

3 She demonstrates this, showing how authors present arguments which can be read as implicitly sarcastic about previous research by competing scholars.
4 See McKinstry's 'A-Z of politically correct madness', for example, in the *Daily Mail* (2017). Many of the comments have been deleted, much like exchanges with Karl Pilkington and Stephen Merchant of Victoria Wright (a disabled actress and writer) who, with Karl Pilkington and Stephen Merchant, was ridiculed for her "big 'ed", and compared to Bo Selecta, a comedy figure played by Leigh Francis wearing a large mask, something which resulted in more 'verbal abuse and threats of violence' in her everyday life (Scott and Champniss, 2009).
5 Referring to cultural, rather than economic inequalities in attitudes towards disabled people, a call for recognition for a full acknowledgement of their humanity, rather than the 'misrecognition' which emanates from prejudicial views.
6 This is a co-authored journal article which goes from plural to singular style when presenting this example, and I am presuming this is Paterson speaking, because I have heard him present this example as a conference paper.
7 It should be noted that the Disability Arts community is a diverse one, and here I am referring to Paul Darke's exposition of the initial goals of Disability Arts. He defines these thus:

> Disability Arts is about the nature of the barbarism of contemporary culture in relation to itself through explorations of the construction of otherness and disability. As most non-disability canonical art practice was, and still is, structured around the cultural hegemonic of normality, Disability Art is a threat to the core aesthetic values of contemporary cultures. Thus, Disability Art is, perhaps, the last great revolutionary art at humanity's disposal that is solely humanitarian and non-ideological.
>
> (Darke, 2003)

8 Quayson tends to use this terminology to refer to impairments, despite presenting a critical analysis of cultural representations of disability, aligned to the goals of both disability studies and postcolonial theory.
9 This kind of attitude can be seen, for example, in the contemporary use of the word 'snowflake' as a means to silence those who are seen to promote politically correct solutions such as better education, and who are noted for their propensity to express offence – see Nicholson (2016).
10 Lee questions the anti-PC ness of this comedy and says that comedy has always been about, amongst other things, 'taboo-busting' and 'somehow bound up explicitly in contemporary cultural negotiations with the ephemeral' (2007, para 8).
11 People may say that this is something that should not be done, especially as this is likely to 'spoil' jokes. Quite simply, I disagree. Although there are, admittedly, forms of comedy I enjoy as 'guilty pleasures' which I choose not to analyse, I regard humour and comedy as a fundamental part of social experience, as outlined, to be dismissed in fear of 'spoiling' a joke, when there is so much to be gained from understanding its place in society, in all domains.
12 See Bucaria and Barra (2016) for a more extended discussion of this in relation to comedy and taboo.
13 As a regular audience member I have witnessed Stewart Lee condemning his audience, as part of his comedy, on this very issue.

3 Contemporary comedy
Subjectivity, genre, and impairment

Look who's talking! – Comedy, censorship and the 'tolerant subject'

Shakespeare demonstrated how much meaning is likely to differ according to who is making the joke and to whom (1999b). Accordingly, he showed some of the ways that humour about impairment and disability has a key role to play in creating shared identities and solidarity within some disabled people's communities, such as that epitomised in Albrecht's concept of 'crip humour' (1999). He also illustrated how this can lead to greater understanding between disabled and non-disabled people. He argued, for example, that disabled people using humour about themselves which acknowledges our 'failure' may help to address and navigate 'tensions' and 'anxieties' in non-disabled audiences, who may otherwise have an 'unbearable weight of empathy which they feel obligated to carry' (ibid., 1999, 52) – perhaps leading us to the conditions of possibility for 'communication to overcome stigma' (ibid., 53). This appears to be true for *The Last Leg*, a British television programme, providing the social context of a television community which is led by two disabled men (Alex Brooker and Adam Hills) and one non-disabled man (Josh Widdecombe), inviting others in to the joke, often about their own impairments and personality flaws. Of course, this may be read according to Stronach and Allan's theorisation where Brooker and Hills' actions are seen as responses to their own acknowledgement of their weaknesses, and as attempts to 'switch the register', 'reclaiming the event for farce, rather than tragedy', designed for 'attracting the laughter of others' (Stronach and Allan, 1999, 32). Further, whilst some of this comedy could be regarded as selfwork, in Stronach and Allan's terms, as both Hills and Brooker often joke explicitly about their physical 'differences', these performances of self are very different from those observed by Stronach and Allan; they certainly do not position themselves as failed 'others' as they joke about each other's impairments, and these jokes and insults are presented as 'banter'. This humour is distributed quite evenly amongst them, with Josh Widdicombe also joking about Hills and Brooker and being on the receiving end of their provocations. Bearing these features in mind, Palmer's theorisation of offence-taking would suggest that even if this programme began by 'switching the register', it is certainly no longer the case, after the show has run for some time (on its thirteenth series at the beginning of 2018). Of particular significance here is 'the relationship between the joke-teller and the others involved in the enunciation – the butt and the audience', which is fluid and relational, with all the presenters taking their turn. Thus, 'the nature of the occasion on which the attempt at humour is made' is always one where both non-disabled and disabled people have equal stakes (Palmer, 1994, 164). In many ways, then, *The Last Leg* can be seen to place the 'tolerant subject position' at its core, and create humour about it, as the joke is perhaps one which we can all share in, disabled people and non-disabled having the 'last laugh' about disability together.

I have begun to show how humour has been, and can be, used as both an offensive weapon against disabled people, as a shield (Koller, 1988) to protect ourselves and others – and also, perhaps most fruitfully, as a place where we can all find common ground, possibilities for resistance, and forms of identification where these were previously scant. Even cursory analysis of recent trends in comedy, and disability and representation, especially the popularity of anti-political correctness, has suggested that there is a strong desire to make jokes about impairment and disablement, and that there is a large audience for this, even if the ways in which this is done vary widely. Important concerns which arise are those about who delivers the punches and in which direction they fly.

Television and the tolerant subject, and the shaping of 'offence'

It is clear that comedy which centres the 'tolerant subject' (Mallett, 2010, 6, following McRuer, 2006) has been a popular focus over the last two decades, seen clearly in the preoccupations of *I'm Spazticus* and *The Office*, and also in *The Last Leg*. The positioning of this figure can be seen to operate in the responses of innocent bystanders to pranks, focusing on their ambivalent and embarrassed responses in *I'm Spazticus* sketches, in the actions and discourses of the pathetic character of David Brent in *The Office*, and also in the popularity of *The Last Leg's* #isitok hashtag, which plays with our social boundaries and their transgression (see Ryan, 2016, or Winch, 2012, for example). It also operated in *Little Britain* (see Lockyer, 2010a), for a range of analyses on this show), a programme which predated *The Office* by a year, being broadcast on radio from 2000, and then on television until 2003. The characters of Lou Todd and Andy Pipkin are of particular note here, with Andy testing his companion Lou's 'tolerance' and selflessness to its limits, often deserting his wheelchair to do very physical activities when Lou has left to do brief errands (such as using his wheelchair to climb into the lion's enclosure while Lou gets them both an ice cream).

To explain the idea of the 'tolerant subject', I will draw briefly on *The Office*; as Mallett (2010) has demonstrated, the character of David Brent, played by one of the writers Ricky Gervais (the other being Stephen Merchant), exemplifies this figure. The audience are encouraged to sympathise with discriminatory ideas against women and disabled people because the character of Brent is placed centre stage, and we continually witness his half-hearted and futile attempts to understand and re-present his place within discriminatory processes and practices. This is a portrayal which is balanced well with the contrasting masculinities and struggles of Tim (Michael Freeman), Gareth (Mackenzie Crook) and (occasionally) Chris Finch (Ralph Ineson). As Brabazon demonstrates, the narratives are powerful in depicting how these men's trajectories show the 'brutality of their daily failures and humiliation by displacing them onto the disempowered' (2005, 114) (although this applies less to Tim, who only tends to take his frustrations of his underachievement and his irritation at this working environment out on Gareth). As Brabazon states, it is once again 'men directing the narrative' (ibid., 103). She argues that 'women, gay men, black communities and people with disabilities are continually ridiculed, categorized and implicated in the patriarchal project' (ibid., 113). As suggested, this male-directed narrative is so thoroughly imbricated with the oppression of bodies which are 'other' to the male, white, non-disabled, heterosexual identities, it returns our primary attachment to Brent, and the plight of the men who are so central to the office structure and storylines. Indeed, Gervais has remarked that *The Office* is 'all about white, middle-class angst, male angst' (McLean, 2016, para 5).

Mallett (2010, 6, following McRuer, 2006) has argued that 'David Brent reveals by a mechanism of excess, the provisionality of the tolerant subject position, with the comedy coming from the failure of that positioning', suggesting that the audience are also implicated in the failure of this 'tolerant' subject position. Both McCruer and Mallett theorise that this subject position emanates from neoliberal capitalism, which is 'less rigid' in its global reproduction of (deepening) social inequalities, and that such economies require a 'system of unacknowledged compulsory ablebodiedness' (ibid., 6).

Brent is, it seems, the epitome of this 'tolerant subject' who feels he has to be seen to be 'visible and spectacularly tolerant' (McRuer, 2006, 2, also cited in Mallett, 2010) in the everyday arbitration of identities which he (clearly) sees as 'other' to the heterosexual and non-disabled norms he perceives himself to embody. In an era where processes of individuation (Beck, 1992) led to the type of crisis of subjectivity theorised by McRuer, this predicament can mean we struggle to understand diversity, and the claims made by less-entitled 'others'. It can be seen that many of us are unsure of our responsibilities as human beings whilst being confronted with the overwhelming choices and pressures to act as moral and ethical agents who have to attempt to gain knowledge, awareness and understanding in a vast, yet confusing ocean of information and experiences we have never had. These processes are exacerbated further by the increasing fluidity and fragmentation characteristic of late modernity (Bauman, 2000), especially in respect to the increasing uncertainties, chaos, and 'privatisation of ambivalence' (Bauman, 1993; Marotta, 2002) which are reproduced within 'liquid modernity', a stage of societal organisation where the certainties of former 'solid' forms of modernity have gone, and where the liquidizing powers have moved from the 'system' to 'society', from 'politics' to 'life-politics' – or have descended from the 'macro' to the 'micro' level of social cohabitation.

(Marotta, 2002, 40)

With the individual as the site for the resolution of dilemmas of diversity, who has to navigate the politics of everyday life, the figure of Brent, as the 'tolerant subject' is one which is seductive in its appeal to the privatised uncertainties and ambivalence which we all face. Significantly, Mallett (2010) suggests that the comedy in *The Office* (and similar depictions of the crisis of the 'tolerant subject') is created by these deeply flawed performances of tolerance, thus disrupting the discourses of tolerance and diversity which we find aligned with alternative comedy and ideas of political correctness.

Reflecting Brent's crisis, the audience can easily recognise the increasing uncertainties, risks, and inequalities of a globalised society (Beck, 2007), and most, if not all, audience members are likely to identify deeply with 'the indeterminacies of global ethics' (Brassett, 2009, 223), which Gervais's work appears to be embedded in, situated within the ubiquitous landscape of post-industrial office culture. As Beck explained in his theory of 'risk society' and increasing individuation, as applicable to social risks as environmental dangers:

> The place of the value system of the 'unequal' society is taken by the value system of the 'unsafe' society. Whereas the utopia of equality contains a wealth of substantial and positive goals of social change, the utopia of the risk society remains peculiarly negative and defensive.
>
> (Beck, 1992, 49)

Indeed, it is perhaps this appeal to a righteous sense of self-limitation and defensiveness which lies at the core of comedy which centralises the figure of the traumatised and misunderstood 'tolerant subject'. Given the positioning of disabled people as marginal or external to this system, through 'compulsory ablebodiedness', and the existence of this 'tolerant subject position' in the minds, and probable dispositions, of the audience, empathy with David Brent is likely to be high, especially as he can be seen to struggle with his efforts to be tolerant on many fronts (equally getting it wrong and offending most people around him). In some ways then, we can conceptualise David Brent as 'everyone', or 'everyman'. Even though the punches tended to fly down at 'others', identifications can easily be made with him by non-disabled and disabled members of the audience, and members of other marginalised groups, indeed anyone who has any uncertainties or ambivalence about how to be an ethical person in the world. Reflecting back on Palmer's variables of offence-taking, the structure of jokes founded on our recognition of this figure appears to be recognisable to all, i.e. his situation can be 'considered as a representation of the world external to the joke' (Palmer, 1994, 164), or as Scannell theorises, a good example of the 'we world' creating a form of communication which is shared by all, a 'sociable world-in-common between human beings' (Scannell, 2000, 19); even if we have had the good fortune to have worked in or visited an office like this, there can be few who see this show who have not experienced the post-work cultures of the contemporary era epitomised in the show.

Conversely, as suggested, *I'm Spazticus* was a prank show which tested the limits of tolerance more explicitly, where the audience were encouraged to laugh with the disabled pranksters at the expense of non-disabled passers-by/bystanders. Genre seems to matter here, as the prank show provided a clear reversal of the usual social hierarchies which shattered the expectations of the (non-disabled) 'we-world' and thus, delivered an explicit 'message' about non-disabled people's assumptions of disability. It could be conceptualised as a 'for someone' structure, and was possibly feared by broadcasters as a form of narrowcasting. Indeed, the prank show might have attracted a larger audience or further series (it ran for just two years, 2012–2013), if it had adopted a more polyphonic structure, where the punches flew in all directions, and more equally; despite some self-deprecation it punched up at non-disabled people. A sketch from one episode of *I'm Spazticus* was criticised for fooling unwitting students into thinking a 'blind man' had assaulted a nude life model in their art class; this was subsequently withdrawn (reported by the BBC, in April 2012). Gervais's and Merchant's comedy has the same primary purpose of playing with non-disabled people's awkwardness as *I'm Spazticus,* but it has not been found culpable of offending anyone, or of breaching regulations, despite Ricky Gervais's comparable 'mong-gate' incident a few months earlier (see below).

The difference between the two shows is perhaps indicative of fears about the limits of tolerance for the 'model viewer' and the greater risks attributed to stories which centre those deemed 'other' to the 'everyman' figure. The *I'm Spazticus* sketch that used a disabled person to provide a direct mimetic challenge to one of the primary stereotypes of blindness as sexually deviant and excessive (see the explanation of Fenichel's work in the Introduction, and Wheatley [2010]) was withdrawn, after being taken at face value, despite its clear attempt to 'evoke' this common type of disablist misrecognition. Significantly this was considered as poor taste due to the trauma of the students who were not in on the joke (BBC, 2012). Conversely, the use of an ostensibly radical, mimetic strategy, was attributed to Gervais by Ofcom in respect of Gervais's use of disablist language in a performance (MacDonald, 2012), despite evidence to the contrary. He spoke about singer Susan Boyle thus:

> She would not be where she is today if it wasn't for the fact that she looked like such a ******* mong.
> (McDonald, 2012, para 4, author's asterisks)

This verbal attack has shown that, like the *I'm Spazticus* sketch, there was potential trauma to Susan Boyle, people with Down Syndrome, and other people with learning difficulties who often have to face such name-calling. As such there was no evocation of disablist misrecognition which might parody and illuminate the harm of conventional name-calling/hate speech, just a straightforward perpetuation of it. However, genre certainly has a significant role to play; one could argue for example that a prank show featuring non-disabled people playing pranks on disabled people would never be broadcast on contemporary television, and a panel show of non-disabled people regularly making fun of disabled people would also be unlikely. It may even have been possible that Ofcom would have been censorious if this had been a line from a different kind of show. Clearly fictional comedy is something of an exception for such hierarchical forms of 'transgressive' humour on television.

Genre matters

There has been a tendency in academic literature on cultural representations of disability and impairment to discuss representations of disability and impairment as though meanings are the same across genres. Equally, there is now a wealth of analysis of single impairment or disability representations, which focus on the meanings of specific media texts or literary works, in journals such as the *Journal of Literary and Cultural Disability Studies* (Liverpool University Press, since 2010). I am proposing that the analysis of impairment tropes needs to be discussed in relation to a consideration of genre, particularly as it is easy to discern a pattern in how many stereotypes arise according to genre; a clear example of this can be found in the figure of a wheelchair user (invariably male), or man with another mobility impairment, and his place in drama (see Norden, 1994, Darke, 1998, Wilde, 2004c). Similarly, Cheyne (2012) has also written of the need to examine genre in her introduction to literary depictions of disability, demonstrating how popular media tend to be avoided as texts for critical analysis – clearly a key area of concern in their potential for influencing contemporary attitudes.

Overall, analyses emphasising the ways in which pathological imagery has fed stigmatising and discriminatory attitudes has also tended to neglect issues of genre, particularly in the earlier stages of analysis in this area. If we examine Klobas's (1988) work which centred on impairment group stereotypes, for example, the way in which genre changes meaning tends to be obscured; although she analyses particular depictions within specific films and television shows, the focus of her study is on the generalisation of disabled people's portrayals by impairment groups. Although there has been a burgeoning of work in the area of cultural representation and disability since Klobas's study, there is a tendency to focus on particular impairments, often analysing a single film, show or piece of literature, or to use an impairment-based critique more generally (see Murray, 2008, on autism), rather than analyse disablement by genre. This kind of work has provided us with a deeper understanding of specific disability discourses, or impairment representations, but we still have limited knowledge of how that may or may not be typical of the genre. I have previously compared portrayals of mental health in two romantic comedy films, emphasising the visual and narrative strategies used, suggesting that particular genres of film, such as 'smart film', are likely to support more multi-dimensional portrayals, when compared to more traditional romantic comedies, or even 'nervous romances' (Wilde, 2018b), but portrayals of disabled people within the romantic comedy genre remain under-explored (a theme which is examined in the next chapter).

As Altman has proposed, a genre-based approach has the capacity to acknowledge the diversity of viewing experiences, their differing interpretations, and the 'relationships between those users' to 'actively consider the effect of multiple conflicting uses on the production, labelling and display of films and genres alike' (Altman, 1999, 214). As such, not only does the study of genre and sub-genre, and impairment and disability, provide a greater understanding of how meanings are constructed within specific social and cultural contexts, it is also crucial to understanding how meanings evolve, both in film-makers' intentions and in the understandings of their audiences, and the interactions between them, especially in charting processes of genrification (ibid., 62–68). Significantly, although the importance of the study of genre has been demonstrated in work on race/ethnicity and gender (e.g. Williams, 1991; Bell et al., 1995; Grant, 2007), research on genre, impairment, and disability is scant. A recent report which includes the examination of genre in its study of inequalities within film does not explore how genre interacts with either disability or LGBQT portrayals (Smith et al., 2017) in its examination of other forms of inequality in the film industry, e.g. the low numbers of characters or actors from these communities.

I am contending that an understanding of how genres evolve, and the development of specific tropes and modes of address within them, will illuminate the shifting conditions of possibility for representations of impairment and disability, a discussion which will be a significant part of each of the genre-based chapters which follow. Altman's brief analysis of feminist film theory and the relationship of the (shifting) concept of 'woman's film' to woman's film provides a useful comparison, with the former applied to genres such as the melodrama (Altman, 1999, 72–77) and the latter as a 'substantive' category applicable to all films. This is a good and comparable example of how film criticism and genres feed into one another, evolve, and change in cycles which lead to new phases of re-genrification, shifts in representation, and changing ideas of women's media (who produces it and so on). As Altman argues, 'the evolution of genres through semantic or syntactic shifts deserves far more attention' (ibid., 225), and nowhere is this more true than in understanding the evolution of meanings attributed to disability. As Carpenter (2011) has suggested, disability is often taken unproblematically as an ableist metagenre which is usually applied (uncritically) to all film genres (discussed further in the conclusion). And given the troubled, yet potentially liberatory role of comedy and humour in disabled people's lives discussed so far, comedy and humour is an especially good place to explore the common basis for the genres throughout this book. For the purposes of closer analysis, this is limited to the genres of romantic comedy, satire, and gross-out; but I will first outline some broader issues of impairment stereotyping, genre and meaning-making, by examining one impairment group in particular, demonstrating the value in comparing portrayals across genres.

Meaning-making, impairment stereotypes and humour (some examples)

Klobas's observations on people of 'small stature' commonly being depicted as being part of a large band of others with (ostensibly) similar impairments (solely by virtue of them being smaller than people who are of average height) provides a useful demonstration of the importance of genre. Film and literary depictions such as *Willy Wonka and the Chocolate Factory*, *The Wizard of Oz*, and *Snow White* means that the 'gang' imagery is likely to occupy a foundational place in many people's understanding of people with restricted growth.[1] These are well-known twentieth-century images, often drawing on pre-existing stories and tropes which have been used to generalise impairment experiences (across different medical conditions), but have been invariably linked to a limited range of personality traits and associated social expectations. These 'gang' centred narratives of people with restricted growth, present across many historical eras (Backstrom, 2012; Kruse, 2003, Barnes, 1997), have added to the essentialising tendencies of portrayals of people of small physical stature. As Stone suggested of Snow White, 'dwarfs' have invariably been used as characters who denote 'other persons not normally encountered' (1975, 48), and so people with restricted growth, often portrayed as part of such collectives, still tend to be represented in ways which generalise fictions such as these, rendering all 'small people' as the same, robbing them of their unique personhood. This has worked to position them within a very limited range of characterisations, perhaps most regularly as 'comic sidekicks or magical freaks' (an interview with Gillian Martin, cited in Benedictus, 2010), or even as evil (Barnes, 1992).

Hence, it is probable that a contemporary dramatic story of a group of people with restricted growth told, straightforwardly, in this manner, would seem to invite audiences to trust these tired and damaging old tropes. Using irony, perhaps, the portrayal of people with restricted growth in 'gangs' could be regarded as a deconstructive strategy if used as a pastiche of the dominant imagery of (early- to mid-) twentieth century film depictions. However, avoiding this formulaic form of portrayal of a group of people with restricted growth may be seen as a wise decision by contemporary broadcasters or film-makers, especially as a greater awareness of discrimination might be seen to threaten the reputation of film-makers who choose to create a new gang of 'small people'. Significantly, Gervais's *Life's Too Short* is focused on Warwick Davis as *the* central character, perhaps parodying this collective trope, alluded to in some of the scenes which are about Warwick's (fictional) actors agency 'Dwarves for Hire', where he often generalises his clients as talentless worthless actors (see YouTube, 2011) and propagates the idea that they lack the competence and gravitas to play a heroic protagonist, historical figure, or a romantic/sexual role.[2]

Such collective images can be seen as even more damaging if audiences fail to question the infantilisation of people with restricted growth (Shakespeare et al., 2010) – a single childlike figure is problematic, if linked to height, but a posse of infantilisated people is likely to consolidate the idea. Even though the depersonalising traits of this approach may have gone un-noticed beyond the academic sphere, a greater acknowledgement of the need for diversity might lead the audience to question, and writers and directors to avoid, such 'gangs', particularly if film-makers are setting out to show how disabled people can and should be treated seriously as persons in their own, individual right. It is also notable that gangs in all these films were also cast as helpers of one kind or another (to Willy Wonka, Dorothy, and Snow White), suggesting subservience to other characters and social forms of diminishment, rather than depicting them as individual people with unique forms of agency, and needs of their own.

Although such portrayals of groups of people with restricted growth are less evident now (being most likely in remakes of the original films) especially (as suggested) due to appeals for diversity in films, and the reputational risks involved in reproducing discriminatory imagery, contemporary equivalents persist, most notably in fantasy films, such as the *Harry Potter* series, *The Hobbit* trilogy (arguably), and films featuring the minions . These latter creatures are diminutive animated figures first seen in the *Despicable Me* franchise and the spin off and prequel *Minions*. As the name 'minion' suggests, these little creatures live to serve their superiors, much like the human gangs of 'dwarves' (if not those in *The Hobbit*), Oompa Loompas and Munchkins who came before them. Magowan (2015) has also pointed out that all the minions were male, again mirroring the predominantly male composition of the Munchkins (*Wizard of Oz*), and the all-male crews from Willy Wonka's Oompa Loompas, and Snow White's seven dwarves (all versions). Their creator, Pierre Coffin, has described the minions as 'galumphing pods of ridiculousness' (Chemaly, 2016), which are designed to make us laugh. Animation is likely to be seen as a less pernicious form of disablism when the humour is aimed at animated and fantasy figures, rather than real humans, but this tends to underestimate the disposition to produce affect in the audience as if they are fellow beings, explained here by Jenkins (2013, 576) in terms of the

> prick or tickle one may get from sensing as alive what they know is not, from crying for a never-has-been, from identifying with an imaginary personality, from laughing with a mouse, from mourning with a spoon.

However, these similarities with portrayals of gangs of 'dwarves' has gone largely unnoticed in criticisms of disability portrayals, despite the propensity to group caricature – with the exception of Manoharan and Jones (2015), who attempted a comparative analysis of the structures of a minion and the human genome. Nonetheless, the idea of portraying people with agency has been a regular occurrence in recent film and television depictions of people with restricted growth, which, increasingly, have also featured women. Despite this, and the persistence of 'magical/mystical' portrayals of people with restricted growth (Rose, 2011), perhaps an explicit acknowledgement of the need to move away from such caricatures was made in 2003, when Peter Dinklage played Finbar, the central protagonist of the film *The Station Agent*. This was one of the first of these 'changed portrayals', a narrative based on Finbar's life after he inherits a former railway station. The title seems to be a word play on the representational changes presented by the film and the premise for the story being told, with the greatest shift in characterisation being the character's capacity to find a 'third way' of representation, avoiding the conventional choice of writers and directors to 'play your difference for all it is worth, or [you] retreat into solitude' (Malcolm, 2004, para 4). Notably, refusing a redemptive storyline so common to narratives of disabled men (Wilde, 2004b), Finbar's story focuses on more universal themes. As a character who is self-sustaining and makes his own decision to live in isolation from others whose attitudes to his 'difference' have blighted his life, but is willing to trust and make friends with others, his experiences and everyday difficulties probably resonate with most members of the audience. He later became one of the leading characters in *Game of Thrones*, a television drama series which also showed him as an active agent. Despite being within the fantasy genre, this role, and the medium of the series, also enabled more complex characterisations over time, often using humour to acknowledge, highlight, and challenge the disabling circumstances which emanate from discriminatory attitudes towards him. However, the persistence of the comedic values attached to smaller height are clear, with Dinklage commonly cast in roles which play on jokes about his height, including *Death at a Funeral* (both versions), and *Three Billboards outside Ebbing, Missouri*.[3]

While the move to representations of individuals is clearly a key strategy to representational change for restricted growth, it is clearly not sufficient, and certainly not a guarantor of more progressive and informed imagery, as several recent television programmes have shown. *Life's Too Short*, for example, does not focus on the magical or gang-related themes, choosing to emphasise the fictionalised personality of Warwick Davis. It also demonstrates common types of social and cultural barriers facing people with restricted growth; the show might also be seen to prioritise a more multi-dimensional characterisation, even setting him against other people with restricted growth fighting for the same jobs. However, given the weight of previous depictions of people with restricted growth, and the use of humour against them, it is unsurprising that some have criticised the decision to make him a very unlikeable, unkind, and deluded character who is often placed in size-contingent scenarios for laughs (such as having his head down a toilet or using a dog-flap), which render him little more than a 'minstrel' (Lacob, 2012). Although Gervais has defended this depiction as contesting taboos (ibid., 11–14), the idea of 'pushing boundaries' again suggests that the cultural representation of people with restricted growth has changed in favour of 'political correctness' which, given the films and shows discussed, is clearly not the case. It perhaps would be the ideal to welcome what might be seen as negative portrayals (e.g. unlikeable personalities), but as this is much like the wide array of other disabled characters in the mediascape, particularly men (Wilde, 2004b), it is problematic when so few likeable characters have existed or co-exist in other media.

As suggested, the magical tropes persist, despite shifts towards individual, and sometimes fuller, characterisations, so the legacy of the gangs is still apparent, and contemporary portrayals are likely to bear the traces of these uncontested images. If film-makers were to re-present these collective images in a new form, this would clearly differ according to genre. 'Issues' tackled in drama, for example, are often read as politically encoded messages, and can to be taken less seriously as a result (Gavin, 2000). Gavin has argued that 'audiences understand messages as "lessons", as didactic exhortations to behave in a certain way – the morally correct way' (ibid., 91), so they are likely to interpret defensively and resist, whereas comedy provides greater opportunities to present an alternative way of seeing, especially where it is 'not smashing you over the head with a message' (ibid., 85). Conversely, reading 'against the grain' (Culler, 1982, ii), the use of a comedic depiction of a group of people with restricted growth in a group might take a variety of different meanings in a film or TV comedy. It could be especially valuable in challenging deeper cultural narratives of 'dwarves' in a satire of restricted growth and 'magical' traits. Comedy may have the greatest power in shifting viewers to reconsider these collective images, even showing the symbolic violence that is perpetrated in the depersonalisation of their characters. In Chapter Six, for example, I argue that mimetic strategies such as those suggested by Irigary in relation to women have been used successfully in comedy to imitate and unsettle common stereotypes, to destabilise meanings attributed to people with learning difficulties, creating a 'strategic essentialism' to undermine beliefs about them, simultaneously exposing the prejudices of the audience; this is seen most obviously in the films of the Farrelly Brothers. Potentially paving the way for attitudinal change, such strategies might also vanquish the conventional binaries that depictions of restricted growth are set in, adding to the cultural criticism of disabling discourses that we have begun to see in (for example) *The Station Agent* and in *Game of Thrones*. Given the prevalence of the images discussed, the most significant binaries in the case of restricted growth can be seen in the clear divisions between normal/abnormal, group/individual, magical/familiar, and mature/childlike. Although some of these dualisms are (arguably) contested in Channel 4's *Seven Dwarves*, and US shows such as *Little People, Big World*, both in the reality/documentary genre, they received a mixed reception, much of which questions the appeal to voyeurism (Caulfield, 2011).[4] I am suggesting that comedy, at best, seems to have the greatest power in both exposing, and overturning, characterisations which have been very resistant to change whilst simultaneously problematising the voyeuristic stare.

Alongside the development of different forms of representation in other genres, then, we can see how the depiction of a gang of people, and individual figures, with restricted growth will vary significantly according to media form, mode, sub-genre, character, and positioning within the narrative. Indeed, context is crucial to understandings of how meanings are constructed. Significantly this is also, to a large extent, dependent on the form of comedy; parody may achieve these ends where other forms of comedy, such as slapstick or anti-politically correct (anti-PC) comedy may buy into and perpetuate traditional stereotypes. This illustrates the points made by Gavin (2001, 91) in respect of the need to pay close attention to the ways in which meanings are 'opened up' and' closed off'.

I have outlined the importance of contextualising the analysis of cultural meaning within the characteristics and expectations of specific genres, or modes, a theme which develops further throughout the book. In terms of film comedy, put simply, laughing *at* or *with* disabled people and others is expected in a comedy film, but may take on greater significance within other genres, such as melodrama, where a disabled person is used in comedic ways, perhaps for 'light relief', serving to mark their difference from the serious business of the non-disabled characters (such as *Three Billboards Outside Ebbing, Missouri*).

It is the shaping and circulation of these matters of meaning which is a key concern throughout the analysis of comedy, genre, and disability in the following chapters. As such, throughout the remainder of the book, analysis will take forward several of the themes discussed, particularly the ideas of the 'tolerant subject', who speaks about whom, and how seriously they are taken. However, analysis of film narratives will be synthesised with a consideration of aesthetics, and be grounded in film studies, in a quest to understand cinematic comedic constructions of disability and impairment and to engage fully with the complexity of humour and polysemy. Such an enterprise is essential if we are to avoid one-dimensional (e.g. right or wrong) or overly optimistic explanations of the transgressive possibilities of comedy, e.g. diagnoses of negative (Barnes, 1992), 'dodgy' (Montgomerie, 2015), or 'ironic' forms which are dependent solely on the unacknowledged position of the analyst's reading. Furthermore, we need to continue to examine the dangers of comedy representations whilst engaging fully with the conditions of possibility for new representational forms and challenges to normalcy.

Notes

1 This is the term I will use in this chapter, in accordance with the UK Restricted Growth Organisation: http://rgauk.org/ (accessed 8 March 2018).
2 Whilst this may be regarded as a reversal, in that the Warwick Davis character is now at the centre of the stories, Ricky Gervais and Stephen Merchant are also in

this, with Gervais playing a character resembling David Brent (and his own twitter persona). It is more than likely that the audience will draw on their stereotypic knowledge of Brent which is likely to undermine Davis' vice as the central character, particularly when Gervais and Merchant were the writers.
3 Frances McDormand, the leading actor in this film, spoke of the need for an 'inclusion rider' when accepting her Oscar award for her role in this film (see Belam and Levin, 2018). The inclusion of Dinklage in this film, and the playing on the comedic value of his height (e.g. in jokes made about his visit to the 'little boys room') is a good example of how efforts to guarantee diversity in cast and crew are not sufficient provision for changing disabling imagery.
4 There are also other, similarly themed programmes such as 'little women' shows, depicting relationships within friendship networks of 'little women', e.g. https://www.mylifetime.com/shows/little-women-atlanta.

4 Romantic comedy and disability

The romantic comedy genre – definitions and traits

Romantic comedy, commonly referred to as rom-com, is a genre which has come to occupy a dominant role in cinema, especially within mainstream films. Romantic comedies have a long cinematic history, having been a 'cornerstone of Hollywood entertainment since the coming of sound' (Grindon, 2011, 1). Romantic comedy was also a feature of silent films, such as *Sherlock Jr.*, and *City Lights*, the latter of which features a blind character/flower seller (Virgina Cherrill) as the love interest of the Little Tramp (Charlie Chaplin). As a genre which has endured throughout the history of film, there have been a number of trends and types of romantic comedy, e.g. the screwball comedy which was popular in the 1930s, featuring the theme of a battle of the sexes, disruptive situations, unsentimental perspectives and a 'visual equality of the characters' (Grindon, 2011, 36). Indeed, Grindon identifies 'nine cycles' over time, concluding that the genre's continuing appeal is to be found in the presentation of 'conflicts central to the experience of the audience' (ibid., 65).

Contemporary romantic comedy in European/American films is often considered to be 'slavishly formulaic' and 'essentially calculating in its execution, cynically manipulating an emotional and sentimental response from the viewer' (Abbot and Jermyn, 2009, 2).[1] Jeffers McDonald's 'master definition' of contemporary romantic comedy is:

> A film which has its central narrative motor a quest for love, which portrays this quest in a light-hearted way and almost always to a successful conclusion.
>
> (2007, 9)

She draws our attention to the way that this definition is potentially inclusive of non-heterosexual forms of romantic love and does not mean that such films have to be 'funny' (ibid., 10). It is also notable that she says that ending 'well' is probable, but not necessary, and that a common feature of rom-coms will be narrative elements which provoke 'mixed emotions' (e.g. sadness and tears). Her master definition includes a useful classification of 'three key components' of the genre. These are seen to fall into three main areas: visual characteristics, narrative patterns, and wider ideology. She argues that visual characteristics will include

> setting used in an 'iconographic way'
>
> (2007, 11)

demonstrating how these are often urban, using props such as those symbolising weddings, and featuring

> 'flowers chocolates, candlelight, beds',
> 'costume (the special outfit for the big date)', and
> 'stock characters' such as 'unsuitable partners'
>
> (2007, 11)

This type of visual language for romance is easily discernible in a number of well-known rom-coms, perhaps most obviously in *Four Weddings and a Funeral*, where we are rarely outside the domain of such settings, as the film charts the lives of the central romantic couple within a wider a group of characters (who all seem to have almost the same network of friends) over the course of four weddings and a funeral. As such, many of the scenes are set at weddings and receptions, often in glamorous costumes, also with a number of scenes which are set in bedrooms, and with central obstructions to romance in the form of stock 'unsuitable partners' (on/off girlfriends, and an older rich husband).

Indeed, this and most other rom-coms fit the narrative structure of this film where a man meets a woman, loses her, gets on with his life in the manner of acceptance, only to find her again, and, presumably, finds lasting happiness. Following Shumway (2003), Jeffers McDonald (2007) states that the overall narrative of the romantic genre is that boy meets, loses, and regains girl, indicating that this is true for conventional romantic comedies, and suggesting this may differ for those with more complex narratives and a less heteronormative focus. She argues that another frequently occurring facet of the narrative is the 'meet cute', where the central couple 'encounter each other in a way which forecasts their eventual union' (2007, 12). Other common features she lists include the tendency for one partner to leave at some point, or to pretend to be someone else, and there are frequently scenarios where 'dignity' is sacrificed for 'public humiliation' (ibid., 13) in the name of love.

The latter trope often comes close to the type of behaviour which might be considered stalking in a real-world situation, e.g. finding, then following, an 'object of affection', typically female, and refusing to take no for an answer at the start, or in the continuance, of a relationship, in the face of the unwilling partner's desires and expressed needs. Lippman (2015) uses findings from her audience research on this topic to argue that stalking types of behaviour have become normalised in many romantic comedies. She shows how 'persistent pursuit' is supported and legitimised when placed in the romantic genre's narrative structures. She also demonstrates a marked difference in the affective responses of the audience according to the passion and commitment of the male protagonist's determination, and rejection responses typical of the rom-com compared with the placement of stalking behaviours in portrayals marked as 'scary'. Fear was generated by the 'scary' narratives of stalking, these portrayals being differentiated from the rom-com by pursuance by a man who is portrayed as 'psychologically troubled' and the levels of desperation shown of the woman's attempts at escape (Lippman, 2015, 6). Her examination of the responses of viewers to a number of romantic-comedies found them to have 'a clear and negative impact, in that they can lead people to see stalking as a less serious crime than they otherwise would', whereas the 'scary' depictions of stalking, which generated feelings of fear, led to greater judgements of stalking as a serious crime (ibid., 19).

Thus, it is Lippman's contention that 'romanticized pursuit behaviours commonly featured in the media as part of normative courtship can lead to an increase in stalking supportive beliefs' (ibid., 1), upholding 'stalking myth endorsement' (Sinclair, 2006, as cited in Lippman, 2015), an attitude comprised of erroneous beliefs which minimise the effects of stalking actions and misattribute blame.[2] Lippman shows that the reception of 'scary' variants of stalking in other film genres generates very different responses, and that stalking framed as scary (e.g. in thrillers) tends to lead to the rejection of stalking myths. It is argued, in turn, that romantic comedies may perpetuate assumptions of 'gendered aggression' (Lippman, 2015, 22), and 'victim blaming', particularly of women, though she argues that this is highly contingent on 'perceptions of the perpetrator' and the appropriateness of the stalker's behaviour (ibid., 22).

Lippman draws on the work of Green and Brock (2000) to suggest that the meanings attributed to these portrayals of stalking, and of love, are influenced to the degree of 'transportation' experienced by the viewer. They define transportation as absorption (ibid.), denoting a 'psychological closeness', having similar effects to perceptions and expectations of realism, in terms of 'media priming' (Lippman, 2015, 7). Put simply, the more a viewer is transported by the story, the more consistent their beliefs will be with the themes addressed in the films, and the discourses within it. If this is true on a wider scale, then, a heavy viewer of rom-coms is more likely to hold highly gendered views on appropriate courtship behaviour and gender norms, which fuel further expectations, especially if they watch those which replay these stalking myths. And, given the narrow demographic of those who tend to be placed as romantic leads (typically, white, heterosexual, middle class, young, non-disabled, with a slim build – see following pages), further questions are raised about how discourses of romance and love feed into diversity, ethnocentrism, ableism, and other prejudicial attitudes.[3]

Although Jeffers McDonald lists all these traits of romantic comedy under the dimension of narrative, structure, and tropes, it is clear that some of these elements feed straight into potential ideological biases; for example, would

Ted (played by Ben Stiller) in *There's Something about Mary* (see Chapter Six), – a typical 'putz', a type who tends to elicit 'rueful identification' (Taylor, 2015, 63) – be received by the audience as *the* deserving romantic choice between potential suitors if he had been disabled? Or would we be more likely to draw on stereotypic knowledge of disabled men as evil, sinister or pitiable, putting him on the scary or invalid (sic) category? Even if he is likeable as a disabled person, will his 'putz-iness', depicted variously in physical 'imperfections', and as someone who 'bungles', is an 'inept or ineffectual person' or is seen as a 'blunderer', 'dope', 'nerd' or 'drip' (ibid., 69) be eclipsed or transformed by dominant ideas of disabled identities which are defined in terms of deficit, difference or pity? In other words, is the transgression of idealised (hegemonic) masculine norms, such as competency, strength, athleticism (see Connell, 2005, for example) attractive or 'relatable' only for those who are a close fit to ableist, white norms in most other respects?[4] Whereas Ben Stiller as Ted, Ricky Gervais (who self-consciously constructs David Brent as a putz), and other bungling white, non-disabled men may elicit affection and attraction, or identification, for viewers (see Taylor, 2015, 68), conventional tropes of disabled men as creepy, bitter, violent, or pathetic (Wilde 2004b) are hardly likely to place them in, or near, the endearing category of 'putz'. Furthermore, the dominance of such stereotypes of disabled men will take on a far more sinister dimension when combined with the expected stalking myth behaviours of the conventional leading male of the rom-com, especially when they have obvious impairments, manifested in wheelchair use or facial 'disfigurement' (Wilde, 2004c).

Even characteristics such as the 'meet cute' could be seen as ideological, encouraging the audience to spurn prosaic, mundane forms of love in favour of exoticised improbable forms. This is typical of the 'screwball' form of romantic comedy, where the main protagonist's life is 'subverted', 'usually by an anarchic female' (Jeffers McDonald, 2007, 25–26), in ways which suggest some form of karmic destiny. Such stories are likely to make our own most exciting or eventful love stories seem dull, perhaps increasing our desire for vicarious and simpler pleasures on screen. As Beck and Beck-Gernsheim argue,

> lovers tend to love the idea of loving more than confronting the banal facts about the person they have chosen to adore. Idealising someone is easier at a distance.
>
> (1995, 190)

I am suggesting that these features fuel, and are inextricable from, the third component of romantic comedies identified by Jeffers McDonald, the domain of ideology, the area which lends itself to the genre's reputation for conservativism. Jeffers McDonald argues that the couple are shown to be of central importance, invariably supporting ideologies of monogamy (2007, 13). At the time of writing she stated that no rom-coms had tried to portray monogamy as an 'outmoded concept' (ibid.). This is no longer the case, as there have been a number of films which have been founded on this challenging this premise; these include *Appropriate Behaviour, 500 Days of Summer,* and *Trainwreck*. Gehring has demonstrated that such subversions are more likely and more easily accommodated within the framework of screwball comedies, as a genre which, though closely aligned with romantic comedy, is seen to emphasise comedy over romance, whereas romantic comedy is seen to place romance, and one couple, at the centre (Gehring, 2008, 2–3). Conversely, King (2002, 3) sees the romance of the rom-com as subordinate to comedy i.e. as an 'adjectival take (romantic) on the non-object (comedy)', even though he considers romance to be 'the main and foregrounded element of the narrative rather than occupying a secondary position' (ibid., 51); this perhaps supports Gehring's point that romantic themes are less open to transgression in the conventional rom-com.

However, even where heteronormative heterodoxies (see Beasley et al., 2015) are explored as a central premise for the film's story, particularly the creation of alternative family and friendship forms which are not contingent on a lifelong commitment to a spouse or partner, contraventions of the expected model are usually contained, promoted, and underwritten by narrative resolutions that confirm the triumph of 'love' against all odds (see Cadwallader, 2012, for example). Most of these stories have invariably presented the depiction of romantic love as a relationship which is founded on a monogamous basis, between (cis) men and (cis) women who tend to be white, heterosexual (Cadwallader, 2012), and non-disabled, themes which will be explored a little further in the next section on diversity in casting.

In many ways romantic comedies can be seen as one of the most conservative and predictable genres (Deleyto, 2009; Jeffers McDonald, 2007). This is unsurprising when one considers the desire of film industries to maximise profits by targeting as wide an audience a possible (Altman, 1999; Deleyto, 2009), by delivering a product which is recognisable as a romantic comedy, pandering to audience expectations such as recognisable structures and happy endings. In Scannell's terms (2000), then, the proclivity of the film industry to produce narratives which are almost indistinguishable from each other can be seen in terms of intentions to conform to the 'for anyone as someone structure'. Simply explained, this structure has been seen to be crucial to drawing large audiences, being theorised as 'always, at one and the same time, for me and for anyone' (ibid., 9), thus perceived to be usable by everyone, appealing to mass and multiple audiences, notwithstanding the lack of diversity therein. Further, to the embedding of rom-coms in such structures, Deleyto (2009) argues that the conservatism and homogeneity of those films which are seen to fall into this category are due in part to the way that the genre tends to be crudely defined in a somewhat circular manner by critics and genre theorists:

> Only those films that include conventions and a certain 'conservative' perspective on relationships are romantic comedies and therefore,

romantic comedies are the most conventional and conservative of all genres.

(ibid., 3)

She goes on to show that the types of definition put forward by Jeffers McDonald work to neglect films which fall outside such narrow remits, typically those which may proffer alternative ideological schema, or more complex conventions. Thus, films which have significant traits of romance and comedy tend to be overlooked as romantic comedy, if, for example, they are aligned with other genres, or films that are considered to be aligned with 'art' films; *Before Sunset*, is one example she provides of 'pure cinema' which contains elements of romantic comedy (ibid., 2).[5]

Wider questions of genre

As useful as Jeffers McDonald's framework is for analysing how generic elements fit together in a number of films, Deleyto calls for a more expansive understanding of romantic comedy, accommodating more 'problematic texts' (2009, 2). She argues for consideration of romantic comedy in films which might be identified with other genres (such as *Out of Sight*, ibid., 1–2), a crime comedy with romance, or Western films which include romance, such as *Rio Bravo* (ibid., 4), and also for those deemed to be 'non-genre' films, usually associated with other cinema traditions such as 'pure cinema' (e.g. *Before Sunset* as suggested). Using these examples, she appeals for consideration of such films 'in relation to romantic comedy' (ibid., 2) rather than *as* a romantic comedy. She argues that the association of genre films with (less worthy) forms of popular culture has not been helpful in the development of more sophisticated approaches to romantic comedy, especially in understanding the role it plays in the analysis of romantic comedy beyond narrow genre, and more 'ideologically determined', conventions (such as those proposed by Jeffers McDonald). She also explains that Neale (1992; 2000) has shown that contemporary practices in genre theory have been adversely affected by auteur theory and an over-emphasis on text rather than 'systems of communication and expectation' (Deleyto, 2009, 5), and agrees that these are significant in the analysis of how film genres work. However, focussing predominantly on 'films as texts' and 'as cultural products', Deleyto questions the concept of genre and the boundaries which have been constructed between them, showing, for example, how films outside of conventionally recognised genres have contributed to the evolution of the genres themselves, which would not 'have been the same without them' (ibid., 17). Using the approaches garnered from chaos theory, and the theories of Derrida, Lakoff, Altman, Wittgenstein, Bakhtin, Schatz, and Saussure, she highlights (following Altman, 1999) how most genres are inherently mixed, arguing that all films can only share 'family resemblances' (Deleyto, 2009, 7, after Wittgenstein, 1963) having no single 'essential property' (Deleyto, 2009, 9). She shows how a genre's dynamism and evolution comes from 'instability and spontaneity' (ibid., 8), shaping it into the form of a 'jumbled structure rather than a preconceived design' (ibid.). Considering all this, she argued that the concept of genre itself is best understood as an 'open shelf' rather than a 'closed bag' (ibid., 16), emphasising participation in a type, rather than belonging to a category. As useful as this is likely to be, there are still judgements of extent which need to be considered; as King (2002, 51) argued, romance tends to be 'an obligatory feature of most popular genres'.

Referring to the difficulties in defining genres, Martin made a suggestion which is helpful here, suggesting that the romantic comedy might be thought of as 'a film that has something to do with love, and that tried to make you laugh somewhere along the way'. But he also argued that we need to 'chase the genre's self-definition in flight, as it happens' (Martin, 2013, 17), due to its character as a continually evolving phenomenon which is put in new contexts, and moves on to explore new scenarios. Similarly, Abbott and Jermyn see the romantic genre as a disputed one, 'marked by numerous different inflections rather than clearly defined generic boundaries' (2009, 3). Indeed, they demonstrate that the genre has become the object of many parodies since the release of *When Harry Met Sally* in 1989. Nonetheless, Mortimer (2010) points to the persistence of formulae in the genre to protect popularity and profits, which leads us back to the type of expectations expressed in Jeffers McDonald's 'master definition'.

Seen in this way, and like comedy more generally, romantic comedy tends to be seen as an unworthy, trivial genre by film critics, and within the study of film (Abbott and Jermyn, 2009, 2). Further, Martin (2013) has demonstrated how rom-coms are even relegated to beneath the purview of those focusing on 'vulgar auterism' and suggests that there is a masculine bias to this area of study. Martin explains that the study of 'vulgar auterism' has a focus on popular cinema (or sub-popular, e.g. video on demand), which is invariably dedicated to 'male-driven, violent action genres' (ibid., 18). The neglect of romantic comedies is likely to be associated with their reputation as a woman's genre, but Martin argues that this is qualified by the 'aesthetic alibi' that 'physical action is somehow more "cinematic" than actors delivering sparkling dialogue', contending that this approach and focus 'replays an old auterist fixation with the visual' (ibid., 18).

Whilst Martin's opinions on auterism might easily be contested, on a number of grounds – not least in the roles that writing, ideas, politics and philosophies of film might play in the work of 'auteurs' – romantic comedies tend not to be associated with aesthetics, other than the types of iconography proposed by Jeffers McDonald (2007), with rom-coms being associated with 'chick flicks' and the transmission of female perspectives on life in general, and relationships in particular (Cadwallader, 2012). Cadwallader (2012) explains how rom-coms are positioned as a woman's genre, as a window on women's approaches to relationships, in much the same way that pornography is associated with men. However, Taylor (2015) has argued that there are a number of misconceptions about women and comedy, including the idea that there is an 'overrepresentation of female perspectives' (ibid., 73) in a domain which is centred on male protagonists. Taylor contended that there is a 'double cultural prejudice: that women either are not or should not be funny' (ibid., 72). She showed how there are similar 'risk aversive' (ibid., 74) attitudes towards women in comedy as there have been to disabled people, seen in the censorship of women in comedy and limitations on their participation. She demonstrates how these have included conscious efforts to limit the number of women in comedy and to censor their humour, particularly comedy which lampoons sexist forms of culture such as Robin Thicke's *Blurred Lines* video (discussed in Taylor, 2015, 63). Much like my arguments about the centrality of the white non-disabled male as 'tolerant subject', and the undue forms of censorship and restriction imposed on disabled people, and even disabled characters in similar roles, Taylor argues that such protections of the status quo lead to lesser forms of character development and cultural capital being afforded to women within film narratives.[6] In turn, this is likely to result in the deepening of social inequalities, reducing the power for those deemed as 'other' for 'defining situations' (ibid., 74) which constitute the world of cinema. Further, despite any 'diversification' in rom-coms (Krutnik, 2002, 130) these are not, by any means, the only inequalities in casting and narrative content of romantic comedies, as the cursory examination of casting and diversity of leading roles which follows illuminates.

Diversity, casting and patterns of love

In addition to the ways in which romantic comedies tend to strengthen the agency of the male protagonists and their comedic discourses and persona, the biases suggested earlier are very evident in compilations of 'Top Romantic Comedies'. There are many such lists which can be found by internet searching, but these listings show few differences in choices of favourite rom-com, and the lack of diversity in their casting of romantic leads as white and heterosexual is overwhelmingly evident.

Race and ethnicity

Of the lists I found from a search of 'top romantic comedies', the only list which was compiled from viewer and critic responses was one on the Rotten Tomatoes website (Rottentomatoes, 2016). Like the other lists, these romantic comedies were overwhelmingly dominated by white actors in romantic leads, with the rare exceptions of *The Big Sick* (starring Kumail, Nanjiani, a Pakistani-American comedian) and *Appropriate Behaviour* (starring Desiree Akhavan, an Iranian actress and filmmaker). There were occasional examples of Black actors as leads on other lists, such as Will Smith in *Hitch*, and Jamie Foxx as one of the lead actors in *Valentine's Day*. Indeed, there is a dearth of popular rom-coms which have two Black actors in lead roles. However, on the

Vogue list (2017) of forty-five rom-coms there are two with Black stars, *How Stella Got Her Groove Back*, starring Angela Bassett and Taye Diggs, and *Top Five*, with Chris Rock and Rosario Dawson. This is unsurprising if we consider Bowdre's argument that 'Black bodies disrupt romantic comedy conventions' (2009, 105); her analysis shows that a number of conventions, such as the 'meet cute', and the 'boy meets, loses, (and) regains (the) girl' (ibid., 106–109) are absent. In addition to the predominance of a limited number of character types in wider culture, e.g. reflecting ideas of the lower intellects, 'hypersexuality' and higher 'natural' musical abilities of Black people, she shows how they are 'comedically overdetermined' as 'natural' comedians. So, like disabled people they occupy a comparatively fixed position in the strata of comedy, this time as the joker, rather than the (disabled) butt of the joke, denying them the full range of humanity (ibid., 107) exacerbated by the positioning of 'whiteness as infinite variety' (ibid., 108), and the naturalisation of stereotypes, within a limited, less discernible range of 'malleability'.

Gender, sexuality and monogamy

Additionally, most of the pairings in these top romantic comedy films were heterosexual couplings, with the exceptions of *Appropriate Behaviour* and *Chasing Amy*, the former focused on gay and bisexual love and identity, and the latter on a lesbian woman as the love interest of a heterosexual man. Although recent films featuring trans gender characters often have storylines where trans gendered people's lives and identities are portrayed, e.g. *The Danish Girl* and *Tangerine*, the portrayal of trans gender concerns in rom-coms has largely been seen as problematic. Furthermore, Miller (2012) has shown how comedy is 'the most popular and well-known mode of representation of trans gender individuals in film' (ibid., 47), including using comedy to make such characters an 'object of ridicule' (ibid., 27) in a number of rom-coms. As suggested, Cadwallader (2012) demonstrates that even where the pattern of monogamous, ever-after love is challenged, or where there is greater diversity in the casting of lead protagonists, it is usual for the narrative structure to work to return us to the naturalness, even triumph, of this heteronormative state of affairs.

Class and impairment

Romantic leads are usually middle-class (Johnson and Holmes, 2009), and rarely disabled. There are exceptions to this, which include a disabled actor in *Four Weddings and a Funeral*, where Charles, the lead protagonist (played by Hugh Grant), has a brother David, who is Deaf (played by David Bower, a Deaf actor). Similarly, Daryl Mitchell is a black disabled wheelchair-using actor who was cast in *10 Things I Hate About You*. But, like these two characters, disabled actors are rarely, if ever, cast in the leading roles. Disabled or

Deaf characters being used as supports/prostheses (Mitchell and Snyder, 2000) for the lead protagonists have become more common, where they tend to support ideologies of normalcy, create comic effect, and build the protagonist's character, as David does for Charles, e.g. through Charles' deliberate mistranslation of David's use of British Sign Language. Although there are few disabled lead characters in romantic comedies, two recent exceptions are to be found in *Me Before You* and *The Big Sick* (if illness can be considered within the realms of disability – see Barnes and Mercer, 1996 for a range of arguments on this). As such, *Me Before You* will be the main focus of analysis in the latter half of the chapter as an example of a recent disability-themed romantic comedy; as an exception for the genre it is of particular note that disabled people were its strongest critics on a world-wide basis (Quinn, 2016). It is also of some significance that neither of the leading romantic leads in these two films were played by disabled actors, even though disabled and Deaf actors have been cast in leading roles in popular films which would fit other genres, e.g. Marlee Matlin in *Children of a Lesser God*, a romantic drama, and Christopher Reeve in the remake of *Rear Window*.[7] This would suggest a continuing reluctance to see disability in the context of the perfect world of the romantic comedy, and a perception of risk in embracing the idea of disabled people as sexual agents (see Sancho, 2003 for a wider discussion of these opinions in her analysis on television and disability).

Age

There is generally an expectation that romantic leads will be young, or look youthful, even though there have been a number of films which have provided love stories for older people since the release of *Something's Gotta Give* in 2003 (Begley, 2015), a film which had its lead characters cast as a sixty-three-year-old man (Jack Nicholson) and a fifty-six-year-old woman (Diane Keaton). However, the predominance of youthful love, and the casting of younger actors, has been especially significant for women who are often classed as older when they are under thirty; Jermyn (2011, quoting Sontag, 1972), has shown that the portrayal of characters who are positioned as 'women of a certain age' can be played by women who are in their early twenties to late fifties. When Stephen Follows (2016) examined a sample of contemporary films from the wider romance genre (over the past thirty years) to investigate the significance of age in casting for romantic leads, by sex, he found that a disparity in ages was common, with men being an average of 4.5 years older than the women, especially where men are the directors (88 per cent of romance films, between 1984 and 2014).

Body and personality tropes

In addition to this narrow range of people and the normalising ideologies which ensue from a young, non-disabled cast with predictable physical features, usually slim with standardised body characteristics, ideal types of both genders are created. These are 'enhanced' by 'beauty work', a largely digital process (with additions such as cosmetics, cosmetic surgery, and hair and dental 'restoration') rendering an image of actors' bodies which (Dickey argues) we presume to be 'real', perpetuating narrow principles of beauty and desirability, whilst creating inaccurate and impossible standards (Dickey, 2014). A number of scholars have shown how the genre perpetuates a number of other oppressive ideologies, whether this is deemed as a reflection on the continuing appeal to the male gaze (Mulvey, 1975) or as a spectacle which is offered instead for the edification of women's pleasures, and focuses heavily on 'looking your best' (Cohen, 2010, 87) through body and material accessories.[8]

Together, these characteristics of romantic comedy work to promote naturalised discourses on 'perfect' bodies – generally slim and youthful, white and non-disabled – and preferred gender roles aligned with ascribed – and ethnocentric – characteristics of femininity and masculinity. Although romantic comedies tend to present and re-iterate a limited number of 'perfect' relationships, albeit in a short-term narrative where the end presents itself as the beginning of the inexorable happy-ever-after life that these protagonists will go on to lead, a significant trope in femininity since the early 2000s has been that of the 'Manic Pixie Dream Girl' (henceforth MPDG). This is a woman who is exceptionally attractive, but quirky and chaotic, with a zest for life (see Tvtropes.org, 2017a), constructed through the perspective of the men who pursue them (e.g. see Zoe Kazan, interviewed in Greco, 2012). Nathan Rabin, who created the term, says it was devised to

> call out a particularly toxic, dishonest and ubiquitous fiction promoted by romantic comedies, namely that women exist exclusively to cheer up mopey male sad sacks, and have no real agency or drive or will of their own.
> (2017, para.15)

He discusses the character of Summer (Zooey Deschanel) in *500 Days of Summer*, as the epitome of this figure. Here, she is positioned such that she subverts common ideals of romantic love and the conventional narrative of romantic comedy through her involvement in a relationship with Tom (Joseph Gordon-Levitt), whilst holding forceful anti-romantic love ethics, values which are overturned when we discover this only applied to Tom, the male protagonist, as she goes on to marry the 'right one'.[9] She concludes that she was wrong in challenging Tom's belief in 'true love', a move which underscores her lack of rationality, possibly suggesting that there are a few other ways that women can say no to a man, other than this, without losing their appeal, fantasy or otherwise. Thus, the narrative is transformed into 'boy meets girl who couldn't possibly ever exist' (Angerstein, 2015), resulting in the transformation of Tom into the best man he could be, ready for Autumn, his next love interest (perhaps suggesting that 'girls' come in seasons of four personality types indexed to a man's stages of self-development). Rabin asserts that the trope of MPDG is also reflected in wider cultural mores, moods, and locations, arguing that it is,

> stitched together from Belle & Sebastian singles and Woody Allen movies from the 1970s and bicycling in the rain and Audrey Hepburn's impossible beauty and Wes Anderson and heartbreak and Nick Drake and arthouse first dates.
>
> (Rabin, 2017, para 24)

Significantly the MPDG is also likely to work to support the unrealistic fantasies of entitled heterosexual men's pejorative views of other women and their imperfections, e.g. as dull, less attractive, difficult (his next girlfriend might be a cold and frosty Winter) and so on, especially if they don't possess such joie de vivre, sunny dispositions, and magical qualities, or show the desire to centre the male's needs and desire. This is underlined by the tendency of the MPDG to be the second 'love' (Tvtropes.org, 2017a), casting shadows on the first, and subsequent, partners, almost literally in the seasonal shifts from Summer to Autumn.

The scope and potential for multi-dimensional portrayals and engagement with disabled characters in romantic comedies

Following Bowdre's (2009, 107) argument about the exclusion of Black people 'from the full range of humanity' throughout the visual and cultural histories of Black bodies, it is clear that most romantic comedies work to deny this full range of humanity to a number of social groups, including disabled and older bodies, despite any advances made in representational diversity. The 'static stereotypes' which ensue confine such characters (and actors) to limited roles, perpetuating the normalcy of young, white, middle-class, non-disabled (and usually heterosexual) protagonists as our central concerns. As she asserts, these depictions are 'thought to be universal narratives whereas films with people of African or Asian descent or Latinos are read as "Black", "Asian" or "Latin" films' (2009, 108).

Despite much 'academic anxiety' (Jermyn, 2014) about rom-coms, several scholars have suggested that they are very well placed to cast critical ideas on contemporary relationships, particularly those involving older women (Abbot and Jermyn, 2009, Jermyn, 2011; Hobbs, 2013). Jermyn points out that women around the age of sixty have increasingly been portrayed in leading romantic comedy roles, thereby thwarting some of our previous expectations of stories of young love, for example the casting of Meryl Streep as Donna in *Mamma Mia,* who eventually reconciles with her former (never-forgotten) love, and also as divorced wife Jane, who eventually returns to her former husband, in *It's Complicated*; notably, both films were directed and written by women, Phylidda Lloyd and Catherine Johnson in the former and Nancy Meyer in the latter. Jermyn has argued that recent films (from 2000) in this genre, including these, have undeniably offered some of the most nuanced, thoughtful and engaging representations of older women to make it to cinema screens since the golden age of melodrama.

(2011, 33)

Given such changes in the depiction of older people in romantic relationships and recent attempts to depict disability and impairment in better ways, e.g. by putting the disabled person's perspectives closer to the centre of dominant narratives (see Wilde, 2017c, for example), rom-coms may also be well-placed to challenge many tropes of disability – especially those which link sexuality to pathology (for sustained analysis of such issues see Shakespeare et al., 1996, and McRuer, 2006). As Jermyn has said, about the increasing number of representations of older romances, moves such as the positioning of older women as leading romantic protagonists

> can perhaps be understood as awkward, tentative steps by the industry towards exploring or addressing some of the discriminatory practices it has itself adopted.
>
> (Jermyn, 2011, 33)

However, perhaps it is significant that stories such as these centre on, and return to, romances begun by older women when they were young, before parenthood, suggesting some reluctance to break with the link between the passion of romantic love, 'perfect bodies', and youth. Another stark contrast between identifications with ageing and identifications with impairment, is that old age is a destination most of us wish to reach, as part of 'our world,' if we are lucky. Disablement is not.[10]

Just as whiteness manifests itself as having 'infinite variety', the non-disabled body also tends to be treated as being 'coterminous with the endless plenitude of human diversity' (Dyer, 1988, 47, cited in Bowdre, 2009, 109) whilst simultaneously rendering impairments as 'adventitious happenings' (Giddens, 1991, 128), detached from the ontological security of the 'our world' (Scannell, 2000, 9) of romantic comedy. Older people can easily be fitted within this plenitude as something we anticipate as part of our lives, without destroying the formulaic or predicable structure of the rom-com. While the centring of the non-disabled 'normal couple' (special but universal) can expand to fit older, gendered articulations of being, it works to naturalise impairment-based representations as 'other', effectively placing such films in a 'normality genre' (see Darke, 1999), which uses disability to support the centring of non-disabled bodies and experience. So, presented as common sense, portrayals of impairment and disability are rendered as forgettable 'seen but unnoticed' phenomena (Wilde, 2004b), resulting in the endless postponement of impairment and disability concerns in most contemporary films. These forgettable portrayals, most obviously seen in the peripheral roles of disabled characters, or the temporary nature of their impairments before the 'redemption' afforded by cure, deserve careful analysis, and are those which are most commonly discussed by scholars due to relative lack of disabled people and characters in leading roles; some of these will be explored in Chapter Five. However, the casting of a disabled character in a leading romantic role provides an unavoidable focus on conventional tropes of disability as discussion of several recent rom-coms, and *Me Before You* in particular, will demonstrate in the following pages.

Contemporary romantic comedies featuring disability

Martin (2013) demonstrates that where the romantic comedy is taken seriously as an object for analysis, there is a tendency to choose from a 'shallow pool of high quality examples', often from a 'distant past' including 'the so-called classic era of the 1930s and '40s' (2013, 18), 'thus giving rise to the illusion of a classical tradition, and artists knowingly working in that tradition' (ibid., 18). He also shows how directors who would now be regarded as auteurs within this 'classical period' – such as Ernest Lubitch, Frank Capra and Preston Sturges – have more resemblances with contemporary directors than most current critics and theorists are prepared to acknowledge, e.g. in connecting to the 'ephemeral zeitgeist of culture' (Martin, 2013, 19). So, rather than choosing a sample of films for analysis which promote a single argument about disability in romantic comedies, as is common in studies of genre (see Martin's criticism of the work of Cavell, for example [2013, 19]), I have chosen to examine the representation of disability and impairment in quite different recent films, in order to examine a range of approaches.

These films chosen are all from the last three years, a period where diversity in film and television has increasingly been questioned and challenged in a number of areas, including race, ethnicity, sex, gender, sexuality, trans identities, and impairment/disability.[11] I will be focusing on *Me Before You* to examine it in some depth, as it is perhaps the closest fit to Jeffers McDonald's 'master definition' of a romantic comedy which made high profits. It can also be seen to reflect the zeitgeist in terms of its reflection of the resurgence in attitudes towards seeing disabled people as burdens (e.g. Briant et al., 2011). Additionally, it is of particular value because it is an adaptation of a novel, which allows for an exploration of how cinematic practices transform meanings of disability, for better or worse. There will be some comparison with films such as *The Big Sick*, useful as a film (not an adaptation but based on a 'true-life' story) which also has a conventional framework in terms of boy meets, loses and re-finds girl, particularly as it has a stronger focus on representational change, especially in terms of 'race'. It also contrasts with *Me Before You* in three main ways; the 'disabled' protagonist is a woman, leading to a different gendered dynamic; her condition would be seen as an illness by many, perhaps leading to different expectations; and we are encouraged to hope for her cure and complete recovery. It was also one of the highest grossing independent films of 2017 (Erbland, 2017).

Reflecting my aim to examine films which fit with clearly defined generic expectations and those which parody or satirise genre expectations and tropes, I am following Deleyto's proposal that we should look beyond films with a comfortable fit to conventional genre definitions (2009). Hence, the films discussed in this chapter can be seen as conventional forms, before the following chapter moves on to a recent satire of romantic comedy and contemporary society, *The Lobster* (2015) by Yorgos Lanthimos. Although this made a profit which was approximately double its budget, it clearly has limited appeal in comparison to *Me Before You*.[12]

It is important to note that none of these protagonists have had impairments from birth, reflecting a wider lack of leading disabled characters in this genre, and also across other genres, even though characters and actors with lifelong impairments can be found in the casts of a wide range of films. Exceptions to the exclusion of leading roles include the casting of Peter Dinklage (a disabled actor) as Finbar McBride in *The Station Agent* and Kalchi Koerchlin's character of Laila in *Margarita with a Straw*. The latter is an Indian film, directed by Shonali Base, about a teenage bisexual woman with cerebral palsy, but played by a twenty-eight-year-old non-disabled woman. Although both films centre characters who have been disabled from birth, neither of these are close to fitting the romantic comedy genre; despite having elements of comedy in both, and romance in the second, they are both regarded as dramas. Other well-known exceptions, in older films, all fall within the drama genre, including *Rainman, Shine*, and *Forrest Gump*, commonly featuring people with autism, and learning or mental difficulties. Significantly, all of these tend to emphasise exceptionality and are less than subtle in suggesting what we can learn from their noble characters; this is perhaps exemplified in *Being There*, and its 'life is a state of mind' philosophy, built on the premise that a presidential aide mistakes a well-dressed gardener, Chance, for a businessman, evaluating his simple and very restricted knowledge of gardening and televisual content for great wisdom and expertise. In many ways these characters can be seen as uncorrupted 'noble savages', a concept which Ellingson (2001, 7) refers to as one which is 'obviously a forced union of questionable assumptions' based on spurious ideas of wildness, nature, morality and civilisation, which renders them as 'others' from every angle. The disabled noble savage resembles the 'magical negro' figure (a term popularised by Spike Lee); this has been described by Seitz (2010 para 13) as a cinematic device which

> is a glorified walk-on role, a narrative device with a pulse, [...] a glorified hood ornament attached to the end of a car that's being driven by white society, vigorously turning a little steering wheel that's not attached to anything.

It is my contention that such figures often serve to normalise the superiority of white, or non-disabled characters, whilst entrenching perceptions of otherness which appeal to ideas of 'raising awareness'. Thus, they construct an issue-based approach to diversity rather than one which seeks to change the homogeneity of stories which are told and the positions of those who tell them. Indeed, it was this desire to raise the issues of acquired quadriplegia which seems to have served as primary motivation for Jojo Moyes, when she wrote and directed *Me Before You.*

Me Before You: curiosity, speculation and the construction of the non-disabled or othering 'gaze'

Curiosity seems to have been the stimulus which drove Jojo Moyes to write the book *Me Before You*, which led to the film of the same name. This is not an unusual source of inspiration (sic) for films which deal with disability as their central theme. Both Moyes' and R.J. Palacio's interest in writing books which resulted in films about disability (Palicio wrote *Wonder*, released in 2017) were provoked by chance encounters with disabled people outside their usual experiences. They both claim to have written the books on the basis of speculation on disabled people's experiences and their imaginings on how they would respond to the lives they would find themselves in if the disabled person was a member of their own families. The catalyst for Moyes' book was a news item about a former athlete with quadriplegia who chose to seek assisted suicide rather than continuing to live as a newly disabled person (Rice, 2016). Similarly, Palacio began writing her book after an incident where she and her children met a child with a 'severe facial deformity'; after her children became frightened by the way the child appeared – to the point that her three-year-old cried and she fled with her children, for the sake of all concerned. She reports being appalled at herself for not having used her children's reaction with a disabled child as a 'great teaching moment' (see National Public Radio staff, 2013).

Similarly, Moyes explained that the idea for *Me Before You* originated from an attempt to understand why someone would choose to take their own life, when you would hope to accept with good grace even if you suspect you may be angry at becoming disabled. She said:

> That fascinated me because I thought about what it would be like to be that man's mother, what it would be like to be the person in love with him, what it would be like to be him. I just knew it was a story I had to tell.
> (Rice, 2016, para 4)

This seems to have been met with a similar desire to imagine what such lives would feel like, when one considers the size of the audience the film attracted, having made over ten times the amount of the budget (of $20 million) by January 2018 (Box office Mojo, 2018).

We might ask how this fits with the industry's reluctance to make 'disability films', given the thoughts of Justin Edgar, a disabled film-maker; he said (albeit eight years earlier):

> There's a huge resistance to disability films. No one came out and said as much, but the general consensus was that disability isn't commercial, so nobody's interested.
>
> (Edgar, in *Birmingham Post*, 2008, para 12–13)

Given the non-disabled status of the former, and the disabled status of Edgar, there seems to be a great similarity with the television shows of Ricky Gervais here, as discussed briefly in Chapter Three. The large appetite for non-disabled authors to tell the stories of disabled people is perhaps perceived by the publishing and film-making gatekeepers as less risky, and more objective than their disabled equivalents, as Edgar's opinion would suggest, but the difference in the positioning of the disabled protagonist as 'the problem', and the model reader/viewer, as one who is seeing through a 'non-disabled gaze' seems crucial.[13]

Certainly, curiosity and speculation are likely to have been the catalysts for many film narratives across the length and breadth of cinema, firing creativity and driving the desire to present a vast array of questions and stories. Whilst this is valuable, and can be seen to attract audiences across all types of film (not least those for 'auteur films' which reflect the preoccupations of their creators), the viewers who watch these films will be those who identify with the questions and themes raised. As a keen member of the audience for *Three Billboards Outside Ebbing, Missouri*, for example, I found the film to be (amongst other things) a scathing exploration of the taken-for-granted racism which pervades both society and the contents of our own heads; in my own case, learned so startlingly early and surreptitiously. A film like this, seen in my youth, would have spoken directly to my misguided beliefs on 'race' and possibly changed them, speaking eloquently, as it does, of the barbarism of white supremacy, and other forms of bigotry, e.g. assumptions made about James (Peter Dinklage) based on his short height and disabled identity. This viewing experience may not be true for non-white viewers, given the comparative marginalisation of black characters. As some criticisms have suggested (Butler, 2018, for example), there is a story of redemption here which focusses on revealing, and possibly encouraging an understanding of, the brutal, and racist character of a police officer, Jason Dixon, whilst the Black and disabled people's personalities are not explored in any depth.[14] This could thus be seen to play to the curiosity of those of us who claim to abhor racism, but are trying to understand the more obvious manifestations of white privilege. Indeed, the story of this film shows the (white) mother Mildred (Frances McDormand) seeking 'justice' and answers to the rape and murder of her daughter (Angela), where she aligns herself, and her mission, with 'Black folks' as other 'victims' of police incompetence and brutality, an alliance which could easily be seen as a narrative based on 'interest convergence'. This is a concept which is theorised to show the convergence of interests between Black and white people, enabling mutual needs to be seen to be served whilst racial hierarchies are maintained (see Bell, 1980, and the development of work on this concept in work such as Delgado's [2015]); in this case racism is challenged but it is the white characters whose stories we are asked to follow.[15] This is perhaps best encapsulated in Mildred's words:

> My daughter Angela was murdered seven months ago, it seems to me the police department is too busy torturing black folk to solve actual crimes.

Whilst a strong case can be made to support films which explore constructions of racism, and disablism, as this can be seen to do – if we discount disablist jokes at the expense of James and the use of 'nigger' and 'retard' as signifiers of the ills of contemporary America, alongside other metaphors of revenge, rape, and cancer (Morris, 2018) – there are compelling questions to be asked about how viewers are positioned as white/Black/Asian, disabled/nondisabled, and so on, in such films, and how the muting of Black and disabled people's experience makes viewers feel (from all social groups). As valuable as the explorations of injustice, revenge and redemption are, it was no surprise to find that the writer and director, Martin McDonagh (a white, British/Irish man), had developed the idea for this film from seeing billboards in a Southern US state, with a message which spoke of 'rage and pain', stimulating his curiosity about who might do such a thing and why (Channel4.com, 2018). Given the discourses of racism and disability which are one of the key features of the film alongside the marginalisation of the Black characters, it is unclear why the character was cast as a white woman, in a story which did not necessitate this (an undeniably powerful performance of the main protagonist, Mildred, by Frances McDormand) and already had two white male protagonists, in Woody Harrelson, and Sam Rockwell. Conversely, the jokes about James' size required a man with restricted growth. Added to this, on an industry-wide basis, are difficulties that non-white, disabled, and (often) female actors are likely to face in entering the networks of the film-making elites; a report on the British film industry found that they uphold a 'culture of nepotism' (Carey et al, 2017), with film-makers often relying on those who they have previously worked with (Brown, 2017).

World-slicing, and the construction of meanings of disability in adaptations

The commercial success of *Me Before You* and *Wonder* would certainly support the bias towards non-disabled writers and film-makers, and narratives which centre the curiosity and points of view of non-disabled people.[16]. By comparison *Stronger*, a biographical film based on the memoir of Jeff Bauman, who had both his legs amputated after he was injured in the 2013 Boston bombing, did not do well at the box office, a marked difference in a year where other disability films did so well.[17] The lack of popularity of *Stronger* may well be due to the subject matter of the bombing, possibly being seen as 'too soon' by the potential audience (Lee, 2017, para 2). But it could also be due to the film's 'avoidance of clichés' (Lee, 2017, para 1), even its counter 'inspiration porn' messages, particularly as the narrative swam against the tide of other mainstream portrayals of disability by spurning hackneyed tales of heroism, thwarting expectations of the triumph-of-mind-over-matter trope. It is also of some significance that *Wonder*, and *Me Before You*, both commercial successes, were entirely fictional, based only on speculation and imagination, whereas *Stronger* could not be enjoyed as an imaginary story, effectively asking its audience to grapple with 'real' themes of terrorism and acquired impairment.

However, these films are *all* adaptations, allowing us to dig deeper into why certain people and things are presented in particular ways through cinema. Using film studies tools, including narrative analysis and attention to visual features and semiotics, basic comparisons between literary and cinematic texts allow us to raise questions about what was omitted or added, and why. At this simple level of analysis, we can raise further questions about authenticity and authorship, allowing some interrogation of the intentions of the original authors, and the subsequent work of screenwriters and directors. It can also enable us to investigate questions of authorship between texts, in terms of who is 'authoring' the disabled characters' voices, and how they have been positioned, e.g. does the disabled person have more agency in the literature or film, and why? Thus, we may learn more about how cinematic practices can create, change, or remove disabling signifiers. In the case of *Me Before You*, Thea Sharrock directed the film, but Moyes was also the screenwriter, which might lead us to expect high degrees of similarity between the original book and the film, points I will return to later in my discussion of the film, and also in the concluding chapter.

Writing on film adaptations, Geraghty has spoken of the tendency to prioritise 'transposition over interpretation' (Geraghty, 2008, 2). She says there tends to be a privileging of narrative scrutiny over other forms of cinematic analysis – of mise en scène, genre, acting, sound, editing, celebrity, all of which are fundamental to the ways meanings are shaped in films. Thus, Geraghty argues for the analysis of the crucial work of 'interpretative and social processes' (ibid., 4) which act to create specific meanings in adaptations. My intention here, as suggested in Chapter One, is to blend narrative analysis with other fundamental elements of film, disentangling the distinct interpretative and social processes which may have fed into disability representations within this particular adaptation, and examining, in particular, its status as a romantic comedy. This is an aspect of the film which has almost been forgotten by those who criticise it as a disability film, seen primarily in terms of the discourse of 'better dead than disabled' (see Gilbey, 2016, for example). I will also examine fidelity to the original, in order to examine variances in the forms of disablism portrayed or constructed according to each medium

As Geraghty says, there is a need for textual and contextual analysis in the consideration of adaptations. The work of 'recall' suggested by Geraghty allows us to locate the film version of *Me Before You* in a variety of contexts; in relation to the original book if we have read it, but also in relation to other films of a similar type, including romantic comedies and dramas which follow similar narrative trajectories, whilst reminding us of the memories and understandings associated with them. The impact of genre and memory is particularly clear here. In looking at how the film makes sense to viewers, it is understandable that disabled campaigners across the world reacted strongly, seeing this in the context of other films which result in the suicide of the character who cannot bear to live as a disabled person, and the idea that it is better to be dead than disabled.[18] Conversely, when I took part in a small demonstration outside a local cinema, we talked to disabled people (and others) who had read the book and had used such recall of romantic/comedy/ dramas to say how the book had appealed to them *precisely* because it had challenged the idea that disabled people were unworthy of love, complaining that this was typical across a range of genres, with few disabled characters as protagonists in romantic comedies or dramas. Geraghty's points on recall reflect some important themes in Film Theory, particularly those which contribute to our understanding of representational strategies, the place of film/genre, memory, and the affective processes of the audience. The work of Giles Deleuze in particularly valuable in these respects.

Vitale (2011a, para 12 and 13), for example, proposes that we conceptualise Deleuze's concept of the *movement-image* as a verb, *to image*, conceptualising images as movement. Taking this approach, images can then be envisioned as slices of the world and refractions of it, emphasising one aspect of the world over others. Images are thus seen as 'imagings' of perceptions, such that we have the *perception-image* brought about by the 'eye of the camera' usually seeming to come from an unidentified viewpoint, or none at all, but sometimes from the point of view of specific characters. A third concept is also theorised – the *affection-image*; this tends to represent a transition, often expressed as bodily change, present in images which present the ability to affect and be affected, most commonly shown in close-ups of emotional change, but also valuable in the theorisation of sound within film and other media. These forms of movement-image are constituents of *action-images*, in their smaller and larger forms. In terms of action-images, in *Me Before You*, we can see that elements such as the close-ups of Lou's (Emilia Clarke) ever-smiling, tender face, as a classic MPDG, lead to affect in Will (Sam Claflin, the leading man) – most notably – encouraging the audience to think that she will bring about big changes of mind about his proposed suicide.

She is also the perfect fit for the *Blithe Spirit* trope, described on the TV tropes website (tvtropes.org, 2017b) as a 'free-spirited Fish out of Water who goes to a strait-laced land and shakes things up there despite the insistence of everyone else that the way things are can't possibly be changed'. Lou suddenly enters a world of wealth, propriety, elegance and seriousness, from a background of poverty and low cultural capital, as a catalyst for impossible change. The choice of the camera shots, use of colour, and tone of dialogue all synthesise to shape the possibilities for audience responses to the signifiers encoded in these forms of imaging, even before a consideration of the wider narrative. As Vitale says of Deleuze's work '[i]mages become different, become other than what they are/were, simply by being woven together differently' (Vitale, 2011a, para 36). I will argue that this is more than evident in this adaptation, giving rise to distinct meanings becoming attributed to impairment and disability from the start, where they could have been constructed quite differently. This is especially true if we consider the differences between film and book, the differential use of the camera according to character, and the correspondences between this film and the features of the romantic comedy genre. Using the insights and approaches of Geraghty and Deleuze as guides, alongside reflection on how the film corresponds with the rom-com genre, I will now examine how disability is woven into this story in a number of ways to create particular forms of spectacle which are uncommon within the characterisations of romantic protagonists in contemporary rom-coms.

Cinematic constructions of disability and impairment in *Me Before You*

One might expect a high degree of fidelity of the film to the original book, especially as Jojo Moyes is both the book's author and the screenwriter for the film. But, rather than finding a greater degree of similarity than other adaptations, I found that there were striking omissions and additions in the film, resulting in very different readings of disability.[19] The central protagonist is Will Traynor, who had a very successful career and extremely active and satisfying life before he became disabled after a road accident. Louisa Clark (Lou) is a poor, unskilled, and newly unemployed young woman who has been using her meagre wages to support her family, who Will's mother employs to becomes his paid assistant; she takes this job due to a generous hourly rate and her desperate need for work. Eventually she becomes Will's love interest, but, before she even meets him, he has decided that he probably wants to end his life, a decision which is portrayed very differently between book and film. Like many 'meet-cutes' there is initial tension, but in this case we are reminded first and foremost that he is a disabled person. When he is introduced to Lou, and told that she will be his companion, his response is typical of the 'Obsessive Avenger' stereotype of disabled men with mobility impairments (often wheelchair-users) favoured by film-makers, theorised by Norden (1994) to be embittered men who seek revenge on others for their unwanted fate as a person with an impairment. When she first looks at him he fakes an 'Elephant Man' response, complete with incoherent growls and twisted facial expressions. Filmed primarily in shot reverse shots between Will and Lou (apart from a segment where there are very swift reverse shots between Will and his mother) the camera spends equal time showing Will's actions and Lou's, putting the viewer in Lou's position as a shocked observer. However, throughout these exchanges Will remains the focus of concern, with the sounds he is making framing the whole scenario. The use of the camera and sound works to create a jarring distinction between the 'monstrous' visual and auditory spectacle we first see and the self-assurance, eloquence, and upper-class accent of the 'real' Will who introduces himself properly after we see the horror on her face, and the rebuke from his mother. His personal (male) nurse assuages the situation, simultaneously acting to clarify Will's personality to any of the audience who may not have picked up on these cues, by saying, 'You're a bad man, Mr T', positioning him as awkward at best. The smile we have already come to expect from Lou, even in adversity, has been wiped from her face.

Amongst many other changes, perhaps the most striking omissions for me were the removal of a number of incidents from the book. Where we clearly hear Will's voice in the book, and can see the way that people and environments disable and infantalise him on an everyday basis, this is played down in the film, reducible mainly to one incident where we hear him asserting the right to make his own decisions as a competent agent in his own life (although we can reflect on his first appearance as a dour, sardonic man, as a result of, and resistance to, his positioning as a child). Although the book is more polyphonic, presenting some chapters from different characters' viewpoints, significantly Will's voice is not one of them, reflecting the questions Moyes set out to explore, e.g. how do his mother and his girlfriend feel? Another significant, and perhaps inexplicable, omission, is the disappearance of the suggested rape/sexual assault of Lou, in the grounds of Will's family's castle, when she was younger. It is perhaps possible that Jojo Moyes' initial inclusion of this in the book was to suggest a comparison of the trauma of sexual violence with the biographical disruption brought about by his impairment. However, his medical condition is portrayed as devastating in the book, much less so in the film. One might question frequent visits to the hospital, and the lengthy, traumatic stays which ensue, as suitable for the rom-com, but beds are a key part of rom-com iconography and this film exceeds the usual quota, even if few of them are host to sexual activities. However, the hospital as a key location was also used in *The Big Sick*, a rom-com which also drew large audiences, demonstrating that this too can be a site for romance.[20]

As suggested, the construction of disability representations, and the conditions of possibility for making meanings from this film, go beyond the usual features of the romantic comedy, with many visual aspects of the film and mise en scène contributing to the shaping of meaning. This includes the ways locations, camera angles, shots, and use of light conspire to make the film a rather monologic vehicle to tell Lou's story, rather than Will's. As such, the focus on either disablement or the arguments for and against suicide are less of a fundamental feature in the film, beyond the overarching narrative. In many ways, the attitudes towards disability, and arguments for and against assisted suicide, slip through, almost unnoticed, in the emphasis placed on Lou, and the story of their love, rendering this typical of the 'normality' genre (Darke, 1998) which uses impairment and disability to reinforce ideologies of non-disabled normalities. Or they would have, were it not for the worldwide protests against the film. There was a danger here that the emphasis placed on Lou and love on one side, and the highlighting of 'better dead than disabled' suicide on another, would obscure the story of impairment and disablement also being told, which is significant in itself.

Mise en scène, hierarchies of normality, and relationship shifts...

A cursory analysis of mise en scène throughout the film shows a clear difference between locations, and the sharply contrasting discourses on Lou's and Will's personalities, their cultural and moral outlooks, and the ways they occupy space. Will is usually portrayed in the spacious surroundings of his family home, which is in a large castle. We can see this as a very obvious primary signifier of privilege and wealth, perhaps symbolic of Englishness, or Britishness at least, possibly aimed at US and worldwide audiences who equate British films with period films (Monk, 2015, 176), which are often focussed on the upper and upper-middle classes, and the 'excesses of bourgeois finery' (Monk, 2015, 180, following Craig, 1991). The castle in the film is Pembroke Castle, in Wales, built in the eleventh century, an impressive stronghold in extensive grounds, which passed through the hands of royalty and the aristocracy for centuries (pembroke-castle.co.uk, 2018). It is not clear whether the Traynor family live in the entire castle, or Granta House on the side of the castle, a house which is actually Wytham Abbey, in Oxfordshire (O'Connor, 2016). Moyes deliberately sought such a location to emphasise the class difference between Lou and Will, as the 'purest example of old money rubbing up against ordinary people' (Moyes, 2012, 486). Even the specially designed annex the Traynor family have created to accommodate Will's needs is capacious, so we get no real sense of environmental barriers within his own home as he is able to wheel himself around easily in his powered wheelchair. These, and other opulent locations, perhaps exploit international audiences by encouraging them to buy into the idea that British people live like this; the film implies that Will's family own the castle, though in reality the majority of British castles are not owned by private individuals or families (see Campsie, 2016, for example).

The portrayal of privilege is crude, particularly the caricature of white working class lives in both visual and narrative aspects of the film. There are sharp contrasts made between her home life and his, including a scene when she introduces Will to her family for the first time. There is no real sense of the barriers to mobility which would exist in a small inaccessible home – they overlook the obstacles to entry and mobility within the house, whilst mid-range camera shots are taken from angles which emphasise overcrowded small spaces . The forms of mise en scène, emphasising poverty – and possibly suggesting squalor – are underscored by other elements of the story, not least her younger sister who is a single parent and her boyfriend, Patrick, who is portrayed pejoratively, as a self-centred 'chav' (vulgar and lower-class) who has aspirations beyond his talents (often seen sporting a 'Young Entrepreneur of the Year' shirt while running); Patrick provides a foil for Will's clear success in all areas of his life, e.g. as a former businessman who had a rich social life and excelled in extreme sports.

The only location where we get any sense of environmental barriers and Will's discomfort is when his wheelchair gets stuck in the mud at the racecourse, a scene which is used primarily to underline the differences between Lou's excessive optimism and capacity for humour, and Will's dissatisfaction and disgruntlement – this scene is more light-hearted in the film, while there is a fuller account of the indignities he feels in the book. A potentially rare moment of the representation of disablement is used to encourage our engagement with her personality, as helpful and kind, rather than with his difficulties. Significantly, the barriers which Will has had to face in his new life are rarely evident in the film. This is one of the main facets of the story which is lost in the cinematic portrayal, while there are more incidents in the book which demonstrate the exclusions imposed on Will, environmentally and attitudinally, not least in Will's complaints about how people treat him differently – this is only touched upon in the film, often implicitly through gestures on Will's brooding persona, perhaps denoting silent anger or embarrassment. The spaciousness of his living quarters gives us no sense of environmental disablement, beyond his own physical functions. Together the naturalness of his ease of access in his home and grounds, together with the minimisation of his voice as a critique of disablement brought about by those around him, effectively mutes the opposition he may feel towards the ways others are treating him, adding the individualistic lens we are encouraged to see though from the start; from the very first scene he is in we see his surly, dismissive attitude of Lou and his mother.

Despite the repetition of this old trope of disabled masculinity, and perhaps most importantly the blatant connection established between his impairment and his surly personality from the meet-cute, the overall structure of the narrative renders him the positive agent of change in Lou's life, as their mutual attraction develops and the Pygmalion-esque story unfolds. This acts as a normality genre in two ways, then. First, the overall trajectory towards Will's seemingly inevitable death by assisted suicide acts to reinforce ideas of non-disabled normality (where dead is better than disabled), not just for Will but also for Lou and the rest of the Traynor family, who are freed to live their lives without the (implicit) 'burden' of care. Second, his part in Lou's evolution from cheery bun vendor to Parisian adventurer is the culmination of a story where she is 'normalised' to fulfil the potential Will deems her to have, and that he affords to her through transfers of cultural capital, moral improvement, and so on; i.e. despite her joie de vivre, hard-working ethics and care for all those around her, he is seen to rescue her from a life he deems 'duller than his', simultaneously denoting his own new worst life as worthless.

The visual and narrative elements outlined so far link closely to broader themes of class and cultural capital, which are central to both the book and the film. As I have argued elsewhere Wilde (2016), this film is at its most pernicious in supporting damaging ideas of how disabled people should be living. It contains a Randian subtext on class. The Randian idea of the 'moocher' (Rand, 1999), conceptualised as someone who is unable to create value themselves and is therefore parasitical on morally superior people who generate wealth, lies at the heart of this story, from Will's fall from his previous high status to economic inactivity, to Lou's family, who are dependent on her – easily deemed 'useless eaters', significantly a label often attached to disabled people (Mostert, 2002). It is Will, who possibly sees his new self as a useless eater, who ultimately rescues Lou from moocher-hood. A key scene in establishing Lou's potential for superior moral worth was when she immediately went to the job centre to get the (high paid) job as Will's companion, after she was laid off at the café she worked in. The conceit of Will's urging that she should make more of her life, and try harder to maximise her potential, alongside the other discourses about the moral imperative to find a job, can be seen to be exposed in Will later bestowing a job on her father. However, this is unlikely to be read as an ideological contradiction to the meritocratic principles embedded in the story, or as incongruous with the Randian morals we are being encouraged to subscribe to, because by this time we are likely to be invested in Will's efforts at her redemption, and the barriers which prevent her from a higher role in life. We are encouraged to be pleased for her to be able to escape the duties of care to her family, through her parents' new-found capacities for being financially independent. Our focus on *her* wellbeing serves to naturalise nepotism in the job market, considering that wealthier people tend to excuse their use of family and network connections as a self-entitlement which comes with privilege (Pareene, 2013). Moreover, this action towards Lou's father is presented as benevolence, as the 'giving back' we might expect (but rarely get) from the upper classes (see Svalavitz, 2013 for example), despite his own (narcissistic) investment in 'freeing' Lou to become more like him.

Will's own fall in status from the higher echelons has no material implications, though the spectre of the moocher seems to lie at the heart of the reasons he is not prepared to accept his life as someone who feels they have no means to create value. This is especially so given his former success in all areas of life, including career, relationships, cultural activities, and sport, and his and others' new positioning of himself as parasitical, in all aspects of personal care. Ultimately Will finds his value by endowing the world with an improved version of Lou, and leaving Lou a financial legacy to become other than herself. There are hierarchies of value being constructed here between disabled and non-disabled, respectable and less respectable, espousing moral values which are clearly attached to wealth, class, and cultural taste.

Related themes which emerge from a closer study of both visuals and narrative include the denigration of working-class males. The embodiment of such scorn seems to take on particular strength in the shape of Lou's boyfriend Patrick – his pride in being twice young entrepreneur of the year is emphasised in the film, whereas his obsession for sport predominates in the book. There seems to be a great sense of mockery attributed to him in the film, in terms of his sporting activities and entrepreneurialism, perhaps best depicted in images of him training with a shirt emblazoned with his entrepreneurial award. His almost brutish masculinity, underlined by this crude athleticism and lofty ambitions unbefitting of his lowly status, are in sharp contradiction to the very same values we are expected to read more sympathetically in Lou's and Will's stories; e.g. we see Will's easier, confident, relaxed and more impressive form of athleticism when Lou peeks at an old clip on his computer, where he is seen to be excelling at extreme sports.

Again, this can be contrasted with Will's subsequent lack of movement and dependence on others, while there is a simultaneous downplaying of disabled people taking up space in the film, not least through the ample space of his living quarters and the provision of all the adaptations he needs. Consequently, rather than drawing our attention to Will's experiences as a disabled person, and the additional barriers he would face if he was less wealthy, we are more likely to be seduced by the beauty of wealth, through these contrasting views of embodied (working-class) ugliness, juxtaposed with our gaze on the beauty of Will and Lou's faces, set within a classic rom-com iconography; a classical music concert, racecourse visit, Mauritian holiday , and a wedding, set in a red-brick Tudor house with extensive gardens, where they are seen to fall in love.

Like the wedding, outdoor locations are used to convey turning points and new possibilities in the story. Will and Lou first venture outdoors into the expansive gardens of Will's home, within the castle grounds, to establish a more dialogical relationship between them. It is out in the open air, in green spaces, that we see Will encouraging her to move beyond the cloying certainties of her 'small town existence' to explore the world. It is also here where we see the growing equality, and increasingly mutual disdain, as well as affection, between them. It is within the ostensibly more democratic space of the natural outdoor environment that the audience first hears Lou mocking wealthy people in Will's company, in the spirit of friendship and trust.[21]

However, the beginning of this mutuality is seen after they have had a disagreement when he sees her repairing the photographs of his past, framed pictures which he has deliberately smashed. He criticises her attitude towards him, saying she thinks she 'knows best' and asks her to spare him the 'cod psychology' she tends to use. After apologising, she points out that he doesn't have to be 'an arse', whilst underlining his agency further by pointing out that she doesn't work for *him*, and is only answerable to his mother as her employer. Perhaps with some remorse, he then invites her to watch a subtitled DVD with him, bringing her into his world whilst simultaneously distancing himself by mocking her lack of cultural capital. She initially refuses his request by saying she doesn't watch those 'kind of films', to which he responds by asking whether it was because she hadn't been taught to read at school. The cinematic 'taste test', often requested of or imposed on women who are the love interest of the male, has become quite familiar, often as a prelude to sex (though not in *Me Before You*), and is often resisted by the female, as we also see in *The Big Sick*, when Kumail (Kumail Nanjiani) insists that Emily (Zoe Kazan) watches *Night of the Living Dead* with him, soon after they meet.[22]

Indeed, Lou also resists. So begins the sparring between them. Sparring is a common trope in rom-coms (Jeffers McDonald, 2007), especially the verbal sparring to be found in screwball (romantic) comedies (Marshall, 2009). This often signifies the emergence of mutual attraction, but Jeffers McDonald points out that the emphasis on sparring in conventional romantic comedies is centred on the relationship between the female romantic lead and the mother of the male lead. This is noticeably absent in the story, given Lou's prime responsibility towards his mother, and her respect for his mother's wishes. This seems significant to the construction of a story where he is intent on following the usual Oedipal journey towards death, a common narrative which is given to disabled men who are portrayed as disempowered, to have no opportunities for miracle cures, or recovery from physical impairments; it is taken as axiomatic that this spoils their masculine identities (Wilde, 2004b). There is an odd difference between the novel and the book in the minutiae of this scene. Although the DVD he picks is not mentioned in the book (described by Lou as being an old film about a 'Hunchback man' who is tricked by his 'unscrupulous neighbours', which seems to be a reference to *Jean de Florette*, made in 1986), in the film he chooses the more recent (2010) *Des hommes et des dieux*. Both films would have provided the audience with metaphors about disability, but the former would have, perhaps more obviously, provided a metaphor for the scapegoating of disabled people which may have resulted in a more political reading. The film's use of *Des hommes et des dieux* provides a better allegorical hint of what is to come in his story, and the way he views it. Simply put, this film is based on the murder of seven Trappist monks of the Cisterian Monastery of Our Lady of Atlas, in Tibhirine, Algeria, in 1996, who become martyrs in the spirit of peace, choosing to stay and face death rather than desert their monastery and community. Although we are not shown the words which start the film in *Me Before You*, which are a paraphrasing of Psalm 82: 6–7 (which changes according to the version of the bible used); 'I say you are gods, sons of the most high [...] But you shall die like men and fall like princes', a message he clearly wanted to get across to her. Significantly the only part of the film we watch with them is where we see a monk being told he has no choice, to which he replies, 'Yes, I do', at which point the camera cuts to a shot of both of Lou and Will, taken from the side, then shot reverse shots, first of Lou from Will's eye line, suggesting he is observing her rapt attention to this dialogue, before the camera switches to examine him focussing close attention to her reaction. There is a swift cut to the gardens outside, before returning to the rolling of the film's end credits, seen over both of their shoulders. Immediately after this Will moves his wheelchair to face her, asking 'So?'. What ensues is an impassioned questioning about how the monks could sacrifice their lives. Within this dialogue she says 'they could have left' and he answers 'but they chose to stay' and she replies that she could understand that it gave their life more meaning. He then asks 'But you don't agree?' Drawing our attention to a blatant metaphor for his state of mind and the questions of her impact upon his potential desire to keep on living, Will finishes this attempt to educate Lou through cinema, and to defend his position towards his new life and death, as a reflection of the noble sacrifices made by the monks. If we were to make comparisons with *Des hommes et des dieux*, then, we could possibly interpret this as 'better death than a desertion of my values', so far seen as a love of athletic prowess, high status, a rich social life, and a career focussed on money-making. After this scene, which points to the decision he has made, he hints that some barriers between them have been removed; he says 'The sky's clearing – shall we get some air?'.

As we might expect from this segue from one scenario to another, the scenes which immediately follow take them outdoors, and, ostensibly, into a more equal relationship. The subsequent exchanges between them are often shot in a way where Lou occupies a more equal spatial position. This is mostly captured in mid-range shots and the use of shot reverse shot, often used to signify multiple points of view and draw the viewer's imaginary into the story (as Ivone Margulies has suggested (1996, 60)). Complementing the move to scenes which are focussed on increasing dialogue and equity between them, and an emphasis placed on both their points of view, more of the conversation is based upon Will's clear desire to know more about her. At first, we see them moving together through the gardens, insulting each other, mostly on the grounds of cultural capital and their differing approaches to, and quality of, life. When he remarks at his shock that she has got to twenty-six without seeing a subtitled film she retorts that she is surprised he has reached thirty-one 'without being locked in a cupboard for being such a snob'. Later in the story, after they have become closer, and he has just recovered from a relapse she has nursed him through, we see her elevated, sitting on a wall, which positions her above Will, who has to raise his eyes and head slightly to look at her. Before we see this, the camera alerts the viewer to the fact that we are again 'in nature' as it pans down from the top of a leafy tree, straight down to her feet. She is wearing green Irregular Choice shoes, a brand of shoes which are a motif throughout the film, emblematic of her quirky fashion aesthetic.[23] After this, the camera uses over the shoulder shot reverse shots, and one long shot of them both, within the landscape of field and trees.

These changes in visual strategy reflect narrative shifts where she begins to claim the moral high ground (and the literal high ground in this scene), even launching a class-based critique of his world, in increasingly critical observations on the shallow superficialities and decadence of the lives of elites (there is a monologue of this type in this particular scene). This may suggest a gradual transference of power and life's riches from Will to Lou. The positioning of her, higher than him, and other visual elements of the scene, in which she is sitting on a wall and delivering her own moral polemic, is of some significance then, considering the tendency of reverse shots to appear fair to both characters, as though we are seeing and understanding both points of view. In this case, I am suggesting that the use of the camera and mise en scène, in an open space, Lou dressed in green within a pretty, green, natural landscape (signifying new life perhaps), repositions her as his superior (physically, spatially, and morally), her smiling almost throughout; this is at a time when we are perhaps most susceptible to engagements and attachments made through the shot reverse shot's appeal to our imaginaries. Despite the growing critique she has of the mores of people within his strata of society, and of his reluctance to 'live boldly', as the film says (its tag line), it is also in this scene where the dialogue establishes the Pygmalion sub-text of Will's desire for her, when he tells her she shouldn't be happy living in that area, and that she has a duty to live her one life 'as fully as possible'. The weaving together of these elements, with other visual aesthetics, encourages the audience to look forward to Lou's future rather than his.

Colour, lighting, and change

Viewer affect is often sought through the use of lighting and colour throughout the film; the saturated colours of the clothes worn by Lou are especially memorable, even though we may often be unaware, or only subconsciously aware, of the psychological effects of the ways in which colour is used.

Speaking of the work of Vincente Minelli, and the relationship to images and the overall affect produced by colour and dance, Deleuze states,

> Colour is dream not because dream is in colour, but because colours ... are given a highly absorbent, almost devouring, value. This means that we have to insinuate ourselves, to let ourselves become absorbed, without at the same time losing ourselves or being snatched away. Dance ... now acquires depth, grows stronger as it becomes the sole means of entering into another world, that is, into another's world, into another's dream or past.
>
> (Deleuze, 1989, 63)

Despite the demonstration of the power of colour in shaping affect, it is a comparatively neglected, albeit now growing, area within film studies (Everett, 2007; Misek, 2010), although theorisations of the use of colour are often linked to specific films or film-makers (see Everett, for examples). The use of colour in *Me Before You* is quite startling, especially for something designed for the 'chick flick' audience, i.e. 'commercial films that appeal to a female audience' (Ferriss and Young, 2008, 2), 'that give women pleasure' (ibid., 17).[24] Lou is staged as the predominant spectacle, linked to parts of the narrative where we learn that her hobby is fashion; she dresses in a way which offsets the colour palette for the film. Invariably she is dressed in bright, bold, and multiple colours, with the occasional use of paler, less saturated colours when she is shown making an effort to be someone more respectable than herself – at Will's ex-girlfriend's wedding (dressed in a pale turquoise), and when he is seriously unwell (pale yellow). Green and yellow backgrounds predominate throughout most of the film, gradually making way for darker romantic scenes, before we reach the disquietingly white canvas of Will's Dignitas room. At his Dignitas bedside Lou is wearing a turquoise cardigan with a butterflies print dress underneath, possibly symbolising her impending metamorphosis after he dies. Throughout there is clearly a deliberate use of colour to make her stand out from everyone around her, and to 'unsettle the mood of the film' as one which is preoccupied with death. As Marine (2015) shows, the audience will always notice saturated colours which do not fit the colour palette of the film, with the resulting discordance drawing closer attention to particular things or people – in this case Lou.

Lou's clothes choices shift in the final scene, in Paris, where she is dressed mainly in muted colours. The changes Will wanted to see in her are clearly beginning to occur, denoted in her appearance and location. She is dressed more elegantly whilst still retaining the quirkiness of her former self, this time in the form of 'bumblebee tights' (yellow and black stripes) he bought her for her birthday to remind her of childhood passions, also recalling the palette of the first half of the film. Otherwise colour is used, as Marine (2015) suggests, to separate time, space, and mood. Greens and yellows are used as background colours in many of the early parts of the film, most obviously in the outdoors scenes, but they are also predominant in Will's living quarters, albeit in paler, less saturated and more clinical, dull hues – so, following Marine (2015) we are more likely to associate lower intensities of life, different moods, and fading life with him. As such, the change in colour tone, but not palette, indicates a more subdued mood in Will's home when contrasted with the vitality of the outside world. Will also tends to wear paler, neutral colours, including white, pale blues and light greys, perhaps denoting his more sombre frame of mind and the (ostensibly) greater elegance attributed to higher social classes (Brooks, 2000; Walker, 2012). In contrast, as suggested, the scene where Lou sits, on the wall, above him, is filled with more vibrant greens, from the trees in the foreground and background, to the grass all around them, and the green of her sweater, skirt, and shoes. Linked to the dialogue about her distinctive multi-coloured character, at the one time where she almost blends into the spring-like scenery around her, the use of green seems to signify fertility and hope, as suggested by the culmination of their conversation, on the abundance of her potential.

Lou's use of disruptive colours to those which are persistent can be seen to associate her with change and possible transitions (Marine, 2015). Marine says he believes colour to be the visual counterpoint between imagery and sound. It can be used to heighten the nature of our desires or to be the final twist of the life. It sets the groundwork for the emotional state of the film.

(Video, 15.03–15.10)

This can be seen very clearly in a scene where Will takes Lou to a classical music concert (the first time he takes the lead in arranging social outings), and she wears a revealing, yet decorous red dress, against a background of smartly dressed people in grey, black and purple tones. She simultaneously stands out, as the most beautiful person in the room, whilst fitting into the elegance of his world. Hence the dress, and her glamour, signals the disruption of his world and the transition into acknowledging her sexual passions towards him, achieved through the use of red, as symbolic of passion, whilst triggering an acknowledgement of his sexual attraction and agency. When they are in the car and she says that they are setting off for home, he asks her to wait a few minutes so he can savour the moment, saying 'I just want to be a man who's been to a concert with a girl in a red dress', suggesting that he has fallen for her, but that this is the last time he will have such feelings.

The music which accompanies this scene is Mozart's *Oboe Concerto in C major, K. 314*. We do not hear very much of this, just a few moments in the concert hall, and then faintly when they are together in the car. This piece of music doesn't appear to have any specific significance, other than to signify her induction into another level or form of cultural capital, although classical music per se is often extra-diegetical in romantic comedies (Classic.fm, 2018). Such music often has additional layers of symbolism, e.g. the use of clarinet concertos in *A Bout de Souffle*, as Godard believed this to be Mozart's last work (Andrew, 1998, 16). Although generous analysis might suggest that Mozart is used alongside the colour of red to denote dissonance and 'heighten the emotional impact' (Brown, 1994, 15), the brevity of the music played and wider narrative would suggest that its placement is to add to ideas of (his) higher and (her former) lower cultural status (ibid., 1994). However, Knauss (speaking mainly of opera, 2012, 118–119) has argued that such concerts are rarely used in romantic comedy, except to convey elite forms of culture, invariably depicting the initiation of the lower-class woman into the man's world (e.g. *Pretty Woman*), where the woman is shown to make extensive or particular preparations for the date, with the onus on improvement. *Me Before You* is no exception – we see Will checking Lou's appearance beforehand, whilst telling her to remove her pale pink (modesty-, or respectability-orientated) wrap, denoting his sexual interest, mitigating her preoccupation with propriety. As Marine says, red is used in cinema to evoke the strongest reactions, and this scene is notably the only scene where red is used in such a bold, dramatic way.[25] As Marine suggests (2015), colour is also used to show the inner-workings of a person's character, both Lou's in her sexual attraction to Will, and also in his direct reference to the colour red, and the clear connections he is making to his sexual past, and his celibate, perhaps asexual future, again a common trope for disabled men (see McIlvenny, 2003 for example, and Wilde, 2004c). Notably, in the car scene, Will doesn't refer to wanting to spend time with *Lou* in a red dress but to 'a girl', clearly denoting his sexual agency in the past tense.

The only real exceptions to the use of bright colour in Lou's clothing are three scenes in the latter half of the film. All of these feature darkness, which may well signpost doom, but such tenebrosity is used in all three to reinforce the growing intimacy between them. This happens first when the hostilities and sparring between them give way to warmth and intimacy; here we can see that it is snowing outside the window of Will's bedroom, contrasting with and enhancing the warmth she is bringing to his life and the relationship between them. Of course, snow at this stage may be taken to symbolise a variety of different things (as a common cinematic, screen, and literary device), from her pureness/chasteness of personality and perhaps the pureness of his final intentions, to the possibility of his impending death; Jones, for example, shows how snow is used to emphasise the 'mutual connectedness of humanity and the natural world' (Jones, 2007, 137). Conversely, snow, as a metaphor for renewal, may suggest a new beginning and 'cleansing' of spoiled lives. However, for me, the contrast between the concurrent increase of intimacy between them indicates that this is being used here to suggest a feeling that it is the two of them against a harsh set of (bitterly cold) circumstances, in itself a comment on disability.

The second scene in darkness is similar in that it suggests that they are finally becoming a romantic couple, basking in intimacy in a hotel bedroom; on this occasion we see them watching the magnificence of a storm through the window, again clashing with the rising heat of sexual attraction in the bedroom and the warmth and comfort of their situation indoors. Although we may see the spectacle of the storm as a symbol of what may come in the drama of their lives, here the film is comparatively subtle. The book seems to have a clearer link to his impending trip to Dignitas, where her decision to close the shutters is met with his refusal and a demand to 'throw the doors open', remarking 'I want to see it', suggesting his desire to confront the harsh realities of death (and life) in a direct, unwavering way. Instead the film veers between camera shots of them on the bed and the storm through the window, choosing to focus more on the themes of romantic love, possibly suggesting some ambivalence, and a wavering of his resolve in the throes of the passion he seems to be feeling towards her.

This use of light is particularly emphatic in the penultimate scene, where Lou goes to see Will, who is waiting to die in a Dignitas room. In quite strong contrast to the actual decoration and more colourful furnishings of the real Dignitas rooms (Gentleman, 2009), this film set is notable for its unremitting use of white; it is at this moment, I think, that the film can be seen to romanticise suicide most clearly symbolising calmness, heaven, or the purity of his death.

Romantic comedy in *Me Before You*: politically correct chick flick as an ode to class privilege

The romantic comedy and romantic drama is usually targeted at a young heterosexual female audience; we can see this writ large within this film. Lou's point of view is central throughout the film compared to the polyphony of the book. This is her story. These (non-disabled) writers/filmmakers are speaking about a woman, for women, about aspirational forms of self-development, and also, perhaps, about disabled men. In this film this is at the cost of men's personalities; there is a repudiation of masculine identities, by class, cultural capital, and physical excesses in romantic relationships (e.g. too much physicality, and too little). Overall, we see a normative form of hierarchical heterosexual relationships, anchored by class and wealth, and excessive and polarised physicalities. In Scannell's (2000) terms this film is not usable for everyone, with various factions of the audience likely to identify themselves outside the 'we world' of this film, including many men, disabled people, and those with few opportunities for social mobility, notwithstanding its use as 'inspiration porn' (Young, 2014) for nondisabled young women.

Many of the ingredients explored so far combine to show that the film is a means to promote Emilia Clarke's career. I have already referred to her character, Lou, as fitting the Randian ideal, helped by the patronage of Will. However, the dominant discourses of masculinity in this film lead to less generous interpretations. Visual and narrative analysis of this film have shown this to be is a story of failed masculinities – especially in their classed and embodied forms. It seems that middle- or upper-class, non-disabled, gainfully employed masculine athleticism is the ideal. This is exemplified in the figure of Lou's father as an inadequate provider who depends on Lou, and has to be given a job by Will to succeed. Further, it is seen in Will's loss of physical functions, which had allowed him to achieve the highest levels in work and play before his accident, and Patrick's crudeness, including an implicit mockery of his working-class physicality seen through Lou's forbearance of his obsession for fitness.

Lou is the predominant spectacle; she dresses in a way which often seems to contrast with the colour palette for the film. As suggested, she becomes more elegant in the final scene, in Paris, a few weeks after his death, where she seems to have effected some of the changes Will wanted to see, being dressed more elegantly whilst still retaining the quirkiness of her former self, with the bumblebee tights making her stand out from the crowd. If we are in any doubt about this Pygmalionesque conversion – the film ends with Lou reading his parting letter to her, narrated in Will's voice, complete with instructions,and loving sentiments. But the last words of the letter seem key to the predominance of ableist values in the story's message about disability: 'I'll be walking beside you every step of the way, love Will.'

The appeal to young women as the main audience is clear – not only does the ending provide the heroine with assurances of love which cannot be taken away, the rest of her story has supported ideas of young women's agency, individuality, and aspirations, while enabling her to be seen as a subject who is playing with femininity, primarily through fashion, whilst feeling they are free from its dictates. Building on the appeal to chick culture, we occasionally see Lou reading 'chick lit'. On one occasion she is staying to care for Will and turns to read the novel as he falls asleep. Providing intertextual identifiers for the chick flick audience, we see that she is nearing the middle of Marian Keyes's novel *Sushi for Beginners*, a well-known book within this genre (Balducci, 2011). Indeed, film viewers who embrace chick lit would probably know that Lisa, one of the protagonists, is negotiating career and life choices in terms of how much meaning and security they provide (ibid., 45–46), much like the questions Will is encouraging Lou to face in her own life, probably adding to viewers' identifications with Lou's story.

Lou's status as Will's companion also allows us a rare glimpse into a leading female character who has to grapple with the uncertainties of occupying the 'tolerant subject position', in circumstances which are new to her, occasionally making quips about impairment as *The Office's* David Brent did. The scene for such humour is set early, before she meets him, in her initial interview with Will's mother:

MRS TRAYNOR: We are talking about complete loss of the legs and very limited use of the arms and hands. Would that bother you?
LOU: Not as much as it'd bother him. Obviously.

This might well be considered to be a quip that punches down, in terms of Palmer's (1994) framework for judging the offensiveness of jokes, but this is mitigated somewhat by Lou's beguilingly kind personality. Overall, the cinematic elements of the film discussed have shown how Lou is *the central* figure in this supposed story about disability. Moreover, she has been shown to bring warmth to a disabled man (in a cold world), introducing light and optimism where there is little, and fun and joy, where there is misery. Will bequeaths enough of his own material wealth, cultural capital, and ambitions – but most important, perhaps, is the bequeathing of his actual self as 'will' (sic). The name seems to be no accident serving as a pun in several ways, as moral self, as rich man and as a dead man. If we pronounce his last name as trainer, being spelled Traynor, he is indeed, in true Pygmalion fashion, a trainer of her will. Sadly, the only real agency we see Will to have exercised is the suicide decision and her future, but the latter actions can be seen to emerge from Will's status as a powerful man in his own past, not from his current position as a disabled man. Essentially his name acts as double entendre to signify his strong agency as very active and successful non-disabled man, and his lack of it as disabled man, where all he can do is make out his will to her, whilst lending his final decisions to the title, putting the 'me' before the 'you' that is Lou, whilst simultaneously portraying his death as a moral sacrifice that has to be made.

Elsewhere, I have asked whether this is really a story about suicide (Wilde, 2016). I have proposed that the most insidious discourses here are about class, cultural capital and *living with* impairment and disability. Inextricably, I have argued, the dominance of these other themes serves to shape *yet* divert us away from disabling discourses, which naturalise disablement and perpetuate ideas of the very limited values of people with impairment, as is often the case.[26]

The cursory comparison of the literary and film text reveals something about how meanings are constructed differently, often relying on specific camera shots, and use of colour and lighting in the creation of audience affect. Accordingly, such explorations can allow us a greater critical awareness for *denaturalising* tropes of impairment and disability, shaping the ways we might respond differently to disabled people, and those around them. In this case our views of Will's life are shaped relationally, but primarily through our desires for Lou's happiness. I have also argued that investigation of adaptations opens up questions of authenticity – even such brief analysis of film texts reveals that aspects of the story on which it is based have left key factors of disablement out which might lead us to the construction of different meanings. Although disablement themes in the film were present, seen mostly in Will's hostile opposition to having decisions being made for him, they were tackled more fully in the book, something which seems inevitable in the centring of Lou's identity.

It is probable that a romantic comedy which is such a close fit to the definition provided by Jeffers McDonald (2007) is likely to tell quite a monologic story, given the anticipated audience of women, even if a 'happy ending' of coupledom would perhaps have enabled multiple viewpoints. However, *The Big Sick* also centres its non-sick character in much the same way, regardless of his masculine gender, suggesting that the positioning of a model reader as non-disabled takes precedence over the primacy of the female viewer and her desires. Given that the locus of our attention is the non-disabled partner, as the primary visual spectacle in both films (Lou in terms of her visual aesthetic, and Kumail as a comedian and general putz), is it possible that we should rethink cinematic expressions of spectacle for disabled characters, in ways which promote identification, rather than dis-identifications, giving due regard to how these are constructed?

When we explore how humour has been used to re-present disability and impairment, it is clear that it is used by both Lou and Will to negotiate their differences and desires. And it is also apparent that Will's agency is pivotal to his eventual suicide, suggesting that the film allows the disabled character to speak, and act, for himself. He is making this decision, which would arguably put the film in the realms of political correctness, as recognising the agency of disabled people is a key dimension of disabled people's campaigns for independence and autonomy. However, the sub-narratives in the film make it clear that he is making this judgement on the basis of physical deficit and a potentially reduced moral worth, e.g. as a non-productive 'burden' to those around him rather than the valuable, dynamic man he had been. A less ableist story might have envisaged a growing realisation of his worth in producing value for himself and other people, not least in employing others and continuing to share life's experiences with others. One might even argue that his former non-disabled self is 'punching down' at his new self. Thus, it is unsurprising that disabled people have reacted strongly to such a crude measure of personal worth, especially when there is no discussion of transitions in identity which can come with the biographical disruptions often brought about by acquired impairments (Bury, 1982). Further, the comparisons made between characters indicate that the film-makers are punching down at those with lower forms of cultural capital – although some of the dialogue (mainly Lou's), and caricatures of the wealthier characters suggest some mockery of the upper classes, the macro-narrative serves to underline the moral worth of social mobility and higher forms of cultural capital.

Although the placement of disabled characters in leading romantic roles can be seen as a progressive step, the propensity to use them as 'the message', and as an emblem of tolerance, the tendency to utilise them as emotional ciphers who are dispensed with, with comparative indifference or disdain, acts to discourage longer term emotional attachments or identifications (Gavin, 2000, 286). Parody of these cinematic norms may well be another matter…

Notes

1 As in the rest of the book, I am referring mainly to Anglophone films, predominantly those distributed in the United States, and the United Kingdom, though the majority of Bollywood (Indian) films follow similar patterns. See Bahuguna (2015) for example.
2 Lippman explains that there is a resemblance between 'rape myths' and 'stalking myths'. Following Burt's (1980) work on rape myth, and Sinclair's (2006) work on stalking myths, she argues that common beliefs about stalking tend to be prejudiced in favour of the perpetrator, who becomes valorised for their expressions of strong love or passion, at the expense of a 'victim' who is often deemed to have 'asked for it', or to have prevaricated, possibly as part of a 'hard to get' game which the victim 'plays' (Lippman, 2015, 4). She also indicates that stalking is often treated as something which causes little harm with little 'serious lasting impact on the victim' (ibid., 5).
3 One such attitude relates directly to the discussion of rape and stalking myths, discussed by Lippman (2015). Although these disproportionately affect women, Crenshaw (1991) has forcefully demonstrated how cultural myths of rape often exclude Black women, relegating them to a lesser position of worth in moral and sexual hierarchies, whilst also demonising Black men. The dominance of white people in these leading romantic roles keeps our eyes and attention on white people, while the tendency to cast non-white actors in more 'deviant' roles persists, despite a growing appreciation of the need for diversity (see Latif and Latif, 2016, for example).
4 Clearly, this idea of relatability is of considerable importance to film, as a medium often used for identificatory purposes (see Smith, 1995, for example), although there is tendency towards universalising experiences and disregarding the unfamiliar, using relatability as the 'sole interpretative lens' as Onion argues (2014, para 8).

Romantic comedy and disability 99

5 This is a concept which has been defined as:

> An experimental film term usually applied to the works made during the first avant-garde which occurred in Europe in the 1920s. Pure cinema enthusiasts were opposed to narrative expression in the motion picture, advocating instead an exploitation of the unique cinematic devices of the medium in order to provide a purely visual and rhythmic experience.
>
> (Beaver, 2007, 39)

6 That is, there is a dual problem here. Not only are disabled people under-employed in the media, with 95 per cent of disabled roles being played by non-disabled people on US television (Woodburn and Kopić, 2016, 19), but there is also a separate (though arguably related) problem in the way that disabled characters are portrayed, regardless of who plays them.

7 A cursory examination of disabled actors in screen media will reveal that most actors seem to get more television work than film roles. See for example Raynor and Hayward (2005).

8 Although there are many criticisms of Mulvey's work on the power of the male gaze to shape representations in cinema, and the subject positions of the audience, her work has continued to play a significant part in Film Studies, as argued in Chapter One. The accusations against Harvey Weinstein in 2017 have also provided disturbing details about the continuing power of movie moguls in Hollywood. Although these have often focused on the sexualised actions of Weinstein towards women in the industry, accounts such as Selma Hayek's inform the reader of how such forms of power are used to prioritise the heteronormative male gaze; amongst other threats and demands she reported, she shows the harm done to her, being made to do a nude scene with two women having sex with each other in *Frida*, for his gratification. Her story shows just some of the ways in which his power (and others like him) censor, marginalise, exclude, or harm those who do not meet such demands (Hayek, 2017).

9 Rabin explains that there is sometimes a male equivalent (Rabin, 2017).

10 Notwithstanding the pride which many disabled people have in themselves and the disable people's community, or the wishes of some to become disabled, usually termed Body Integrity Identity Disorder (see Baril, 2015.

11 Many of these have already been mentioned; further evidence of these concerns can be found on the British Film Institute's website, e.g. http://www.bfi.org.uk/education-research/film-industry-statistics-reports/reports/diversity-reports (accessed 31 December 2017).

12 There are two other romantic comedy films which have featured people experiencing mental distress in their leading roles, *Silver Linings Playbook* and *Greenberg*. As these are slightly earlier films, 2012 and 2010 respectively, and I have compared them in some detail elsewhere (Wilde, 2018b), I have chosen to focus on characters with physical impairments in my sample of films within this chapter.

13 Whether they identify as disabled or non-disabled.

14 There is quite an uncomfortable scene where James and Mildred (Frances Forman, the lead protagonist) go on a date as part of a deal struck for an alibi he gave her. Several comedic references are made to his height, such as his remark that he needs to visit the little boy's room – this worked to raise her eyebrows, and a number of laughs from the audience. In addition to his role as a 'prosthetic' devise (Mitchell and Snyder, 2000) this was one of a series of height-based jokes within the dialogue.

15 I am following the deliberate use of a capital 'B' for Black, to signify recognition of Black as a political category (based on oppression), and the lower case 'w' in White,

to symbolise the tendency for white people to ignore whiteness as a universal norm. See Perlman (2015) for further discussion of debates around such usage.
16 At the time of writing *Me Before You* shows a box office figure of $ 208,314,186, against a $20 million budget. At the time of writing *Wonder* shows a box office figure of $203,280,855, against a $20 million budget. http://www.boxofficemojo.com/movies/?id=wonder.htm (accessed 6 January 2017).
17 *Stronger* made $6,095,583, against a budget of $30 million. http://www.boxofficemojo.com/movies/?id=stronger.htm (accessed 6 January 2018).
18 Often seen in dramas about suicide, e.g. *The Sea Inside*, an adaptation of the life story of Ramón Sampedro, and his fight for euthanasia.
19 There are great discrepancies between the original text (by Christian O'Reilly) and the film *Inside I'm Dancing*, some of which might be attributed to different writers for the screenplay (Jeffrey Caine).
20 As suggested earlier, this is reflected in Box Office figures of $55,849,436, according to http://www.boxofficemojo.com/movies/?id=thebigsick.htm, against a production budget of $ 5 million, https://www.the-numbers.com/movie/Big-Sick-The#tab=summary (accessed 23 January 2018).
21 That is, in a highly privatised world, environments such as fields, moors, and woods might easily be seen as public, shared space, even though this is seldom the case in Britain (see Cox, 2017, for example).
22 This can also be seen as a trope in the hugely influential *Sex and the City* TV show (and films), the overall ethos of which has been described by Lynne Segal as 'soft-vanilla feminism' (Media, 2014, para 8); where Carrie (the leading character and narrator) is often resistant to her most significant partner's (Mr Big) love of old films.
23 A range of shoes which are defined by their name – as shoes that are often colourful, in exaggerated and often themed designs, e.g. ice-cream shoes or animals.
24 Chick flicks are theorised within wider ideas of 'chick culture' by Ferriss and Young (2008), encompassing postfeminist and other feminist ideals.
25 Lou occasionally wears colours on the red spectrum, such as a shiny red raincoat, but this dress is a saturated shade of crimson, the shade most deeply associated with passion and life (Gage, 1990, 110).
26 Many of the films which can be seen to fit the 'normality genre' (Darke, 1998) can be seen to be about other themes, but often work in this way, e.g. the rehabilitation of Ron Kovic, as a Vietnam veteran in *Born on the Fourth of July*.

5 Romantic comedy meets satire
Yorgos Lanthimos' *The Lobster*

It is clear that *Me Before You* set out to explore acquired impairment and its effects on newly disabled family and friends, to raise the awareness of the author and possibly the audiences who see it, especially in terms of debates on the right to choose suicide or life (Barnes, 2016). My analysis of these efforts in terms of awareness-raising is that the centring of Lou, as his non-disabled partner, does nothing to change perceptions of disability or improve the appreciation of the social causes of disablement, simultaneously perpetuating moralistic views of human beings based on their use-value and social status. Given the initial speculations of its writer, the film may be best regarded as an attempt at increasing our understanding of the experiences of those who are close to disabled people; but the film effectively said nothing new about this, with all those around Will being troubled, or burdened, by his needs, even questioning his capacity for independent decision-making – all familiar cultural tropes. Being generous, we might be reminded that disabled people are lovable. Even if his character is not very romantic, this is a rare portrayal of a disabled person as a romantic lead which is likely to seduce disabled members of the audience into seeing it, perhaps more so if he was known to survive. However, the film's artistic conventions worked to show his reduced sexual status and his corresponding new capacities to see beyond the superficialities of sexual attraction, simultaneously rendering him as less sexual but more attentive to the needs of women. Together then, there was little beyond his presence which served to raise awareness of impairment or disability. Indeed, the curiosity of Jojo Moyes about how family and friends 'deal with' impairment centres such characters – in aggregate – as tolerant subjects trying to make sense of 'disability'. I have suggested that satire may be a better way of changing such relationships. It is to this I now turn.

The Lobster as (satirical) romantic comedy

King (2002) distinguishes between satire and parody, with the former being aimed at social and political phenomena and the latter at 'formal or aesthetic' targets (ibid.,107); it can be argued that this film does both in its critique of contemporary society and its parodying of romance. He suggests that satire is a risky medium for a film-maker in that it can cause 'offence to significant numbers of potential viewers' and that less risky films which 'pull their punches' to attract bigger audiences are less likely to deliver a serious political message (ibid., 94). Conversely, he argues, those that are 'harsh and biting' are less likely to make profits (ibid., 94). King also suggests that those which delve into 'darker realms' go 'beyond that which is usually considered to be comic' (ibid.). *The Lobster* is of the latter variety, with humour emanating from the premise of the rehabilitation of newly single people, the methods adopted to orchestrate human relationships, and the absurdity of the world which is depicted. Like all satires, the world of *The Lobster* reflects dimensions of contemporary society, as Hupperetz (2016) has demonstrated in respect of online dating culture. It can also be seen as a satire on anthropocentrism (see Cooper, 2016) and, as I will argue, on our current conceptions of bodily difference and worth. King argues that satire often emerges from 'harsher social-political contexts' (2002, 6). As such, the emergence of a film such as this is timely in an era where disabled bodies are treated with increasing disgust and contempt (Hughes, 2012), alongside cultural/economic shifts which emphasise ideas of bodies being 'matter out of place' (Douglas, 1966), such as the anti-immigration politics of Brexit and Trump. Additionally, though, *The Lobster* can also be seen as a parody in the way it lampoons the tropes of the rom-com.

Unlike *Me Before You*, *The Lobster* did not set out to raise awareness of impairment or disability, even if it may have led some of the audience in that direction. Nor did it place a disabled person at the centre. Further, as suggested, *The Lobster* is not likely to be regarded by many as a romantic comedy by conventional generic standards, set, as it is, in a 'dystopian near-future' arranged around a dualist choice between forms of 'totalitarian love' (Prose, 2015). Lanthimos, the director of the film, is already becoming known as an auteur, with the Institute of Contemporary Arts (2017) describing him as one of the 'most distinctive voices of European auteur cinema', a leading member of the 'Greek Wave', or the 'Greek weird wave' (a new wave of 'messed up cinema', according to Rose, 2011, para 9). So, many would not regard this as a mainstream film, though as Lanthimos' first Anglophone film, it has been located on 'the fringes of the mainstream' (Murray 2016, 46).

Romance, parody, and the world of *The Lobster*

Put simply, this is story where David (Colin Farrell), a newly single man, is forced into navigating a hotel-based world where he has to find a new partner within forty-five days, or he will be 'turned into an animal of his choice', and released into the nearby forest. Like the rest of the corrective hotel's inmates, he is forced into a position where he is driven by the fear of this fate into the selection, and forging, of a new partnership which has to be chosen on the spurious basis of similarity. When asked to choose an animal, should he fail to make a match, he chooses a lobster for its longevity, blue-bloodedness, and lifelong fertility, but later escapes a doom-laden future by absconding to the forest to join resistance group, the Loners. There, he finds a woman he wants a relationship with (Short Sighted Woman, played by Rachel Wietsz). While David is the main protagonist in the film, the story is narrated by Rachel Wietsz, who does not appear until half way through the story. Cooper has argued that this strategy mirrors the voice of Echo in Ovid's story of 'Narcissus and Echo' (Cooper, 2016, 163). This shapes a narrative which is based upon narcissistic relations throughout, with the threat of being turned into an animal rather than a flower; David appears to be positioned as Narcissus to Short Sighted Woman's Echo, especially in his obsession that she should have the same level of sightedness as he does.

The film opens with a scene where a woman drives to a place where she gets out and kills one of two donkeys, a scene we cannot begin to make sense of until we have seen much more of the film; the second scene brings the audience abruptly into the break-up of David's relationship, a more conventional start for a comedy which deals with romance and coupledom. Immediately, despite his newly estranged partner's (out of shot) apology, his primary concern seems to be whether his former partner's new lover wears glasses or contact lenses, and what shoes he should wear; he is looking at his dog, rather than his ex-partner, for most of this scene. This sets the tone for the film, his new and (seemingly) unwanted singledom, and the number of conversations which immediately follow, where we are left to make sense of a range of behaviour and customs, with scant information or background knowledge.

When, in the next scene, we see David booking into a hotel for newly separated people, he is made to choose between rigid identifications as a heterosexual or homosexual man, and then has to choose a 'whole' size of shoes (for the new uniform he will have to wear), a choice which will result in having to wear shoes half a size too small or half a size too big for his feet. Similarly, bisexuality is not allowed due to 'operational problems'. Although these are never explained 'ralphthemoviemaker' (2017) has suggested that this may have been due to an escape the previous year by a (probably) bisexual woman (played by Léa Seydoux), who went on to become the leader of the Loners, who live in the nearby forest and who are planning to sabotage the hotel's mission.

On being shown to his room, David is given a sharp introduction to this new binary world. First, he is given a lesson in the value of pairs, by hotel staff locking one of his hands behind his back and padlocking his trouser belt, making simple tasks, such as changing into bedclothes, difficult with the use of only one hand. The hotel manager (Olivia Coleman) explains to him that 'This is to show you how easy life is when there are two of something rather than one. We tend to forget that sometimes.' This is a theme which is central to principles of the hotel, including a number of compulsory didactic 're-enactments'. These scenarios are performed to show how a man is needed to protect women from rape by others, and another to show how a woman's presence will equally stop a man from choking ('Man eats alone' versus 'Man eats with woman'). As Hupperetz argues, these scenarios (which are unlikely to be interpreted as anything other than skits by the cinema audience, due to their wooden-ness and absurdity, exaggerated by the use of a static camera) reveal the principles of a world of coupling which is based on 'convenience as opposed to one of love and lust' (Hupperetz, 2016, 6).

As suggested, although David's story involves the romantic comedy trope of meeting, and subsequently rejecting, 'unsuitable' partners, the film certainly does not fit the master definition of romantic comedy proposed by Jeffers McDonald. Visually, it has few of the usual trappings of flowers, chocolates, and weddings, although the hotel beds (in the Irish hotel featured in the first half of the film) are used to underline aspects of relationships, sexuality, and commitment, though in a somewhat unconventional manner; bedrooms tend to be used to portray situations of distress, e.g. passionless, non-intimate sex, and the bloody killing of David's dog (his former brother) in a bedroom's ensuite bathroom.

Other iconographic elements are also used in unconventional ways. Whereas we often see close-ups of Lou and Will in *Me Before You*, perhaps bringing us closer to their emotional world, Lanthimos tends to use the camera to *avoid* the audience seeing the interactions. Murray theorises that Lanthimos may be doing this to show us how the characters 'affect each other at least as much through simple bodily presence as they do through finely formed linguistic utterance' (2016, 46), exemplified in the second scene where we know that his wife is leaving him (out of shot), but we only see him, and from the side. We do see 'special costumes' for a dance scene, though this has a significant twist which in and of itself parodies the centrality of the typical couple to conventional rom-coms, where leading females are usually distinguished from other women by depictions of excessive beauty. As discussed in the last chapter, Lou, from *Me Before You*, is characterised as a typical Manic Pixie Dream Girl or Blithe Spirit, by her quirky clothes and superior beauty, symbolized in a revealing and romantic evening dress at a 'special date', always marked out from the others as extra-ordinary; conversely, the women and men in *The Lobster's* hotel are an undifferentiated herd, all wearing exactly the same outfits for their evening of dancing and potential partner selection. All the women wear flowery, plunging halter neck dresses at the ballroom dance, rendering their special, and pretty, outfits as uniformly mundane. These are collections of women and men, undifferentiated one from another, suggesting an 'infinitely renewable supply' of potential partners and the desirability of a 'commodification of social relationships' (Hupperetz, 2016, 4).

The only things that mark their differences out are their most obvious physical characteristics. This significant feature of their new existence is highlighted by their tendency to refer to each other by names such as Limping Man, or Nosebleed Woman (a full list of these type of names can be found in the cast list at imdb.com). Beyond this initial categorisation of others by their superficial physical traits, identification is sometimes made on their most pronounced character, or mental, attributes, exemplified in the character of Heartless Woman (later the killer of David's dog). This resonates throughout the film, David being one of the few characters who appears to have a name. We also learn John and Robert's names; John (Ben Whishaw) is named on the cast list as Limping Man, his main characterisation through the film, and Robert (John C Reilly) is known as Lisping Man. They are the only three who are addressed by, or given a name, apart from Bob, David's dog/former brother. Their first names are perhaps used initially because they bond together on the first day of David's stay, depicting a more authentic personal connection before the competition for a successful match becomes an urgent priority. They may have been given names to identify their centrality to the story, as single men who are all in the same predicament of needing to find a partner (through no 'fault' of their own). Most significantly perhaps, whereas most romantic comedies encourage their audiences to believe in the seemingly inevitable destinies of their romantic protagonists, regardless of their similarities and differences, frequently signified in the eventful 'meet cute', *The Lobster* introduces us to a dystopia, a world of binary attributes, where the most important, indeed necessary, imperative for coupling is the identification of a single shared attribute in a milieu devoid of mystery and romance, but full of potential partners.

So, despite the differences between this and conventional romantic comedies, including the bizarre premise and a range of distancing strategies from the main characters, romance and coupling is the major theme throughout the film. The sense of separation between the characters and the loneliness of their existence, driven further by the fear that they have to choose between coupledom and either existence as an animal or death, is extended through the use of a number of cinematic strategies. These include flat, clipped, usually monotone speech styles, the lack, or limited range of, camera movements in long takes (particularly on unpleasant scenes such as Biscuit Woman's suicide), and the use of repetition. There is also a use of repeated dialogue and extra-diegetic, string-based music – despite the close resemblances of the music used, contributing to appearance of repetition, these pieces are by a number of composers, including Beethoven, Schnitke, Stravinsky, Shostakovich, and Britten. They are often used with slow motion to create distinct, if subtle, metaphors, such as the use of Strauss's *Don Quixote* to suggest knightly fantasy (Cooper, 2016, 168), when David approaches his first dance partner. The use of slow motion is *only* used to address hunting themes, first in this hunt for a partner and also in the later (more literal) hunt for Loners. Nicolaou theorises that slow motion is used in a hunt scene for two specific reasons; focussing on a scene where hotel inmates hunt Loners with tranquilizer guns in order to gain extra days in their hotel stay, he shows how the camera parodies its own actions when it is used to 'normalise the violence' (2016, para 4). These movements are usually depicted as a form of 'dance' in order to show the 'perverted logic of a world which is basically committing genocide against single people', and he argues that the slow motion also provides a 'critique of the violence AND its aestheticization

(2016, para, 4, author's emphasis). Similarly, Cooper (2016) demonstrates that slow motion is used in other, more metaphorical, hunting scenes; these include the hunt for a partner in the ballroom dancing scene, the hunt for shopping items, and also for each other when David and Short Sighted Woman visit the city as Loners, and within a scene where they dance together. The 'aestheticization of the violence' created by both the totalitarian regimes of the imposed coupledom of the hotel (or society) and the forced singledom of the Loners (as a resistance group) is clear in all these cases.

What, and who, is the film about?

Although we are introduced to a wide range of characters looking for a partner, if not for a romance, it is clear that David is the leading protagonist after we are alerted to his predicament from the second scene (even if we are initially left with rather jarring questions about how this relates to his partner in the first scene, who is never returned to). Here, as in other places, the audience has to do the work of meaning-making, instead of relying on tried and trusted formulae and stock characters, which may mean that they are likely to feel less threatened by any 'messages' – Gavin's 'didactic exhortations' (Gavin, 2000, 91) – aimed at them.

In direct contrast to *Me Before You*, which might be telling us to see disabled people as (at best) romantic agents, it is difficult to find a central message here, as the film is open to a number of interpretations; asking questions about love and romance, and offering a number of critiques of wider society, while the fear of becoming an animal, as a fate that might reasonably be considered worse than death, raises questions about the roles of non-human animals in social life, as Cooper has argued (2016).

More prosaically, the idea of the film itself came from a reality show about hotels (Channel 4's *The Hotel*, set in Torquay, England, as cited in Barnes, 2015, para 2). Indeed, when Diane Lodderhouse interviewed Lanthimos about the film, he stated:

> It's about exposing aspects of human life and situations and thoughts that you have… Hopefully people watching will start thinking themselves about those things and come up with their own answers. Whatever we have observed in our behaviour and the way we have constructed this world, we want to make people wonder whether all of those things are true.
>
> (2016, para 6)

Tan shows that it is this 'aesthetic activity of the viewer' and 'puzzle-solving' which provides 'aesthetic pleasure' (Tan, 2011, 91) and the happiness which comes from 'complete surrender' to a story (following Oatley, 1995, cited in Tan, 2011, 91), which might lead us to 'surrender to the film itself' and the 'authenticity of the feelings evoked' (ibid., 2–3). Thus, given the major themes of loneliness and narcissism identified by lead actors Colin Farrell and Rachel

Weitsz (Barnes, 2015), there may be a tendency for the audience to be positioned in ways which make us more critical of why loneliness pervades society (see Monbiot, 2017, for example), and how this links to narcissistic forms of human experience. Or we could be left with stronger thoughts and feelings on the absurdity and harms of classifying people into biosocial and other categories, such as rigid divisions between the values and characteristics of people identified as disabled and non-disabled. Despite the impossibility of defining the film with reference to a single topic, Lanthimos shows that there are questions of love (as a wider social concept) which unite the themes. He has said:

> I'm just trying to find an answer, like the rest of the people, whether there is love, and how do you find it, how do you realize it, and what are you prepared to do for it.
>
> (Asp, 2015, para 14)

Significantly for the purposes of this chapter, the film could easily be considered as a treatise on romance and monogamous coupling, and as a provocation for us to challenge the reification of love and the people around us, especially on the basis of arbitrary bodily differences. Hupperetz analyses the film's relevance to a future which might be dominated by dating apps, discourses of choice, and the increasing commodification of social relationships and body parts (2016, 4). Hupperetz explains:

> The way in which The Lobster's characters can only be identified by their concrete, physical or mental flaws combined due to their reserved communication and the limited amount of text-bound dramaturgy, relates to the process of reification. Both the cinematography in The Lobster (shot by Thimios Bakatakis, cinematographer of Dogtooth) and the characters themselves seem to consider the character's bodies as props rather than persons (Koutsourakis, 96). Emphasizing the physical acting style elevates the role of the body as a medium that draws attention to the most ordinary aspects of human behaviour, stressing the awkwardness of our bodily existence. A striking example of this is the first sexual encounter between David and the Heartless Woman in which they copy the (mandatory) sexual stimulation technique performed by the hotel maid. The fact that they copy the already mechanical action questions the performativity of their identity. As both characters act in a highly passionless and indifferent way, the actors are clearly acting out the performance rather than amplifying their bodily gestures with dramatic expression.
>
> (ibid., 9)

Here, utilising Berger and Pullberg's (1966) approach, she defines reification as 'a state of amnesia in which the individual 'forgets' the human origins of the social world' (1966, 9). She also argues that this is something we might equally see as a critique of behaviour on social media, where the echo chamber created by the partial worlds we control allows us to forget the complexity and contradictions of the wider social world and individual lives. This encourages us to buy into the narcissism of minor differences (Ignatieff, 1995) and to seek to avoid discomfort (Delaney, 2017), minimising understanding of others we deem to be different. This reification of others becomes obvious in the first half of the film, where the inmates are compelled to look for a 'match', invariably with indifference and without passion. The hotel manager (Olivia Coleman) sets this tone from the start. She advises David that he must choose a companion as a partner who is a 'similar animal' to himself, explaining that 'a wolf and a penguin could never live together because that would be absurd'. In so doing, she emphasises the significance of body similarities in a way that delineates those who do not resemble us as belonging to different species, unfit for companionship due to their perceived differences.

The inmates have few options to opt out of this passionless regime, so most go about their search for a partner in an automaton-like fashion. The only exception to the lack of passion is 'Biscuit Woman', although her primary emotion seems to be one of despair. She seems to be attracted to David, but is clearly desperate in the face of rejection and her impending fate, after a series of attempts to gain David's interest – premised on what she can give him, such as company or a 'good blow job', rather than romance, love, or seduction. She also ruminates on how she should kill herself, eventually committing suicide by jumping from a high hotel window – better dead than inhuman perhaps, a twisted echo of the usual 'better dead than disabled' themes which are featured in so many 'disability films', such as *Me Before You*. Her fatal and messy fall from the window serve as foreplay to an attempted relationship between David and Heartless Woman, when he feigns indifference and annoyance at Biscuit Woman's selfishness in an attempt to fake the cold, self-serving cruelty which defines Heartless Woman, a blatantly fraudulent attempt at matching her personality traits in order to escape singledom.

Harris has described *The Lobster* as 'satire so steeped in an understanding of loneliness that it could break your heart if you let it' (2015, para 9); its comedy is dark, often referenced to conventions of love, and the messiness of life, and it seeps through most elements of the film. Comedy is present throughout, from the dystopian premise of a choice of imposed partnership, and unavoidable transmogrification, to the implicit joke about imposed coupledom on an ark-like 'two-by-two' basis to avoid living as a single animal in a 'postdiluvian world' (Cooper, 2016, 164). But it also pervades the micronarratives of the film, from bizarre social conventions, plot twists, and speaking behaviours, to odd conversations and funny one-liners. David's chat-up line to his second potential love interest and eventual partner (Short Sighted Woman), for example, is a compliment on her rabbit-catching skills, which clearly endears him to her. This praise has more comedic power given its complete lack of romance, in the context of a situation where intimacy is prohibited.

Many of the one-liners in the film come from the hotel manager, a woman who both runs the hotel and orchestrates the processing of its inmates. One of the manager's (serious) remarks to a newly formed couple is: 'If you encounter any problems you cannot resolve yourselves, you will be assigned children, that usually helps'; advice which both undermines the philosophy of compulsory monogamous partnering which is being imposed on everyone, whilst parodying the happy-ever-after myths purveyed in many romantic genres, not least the rom-com. When the single residents shoot loners with their tranquilliser gun, one day is added to their remaining stay for each loner, meaning Heartless Woman has over a hundred days left – another dark joke reflecting on the imperative for romance, ideologies of love and care, and the cruelty of matching processes based on instrumental values. Comedy is often present in the visual aspects of the film, even in the dark comedy of the slow motion sequences. In one scene, for example, we see a camel walk by as some of the characters in the forest are talking, an odd and unexpected sight in County Kerry, Ireland, the location for the film, reminding us of the absurdity of their situation.

Impairment, ableism, disablism and bodily difference

Although *The Lobster* is complex and lends itself to many readings, my own interpretation and enjoyment of the film is founded on two things. The first is the counter-hegemonic challenge to cultural ideals of love, and the romantic comedy genre specifically; and the second is the critique it offers for interrogating ideologies of ableism and disablism, especially in its challenges to categorial thinking and the reification of bodily categories. Other than the comedy, and eventual romance, *The Lobster* breaks most of the rules of the romantic comedy formula, and almost seems to go out of its way to do so, not least in its parodying of iconography. As suggested, the beds which in this film are rarely used in the romantic manner which is conventional for a romantic comedy; rather they tend to appear in a number of distressing situations. Further examples include the hotel maid subjecting David to unwanted, but obligatory frottage, leaving him frustrated and powerless; the hotel enforces a ban on masturbation, punishable by the insertion of one's hands in a toaster, so one assumes that the maid's visit is a mechanism to increase his desire for a new relationship. Further scenes involving beds involve the demand for the hotel manager to shoot his wife to save himself, demonstrating the limited extent of his love and commitment to her – a direct challenge to the authority they wield and the philosophies they impose.

Although the first thing which struck me was the focus put on the importance of bodily difference, the film does not seem to be about impairment or disability if judged in superficial terms, nor does the film market itself in this way. Indeed, they have not been explicit narratives in Lanthimos' oeuvre so far, with family often evident as a central theme. Nonetheless, impairment, body functions, and disablement, in a wider sense, have been significant dimensions of these films, with ableism and ideas of 'normalcy' lying at the core of these stories. Elsewhere, I have argued that the story told in *Dogtooth* (in 2010) is 'replete with truly disabling events, often mundane, and increasingly alarming, which echo the ubiquitous and unpleasant disturbances of everyday life' (Wilde, 2010b, para 2). I also argued that, despite the lack of impairment or disability in the film, its focus on the over-protection of children (two daughters) to the detriment of their development, maturation, and social experiences (imprisoned in their parental home by their father) had the power to 'illuminate the many and profound effects of segregation' (ibid., para 4). Social exclusion, infantalisation, worsening health, and segregation are dominant themes which are central to the inequalities facing many disabled people, from those excluded from mainstream education in 'special schools', to those who face profound and deepening forms of social exclusion in an era of brutal cuts to social and health care provision (see Barnes and Mercer, 2005, for example, and also Cooper, 2014, in relation to the impacts of Greek austerity measures, in the period when *Dogtooth* was released). The sense of desperation and isolation facing the children in *Dogtooth* echoes the 'essence of loneliness' which Colin Farrell saw as a major theme in *The Lobster* (Barnes, 2016, para 7), the dimension of the film which Harris (2015) found to be 'heartbreaking'. The story in *Dogtooth* is founded on the idea of freedoms which were contingent on bodily change; the eldest of the two daughters would be allowed to go into the world, as an agent of her own life, when she grew her 'Dogtooth' (i.e. when her father deemed her to be an adult), a subtle reference to wider categorical, biosocial identities.

However, the appeal to bodily difference and associated forms of identity is direct and writ large in *The Lobster*. In the second scene, discussed earlier in the chapter, we witness the main protagonist's obsession with bodily difference and its place in economies of desire, as he anticipates his impending incarceration at the hotel. His first preoccupation in the film, shown in his question about the eyewear choices of his former wife's new partner, is shown to be a recurring concern for him at various points in the narrative. He is short-sighted and seems to think that this is an important aspect of compatibility for a romantic couple, when he is forced by the hotel regime to find important resemblances to prospective partners. Indeed, the obsession with body differences and likenesses is taken to absurd levels when 'Limping Man' inflicts injuries on himself to fake nosebleeds, in order to become a suitable partner for 'Nosebleed Woman', tricking her into a relationship. When asked if he would consider making a match with a woman who was seen limping he remarks that she is not a match because she has (only) a sprained ankle, which is temporary and therefore doesn't qualify as a real limp. He also remarks on the strength of his compatibility with his former partner who had a limp. As odd, and amusing, as the audience may find this distinction, this is an attitude which has common currency in the contemporary world of disablist culture, seen most obviously in the predominance of assessment systems which categorise people by crude physical and mental functions, identifying people as either real and deserving, or mendicants, i.e. underserving scroungers (Saffer, 2018).

The designation of people within such fixed physical and mental categories denies 'them the full range of humanity' Bowdre spoke of, as discussed in Chapter 4 (2009, 107). *The Lobster* uses impairments or other perceived deviations from the normate (physical or mental characteristics) to categorise and invoke biosocial traits as desired attributes and primary characteristics of the self, for matching with others who share them. Clearly this contravenes ideals of normality which are central to preferred biosocial categories in the 'real world', usually rendering disabled people as deviant, a designation which acts as a firm foundation for ableism and disablism. Conversely, Limping Man, for example, fetishizes the desired anomaly, choosing a life based on a faked illness. Ostensibly, taken to its logical conclusion, this places a person who fails to deviate from any norm as 'abnormal'; in the world of the hotel, and with no points of difference to share with another person, an impairment can be seen to protect them from a post/non-human destiny as the animal of their choice.

Occasionally other biosocial categories are used as markers of type, and markers of similarity; one woman defines herself as having a great smile, which would give her a high chance of finding similarities in another resident, based on a subjective assessment of smile quality. This perhaps has another layer of meaning, given the white world of the romantic comedy. This is especially so when we consider that she is one of the few Black inmates in this very white institution, and she chooses her 'very beautiful smile' rather than her skin colour, a denial of most of the social and cognitive factors which come into play in the shaping of human forms of discrimination (see Gilman and Thomas, 2016, for example). The use of her smile could also be seen as the reshaping of an old tradition of survival for Black people; as Maya Angelou has demonstrated, a smile or a laugh has often been a strategy for survival against racism (see Barajas, 2017, for example), an action which has been shown to lessen racist bias in 'impression formation' for some (Senft et al., 2016). In a 'white'-centred social world which affords privilege on the basis of being similar to as many people as possible, identification on the basis of non-white status would be a fatal choice in the hotel if that was taken as the characteristic for match-making, as few, if any, other residents appear to be Black.

Indeed, Cooper sees this quest for likeness as central, describing the film's story as:

> A darkly humorous vision of a world where likeness is the only sought-after foundation for love.
>
> (Cooper, 2016, 163)

She also demonstrates that Lanthimos' recurrent attention on the 'relationship between originals and copies' is one which has preoccupied philosophical, artistic, and scientific endeavours for centuries:

> The pursuit of likeness in this film is part of a generalized system of wanting to be like others, the insecurity of which is palpable precisely because it requires law enforcement: singles can never be allowed to be free because this may set a new norm.
>
> (2016, 167)

Following the theory of René Girard (2013), she explains that coupling is achieved through the 'mimesis of desire', which invariably results in hostility and violence, especially when people all want what other people have (Cooper, 2016, 167). Whereas impairments are highly unlikely to play a fundamental part in the desires we see in conventional romantic comedies, which tend to be based, as discussed earlier, on a narrow set of (impossibly 'perfect') bodily characteristics, this register is reversed within *The Lobster*. Given the unlikelihood of one person having exactly the same health condition, or impairment, as another it might be seen as foolish to seek a partner on the basis of perceived body deficits, but we see characters such as Limping Man prioritising this as his main characteristic, until he faked a more advantageous impairment to couple with nosebleed woman. This emphasis on bodily difference and aspirations to develop conditions which will ingratiate us to others acts to queer the conventional placement of body 'anomalies' as abnormal, where writers render their subjects as external to the story of the non-disabled person which they're trying to tell. Much like the writers of profitable disability films, possibly parodying their vicarious motives, there is curiosity shown by the narrator (Weitz) towards impairment, in musing on what having an impairment, or being near an impairment, is like, before her sight is taken. Further, challenging the dominance of the idea of the perfect body within contemporary media, there is an acknowledgement here that almost all people have differences from standards set as bodily norms; this includes impairments which are not usually regarded in terms of disablement, e.g. hair loss, and eyesight conditions which can be remedied with the use of glasses or contact lenses (Samaha, 2007, 16).

Humour, romance, and desire in *The Lobster*

As a rationale for love and romance, the idea that one would choose a partner on the basis of shared impairments seems absurd, potentially provoking thoughts about why bodily similarity should be used as a basis for romance in the first place. It might also encourage viewers to question categorisation in other aspects of society, e.g. assessments of need, as a foundation for the formation of social groups, or segregation, and so on. Again, drawing our attention to the (unspoken) importance of similarity in the physical characteristics of conventional rom-com protagonists, *The Lobster* flouts the ubiquitous, if spurious, appeal to the idea of opposites attracting in this and other romantic genres. Indeed, the construction of difference may be seen as prerequisite for much of the drama which ensues in typical rom-coms. Hall for example, argues that it is a convention of the Hollywood romance to invent plausible (or, in the case of romantic comedy, humorously implausible) obstacles to the course of what the audience instantly perceives as true love.

(2006, 166)

In many rom-coms the couple are also often hostile to one another on the first meeting (Neale, (1992), an oddly inverted indicator of long-term romantic compatibility. As clichéd as the rom-com may be, the idea that one can make a match on the idea of bodily similarity begs questions of new forms of courtship based on increasing reification (Hupperetz, 2016) and individualisation. Theorists such as Lacan might be used to support the idea that desire is founded on the fulfilment of perceived 'lack', although Ragland argues that Lacan suggests that desire is based on 'concrete conditions that evoke unitary traits' (Ragland, 2004, 146). *The Lobster* parodies the simplistic formulae used in rom-coms, and their reductive approach to romantic love, flying in the face of much philosophical thinking on the topic, which suggest great complexity in the dynamics of attraction and the continual reproduction of desire (Žižek, 1997), in which these films have their own part to play. Thus, the conditions for love in *The Lobster*'s hotel, and the conventional rom-com, are as crude, reductionist and bizarre as one another. As Žižek might say, the particular characteristics, such as the limp or the nosebleed, cannot be generalised as the same to all who have them, despite Limping Man's differentiation between the real and the fake. Further, the appeal to either, a desire based on fantasy of 'opposition' or 'lack' cannot be subjectivised; Žižek (1997) argues:

> Because of the lack of this universal formula, every individual has to invent a fantasy of his own, a 'private' formula for the sexual relationship; for a man, a relationship with a woman is possible only inasmuch as she fits his formula (sic).
>
> (para 7)

Speaking of the identification of a 'factor' which regulates her or his desire, he says,

> this awareness can never be subjectivized, it is uncanny, horrifying even, since it somehow 'depossesses' the subject, reducing her or him to a puppet-like level 'beyond dignity and freedom'.
>
> (para 8)

However, these themes persist beyond the complete reversal of philosophies of romance in the second half of the film, where David escapes to the forest to join the Loners who live rough in the forest. Here coupledom is forbidden, and complete self-sufficiency is imposed, to the point of digging one's own grave and only dancing alone, while wearing headphones. Again, this seems to be a comment on the role of technology in society, specifically on the trend for silent discos in popular culture and the (perhaps spurious) idea that this reflects an atomised society, a 'lonely crowd' (Gross, 2016, para 4), where 'shared isolation' (ibid., para 3) acts to 'silence our social connections' (ibid., 2016, para). The Loner leader explains, with no attempt at humour, 'We all dance by ourselves, that's why we only play electronic music'.

The gore, parody, and dark comedy continue thus in the second half, culminating in the Loner leader's punishment of Short Sighted Woman when she suspects her of having a romantic affair with David. Resultantly, she ensures that Short Sighted Woman is robbed of all sight. As the idea of disability as punishment for wrongdoing is a common trope (see Otieno, 2009, for example), and blindness is often attributed to deviant sexuality (Hayhoe, 2008), this may be read as a parody of the power of omnipotent beings to inflict deliberate atrocities on their subjects, especially given the satirical foundations of the film. But the narrative culminates in a twist, or conversely, its (il)logical conclusion. After his frustrated attempts to find alternative forms of homophily, such as a matching blood type or the ability to play the piano, they effect their escape from the forest to the city (where people only live as couples), and the final scene involves them sitting in a roadside café, David asking to see parts of her body, continuing the fetishisation of body parts which has been the lifeblood of the film. After this he takes a knife into the washrooms to blind himself; Cooper argues that there is an anticipation of his 'Buñuelian assault on the eye' (2016, 173, referencing *Un Chien Andalou*). We do not see what happens to David as the camera cuts to Short Sighted Woman (although she might now be categorised as Blind Woman if naming by impairment continues). As she was also the narrator, and she cannot see the vehicles passing by on the busy road outside, the protracted ending, with a static shot lasting just over a minute, possibly suggests that we should also contemplate the capacities of the cinema to depict the world of its subjects. So, we are left with a number of questions about love, and compatibility. Was this a metaphor for true love taken to its logical extent, given his obsession that his partner should have the same visual impairment as himself as the key indicator of compatibility, a logic which might take us back to the principles of the hotel? Or should we conclude that this is a metaphor that 'love is blind'? Maybe neither. If he has made himself blind he also escaped the probable fate of becoming a lobster, and has queered his narcissistic impulses to become the reflection of his object of desire. If so, this can be read as an act which 'ultimately transcends society's attempts to commodify and regulate the mystery of love' (Prose, 2015, para 14), a deeply romantic ending to an impossible love story. And it is a resolution which is brought about by David giving himself a voluntary impairment which will disable them both.

Whilst this is a move which could perhaps be criticised for the romanticisation of impairment, it could be interpreted as a reversal of blindness as punishment trope, and also of the ubiquitous redemption through cure, rehabilitation, or death narrative (see Darke, 1998: Wilde, 2004b).

Of course, we never know whether he faked his blindness, just as he attempted to fake his brutality with Heartless Woman, especially as Short Sighted Woman-cum-Blind Woman was in a weak position to know. It might also lead us to ruminate on how they would co-exist in a world which is premised on principles which dictate that couples are each other's sole source of help and assistance, one based firmly on individualism. This perhaps returns us to ideas of love for others and the idea that mutuality works well based on inclusive ideas of difference. In this scenario, perhaps Short Sighted Woman might get more love and support if David helped her as a sighted person, enabling them to find less categorical forms of similarity and to forge more meaningful forms of interdependency – unless we assume that they would be rejected as frauds in the city by virtue of their impairment differences. This takes us right back to the hotel, and its rather contradictory idea that relationships based on superficial forms of similarity (such as physical impediments) will provide a bulwark against adversity, fear and loneliness. However, as Prose argues, both the hotel's enforcement of relationships based on likeness and the Loners' imposition of singledom and self-sufficiency, work to make all live 'exactly as' the leaders do, which has 'more to do with power, control, and group identity than with the actual substance of how we think others should lead their lives' (2015, 9).

There is even less room for otherness, or 'radical alterity', in this dystopian world than there is in the communicative structure of the conventional romantic comedy. Conversely, Ilić has argued that Lanthimos' appeal is to raise questions rather than to find answers, and is therefore more likely to maintain the status quo, leaving us with few impulses to act to change 'neoliberal capitalism and its discontents', nor provides any strategies to do so. He contends that,

> it has 'raised our awareness' about social issues – uploaded it onto a cloud which, it appears, we are expecting soon to rain that accumulated wisdom onto the world and rinse all the dualities and polarizations away.
> (2017, 484)

However, putting the debate about how cinema can act as a catalyst for change aside for now, Cooper (2016, 170) suggests that the positioning of animals within the film plays a fundamental role in reimagining our social worlds, not least in engaging with forms of 'radical alterity' through our speculation on the bodies of those we may become. Interwoven with the elevation of bodily 'defects' as a starting point for love, the film encourages us to re-examine why radical forms of alterity are deemed as such. As Graeber has asked of anthropology as a discipline,

> Are we unsettling our categories so as (1) to better understand the 'radical alterity' of a specific group of people (whoever 'we' are here taken to be); or (2) to show that in certain ways, at least, such alterity was not

quite as radical as we thought, and we can put those apparently exotic concepts to work to reexamine our own everyday assumptions and to say something new about human beings in general?

(Graeber, 2015, 6)

The same can be asked of this film. I am contending that the 'we' at the centre has queered the disabled/non-disabled binary. What is more, this disruption of such embedded categories within film is rooted in, and surrounded by, a number of other philosophical questions; no longer is disability a prosthetic device, but a fundamental and interconnected body of the film and the (un)reality it presents. As such, this is an exemplar of a rhizomatic storytelling (Deleuze and Guattari, 2004), creating a multiplicity of questions which resist unity, or separation (e.g. into disability 'issues'). As Deleuze and Guatarri argue:

> A rhizome ceaselessly establishes connections between semi-otic chains, organizations of power, and circumstances relative to the arts, sciences, and social struggles.
>
> (Deleuze and Guattari, 2004, 381)

As such, the film, despite its (probable) niche audience, has a communicative structure which can be seen to speak to us all, whether this is to amuse disabled people on the basis that it has satirised and exposed ideas of difference as a spurious means of social categorisation, or to trouble the ideas of ableist privilege which can be found in conventional rom-coms and cultural attitudes. It has also achieved this without punching down; focusing firmly on social context and hegemonic power, it emphasises (as one might expect of satire) the absurdity of life and of the power structures which serve to define us all.

Significantly, Lanthimos' approach avoids the cause and effect narratives that are common to many film representations of disability, to romantic comedy, and indeed to any film which may be seen as an example of the 'normality genre' (Darke, 1998). Koutsourakis (2012) compares Lanthimos to Lars von Trier and Béla Tarr, in their use of a fragmented structure, and a 'performative' focus 'which privileges gestures, postures and attitudes over concrete character and plot development' (2012, 85). This has been named the 'cinema of the body' by Deleuze (Koutsourakis, 2012), where 'performativity replaces narrative causality' (ibid., 85). Koutsourakis shows that the result is a 'posing of questions rather than offering answers' (ibid., 87), which encourages thought and reflection in the audience, generating what Rosenbaum has called a 'cinema of doubt' or 'uncertainty' (Rosenbaum, 2017). Perhaps most significantly, he argues that one of the reasons for placing the emphasis on bodies' 'corporeal realism' (Koutsourakis, 2012, 106), 'social gestures [...] and the micropolitics of everyday life' (ibid., 2012, 104), is to rediscover what is 'smoothed', reduced, or invisible within processes which work to 'minimise the complexity' of life, inherent within contemporary cinema, particularly Hollywood (ibid., 104). I suspect, given this comparison of two very different films, that the issues raised by the cinema of doubt, ambiguity, and corporeal realism have much to offer to the imagining of new cinematic strategies, and to raise questions of what it is to be human, a theme I will return to in the conclusion. Indeed, Murray suggests that,

> artists make interesting things happen when they refuse to respect the allegedly natural character of a consensually agreed way of being (and being with others) in the world.
>
> (2016, 45)

Bearing in mind Koutsourakis' point that Hollywood tends to simplify stories told for commercial purposes, ensuring processes of 'commodification' meet the needs of diverse audiences (ibid., 2012, 106), I now turn to a genre which places the body at centre stage.

6 The gross-out genre, the Farrelly Brothers, and disability
Mapping representational change

Gross-out, impairment, and political correctness

There is evidence of gross-out films through the history of cinema right from the silent era, and some of the origins of contemporary gross-out cinema can be seen in other genres, such as horror, pornography, and 'gorno' (a 'portmanteau' of gore and porno (Cromb, 2008, 18), but it is usually seen as a relatively recent form of comedy, emerging in the 1970s with John Waters' *Pink Flamingos* (1972) and John Landis' *National Lampoon's Animal House* (1978). Gross-out's raison d'être seems to be the need to transgress common understandings of normality and to provoke disgust (King, 2002). These transgressions usually involve the shocking use of body fluids such as semen and vomit, bodily functions such as defecation, or the depiction of people with non-normative body types, often fat, and frequently naked. In *Pink Flamingos*, for example, Divine (aka Harris Glenn Milstead, a cult figure who appeared in most of John Waters' films) was seen to eat 'fresh' dog faeces which she picked up from the ground. These actions had the appearance of being filmed in one take (Harrington, 1997), potentially heightening the shock for the audience. Reflecting a tendency towards revealing taboo sexual topics, and the disposition for using naked body parts gratuitously in many such films of the 1970s and 1980s, *Porky's* (1982) has a scene in which a sports coach, aptly named Beulah Ballbricker (Nancy Parsons), pulls at a penis (belonging to Tommy Turner, played by Wyatt Knight) which she sees protruding through a peephole; he had placed it there after attempts to see the girls showering were thwarted by the obstruction of a large naked girl. These kinds of events tended to occur in shockingly inappropriate situations, serving to mark behaviour and the protagonists as 'matter out of place' (Douglas, 1966, 44).

As a form of comedy which is designed to provoke disgust and shock as well as laughter, which is explicitly triggered by the appearance of body fluids or the public performance of bodily functions which are expected to occur in private, gross-out films do not seem to present themselves as the most 'positive' vehicle for changing pathological images of disabled people and the promoting new images of disabled people's experience.[1] Neither are they likely to proffer alternative images of disabled beauty. Given the focus on abject bodies, gross-out is more likely to be seen as a pathologising genre, particularly when one considers the history of comedy and disability, and the ways in which humour has been weaponised against disabled people. However, since the late 1990s gross-out has been used increasingly as a comedic strategy in media which highlights social practices of disablement, playing with ideas of disabled people's difference, often positioning disruptive bodies or minds as central to 'the joke' at the level of both micro-interactions and broader macro-narratives of impairment or disability.

As suggested, gross-out emerged as early as 1914, in *Nell's Eugenic Wedding*, a lost film which, according to a contemporary review, contained one scene of a man vomiting after eating soap.[2] However, it tends to be associated with a more recent period beginning in the 1970s after the repeal of the Motion Picture Production Code (Hays Code). It has been exemplified by the work of John Waters, from the 1960s onwards (Harvey, 2000), and Todd Solondz (Hanitch, 2011, 24), from the 1990s (see below). Recently, elements of gross-out have also been a feature of television comedies, most notably *Little Britain*, and in Ricky Gervais's work, despite his dismissal of the genre as formulaic.[3]

Although I will be arguing that the Farrelly Brothers were the first filmmakers to embed alternative, and more political, understandings of disability in their oeuvre, themes of impairment had been addressed in the work of these earlier directors, including Waters' *Mondo Trasho*, a story which results in foot amputation and their subsequent replacement with prosthetic bird-like feet. However, the use of gross-out as a more explicit comedic strategy to question or overturn social expectations of disability became more frequent in the 1990s, as increasingly troubling ideas about the place of disabled people in society became more common. Nonetheless, King suggests that these films often 'have it both ways', working 'to provoke its own potential "PC" critics while also to some extent inoculating itself against their attack' (2002, 75–76), often by using discriminatory attitudes and language to reveal the absurdity and harms of such views. Indeed, the challenge to 'orthodoxies' of 'subjects that should not be the subject of comedy' (ibid., 75), which was a hallmark of the Farrelly Brothers' work (as well as those who came before them), was adopted by a number of writers and comedians who came later, with or without such inoculatory reversals. Further, much of the legacy of gross-out films goes beyond cinema, and can be seen in the increasing use of gross-out and anti-PC comedy on television from the late 1990s. I suggested earlier that the anti-PC work of Ricky Gervais exemplifies the use of comedic inoculations, but we are invited to laugh at misogyny, ageism, and disablism, in supposedly empathetic portrayals such as *Derek* (Dean, 2014; Landreth, 2014),[4] where the eponymous lead character has an ambiguous impairment status, presumed to be disabled by some viewers, despite Gervais's claims to the contrary (Lawson, 2013).

Little Britain's character Mrs Emery (David Walliams) also has a presumed, but unknown, impairment. As a character who is oblivious to her tendency to urinate frequently in public, she exemplifies gross-out content. The disabled identity which is implied here reflects a wider recent trend to present ambiguous portrayals of impairment, often combined with gross-out, where such disruptive body types simultaneously denote and disavow constructions of impairment and disability. Simultaneously this generates uncertainty which is likely to leave the authors 'innocent' of disability stereotyping, whilst allowing them to use impairment, especially mental illness (Mrs Emery), or learning difficulty/disability, as a prosthetic narrative device to engender laughter, usually at the disabled character's expense (Lockyer, 2010).[5]

Referring to comedy in popular culture overall, Harvey has pointed out, in relation to the risk-taking and taboo-crossing characteristic of gross-out, that by the beginning of the twenty-first century, Waters' 'once-singular edge has become everybody'. He goes on to argue:

> For comedy these days, 'politically incorrect' is as safe a label as 'pasteurized' on milk; its absence might raise more hackles. Waters' talent for disturbing the status quo looks a tad so-five-minutes ago, now that outrage is the new norm.
>
> (Harvey, 2000, 34)

Indeed, more recently Mumford has argued that the 'comedy of outrage' is now 'wearing thin' (2017, para 6) and that audiences need films and comedy which are 'smart, relevant and socially conscious', expressing a need for more 'politically aware' comedy in the age of Trump (ibid., para 14). However, Mumford's recognition that there are an increased number of films which 'open [...] comedy to new voices' (para 10) and more diverse themes, such as inter-racial partnerships between healthy and sick people (*The Big Sick*), does little to recognise the enduring, if rather cyclical, popularity for such comedy, and he significantly underestimates the political content encoded in some 'outrageous' films, suggesting that gross-out and political correctness are mutually exclusive.

Conversely, I will show how gross-out films have offered a crucial site for the contestation of disablist values. The uncomfortable associations made between gross-out, prejudice, and disablement were first seen in mainstream comedy films written by the Farrelly Brothers, pre-dating the work of David Walliams and Matt Lucas (*Little Britain*), and Ricky Gervais by over six years.[6] Often unacknowledged as new ways of portraying disabled people, and sometimes criticised for perpetuating bad or stigmatising portrayals (see Byrne 2000; Richardson, 2016), these particular gross-out films were amongst the first to transform contemporary images of disabled people in film and broadcast media, not least by creating ambiguity and debate about why disability is considered funny. They can be seen to have encouraged the audience to turn their attention to ableist (Campbell, 2009) constructions of impairment whilst revealing them as the misleading tropes that they are. Although some attention has been given to the gross-out genre (see King, 2002, and

Richardson, 2016 for example), it has not been taken very seriously, even less so the place of disability with it, with few exceptions.[7]

Crucially, these images were embedding new perspectives on disability within a cinematic genre, or perhaps more accurately, a mode (King, 2002) which is expected to appeal, primarily, to a young film-going audience (ibid., 73). This is significant because young people made up a large portion of the cinema audience in the later 1990s (Livingstone and Bovill, 1999), continuing to be an important group for mainstream films in particular (Tyneside Cinema, 2013). Further, King (2002) also points out that gross-out films are aimed at young men as the key target audience. This is of some significance when considering the prevalence of 'negative attitudes' towards disabled people amongst young people, as a report by Scope found that men aged eighteen to thirty-four were more likely to have these attitudes and were also the least likely to have social interactions with disabled people; twenty-one per cent reported avoiding communication due to their lack of knowledge on how they should talk to disabled people (Aiden and McCarthy, 2014). Before I examine the challenges the Farrelly Brothers films presented to this and other audiences, I want to explore the ways in which the gross-out genre transgresses cultural ideals of the body, and the important role of disgust in the transportation/absorption (Lippman, 2015, 7) of viewers.

The gross-out genre, the body, and disgust

As incidents or events which happen occasionally in the course of wider storylines, rather than being a defining feature of the whole film, gross-out comedy often takes a hybrid form, usually in conjunction with romantic comedy or comedy horror genres (King, 2002). Gross-out has also been compared to 'gorno', reflecting the close resemblance of the two. Paul (1994) saw gross-out as an anaesthetic brought about by the comedy and horror of the 1970s and 1980s, which was shaped by the ambivalence between individual and community values that characterised political tensions in this period. It has also been used to support other genres whose main aim is to critique normativity, most notably in drama and satire. This is perhaps at its best in Solondz's *Happiness* (Richardson, 2016, 182–187), a film which centres human despair within ostensibly conventional and superficially stable family structures, and (as such) questions the perception of conditions of exceptionality attributed to acts usually deemed immoral, such as obscene phone calls and paedophilia. A notable scene is one where Allen (played by Phillip Seymour Hoffman) is shown sticking postcards to the wall with his semen. He is one of several characters whose life is marked by desolation, the regret of bad decisions, and antisocial habits.

Whatever form these gross-out hybrids take, the rule-breaking which occurs can easily be seen to challenge cultural ideals and assumptions of 'normal' everyday life. King (2002, 64–65) discusses such transgressions in terms of the Bakhtinian concept of the 'carnivalesque', where all the social and cultural hierarchies we know, and tend to conform to, are changed, become more dynamic, and are often reversed or turned 'inside-out'. Bakhtin argues that the carnivalesque body (particularly 'lower' and 'female parts') is seen as 'less rational' and 'controllable'; this, and bodily 'degradation' are associated with the 'unofficial aspects of the world, unofficial in tone (laughter) and in content (the lower stratum)' (Bakhtin, 1984, 315). The carnivalesque serves to contest the more serious and rationalised dimensions of everyday life, and challenge ordered, idealised, and un-messy conceptions of the body and social order. He demonstrates how the appearance of the body on such unconventional terms in cultural representations works to challenge social boundaries directly, where

> the confines between the body and the world and between separate bodies are drawn in the grotesque genre quite differently than in the classic and naturalist images.
> (Bakhtin, 1984, 315)

The body in all its guises, then, is seen as a fundamental feature of the grotesque, which is said to transgress 'its own limits' (ibid., 26). King also compares such gross-out challenges to 'social convention' with Kristeva's psychoanalytic theorisation of 'the abject' (Kristeva, 1982a, 4). Abjection, here, is conceptualised as an ambiguous form of liminality which lies outside the symbolic order, disrupting conventional forms of subjectivity, identity, and order. King suggests (though does not conclude) that both the carnivalesque grotesque and ideas of the abject are central to the workings of gross-out and that this may imbue this genre of comedy with greater transformative possibilities. This would appear to be especially true for an audience who are drawn to gross-out for its shock value and celebration of disgust, only to find unexpected challenges to hegemonic ideals of non-disabled bodies and gender identities. Thus, the earlier films of the Farrelly Brothers, and even the first series of *Little Britain* (Lockyer, 2010), can easily be seen to mark a radical departure from previous understandings, particularly because they brought audience expectations of the comedic value of disabled characters into sharp focus.[8] But, bearing in mind Darke's theorisation of the normality genre (1998) and the role that disruptions of the 'abnormal' can play in re-affirming and perpetuating conservative attitudes, in this case reinforcing ideas of non-disabled and other forms of normativity, it would be unwise to presume that such transgressions would always work in favour of challenging discourses of ableism, or that they will pose a challenge to the 'non-disabled gaze' or the subjectivities of film viewers. As King (2002) acknowledges, the dialectical exchange between subversion and confirmation can be subtle and complex, as is the case with many forms of communication, across media and different genres, and needs to be considered in specific historical and cultural context.

As both Darke's and King's arguments suggest, there is a danger that conventional norms of bodily propriety and ableist discourse may be reinforced even, or especially, where both of these are contravened in gross-out films. There also seems to be a tendency for such challenges to become less radical over time, sometimes re-iterating the initial stereotypes which they, or others, sought to deconstruct. This is especially evident in the later series, and the US version, of *Little Britain*, characterised by Akass as 'crude burlesque' (2010, 213). It may even be seen to be true of the Farrelly Brothers, in their return to the characters of their first 'disability' film, *Dumb and Dumber*, in *Dumber and Dumber To* (discussed later in this chapter). Analysis of both these examples demonstrates that their writers/directors returned us to portrayals which have little subtlety and leave few opportunities for multiple interpretations, other than laughing *at* disabled characters and 'others'. Further, it has been forcefully argued by some disabled people's organisations and mental health advocacy groups that some of these images of specific impairments maintain the stereotypic assumptions made of disabled people, e.g. the association of mental illness with violence (see Byrne, 2009). However, there is little consensus on this with other writers, journalists, and academics (e.g. Bauer, 2005; LeBesco, 2004) claiming more radical potential, albeit with caution.

As King (2002) suggests, our reactions to this and other transgressive genres can tell us much about the class and status issues of culture; he also suggests that an understanding of the effects of transgression is likely to be found in analysis of the experiences of viewing, particularly in investigating the feelings and 'ambiguous cultural meanings' evoked by the balance between 'disgust and comic pleasure' (ibid., 68) lying at the centre of the gross-out film's intentions. Eitzen's (1999) recommendation for a phenomenological understanding of film seems particularly pertinent to the gross-out genre, with its strong emphasis on the physical and emotional responses of viewers' bodies to film. Not only does this suggest textual analysis to investigate how the 'model reader' (in this case, young and probably male), and other audiences, might be interpellated by gross-out comedy, it also highlights the value of more phenomenological understandings of the film-viewer experience. Eitzen (1999) has also underlined the need for a focus on the 'emotional impulses' wrought by comedy, an argument also made forcefully by Williams (1991), e.g. with regard to melodrama and horror.

An especially important element in gross-out films is that of disgust, so analysis of the way this is constructed through cinema, and how it is experienced and managed by the audience, needs to pay close attention to visual and audio dimensions of film alongside considerations of narrative. Our identifications, disidentifications (Butler, 1993), and counter-identifications with disabled characters in gross-out will invariably be shaped by the use of sensory stimuli, combined with the disgust-orientated traits common to the genre and our attitudes towards the characters involved, e.g.in the visceral responses generated (Cromb, 2008). These aspects of film are especially significant to an intersubjective consideration of how affective responses to gross-out 'disability films' are shaped through the phenomenological closeness and the sensory and other responses of the viewer's lived body, particularly in relation to an aesthetics predicated on disgust and the active presence of disabled bodies (see Hanitch, 2011, in relation to disgust, emotions and the body). Thus, for example, the target audience of gross-out fans may seek identifications primarily *with* those who experience gross-out scenarios on screen, even if such affinities are ambivalent; thus the choice to place disabled characters within these situations may encourage greater identifications with them. Conversely, the frequent attribution of gross-out moments to a disabled character, where non-disabled characters have few, may work to reinforce ideas of disabled people's abjection, or are the perpetrators of disgusting incidents or opinions. Bearing these thoughts in mind, the remainder of this chapter will explore the constitution of both disgust and disabled bodies, as key features of gross-out cinema in the work of the Farrelly Brothers, within a wider consideration of representational transformations and new understandings of disability and impairment.

I will explore the work of the Farrelly Brothers as a valuable vehicle for the examination of disability themes, as influential recent contributors to the gross-out genre. They seem to have particular relevance to contemporary culture, in a post-discrimination legislation milieu, ecause they developed increasingly stronger critiques of disabling processes as their films have developed, thereby testing the limits of the film industry's approach to inclusion.[9] This is especially true up to the release of *Stuck on You* in 2003, perhaps their most explicitly political film. Thus, drawing on online discussions of these films, the potential interactions and engagements of audiences, and their psycho-emotional attachments, with Farrelly Brothers' films will be explored, focussing in particular on the earlier films where the narratives were growing incrementally more radical, to the surprise of an unsuspecting audience. Close attention is paid to the matter of how these films play with and may be seen to manipulate disabled and non-disabled viewers' prejudices and intersubjectivities, and how these are likely to feed into wider audience reactions, questioning whether they are likely to expose or perpetuate the cultural misrecognition of disabled people in contemporary culture.

The work of the Farrelly Brothers

One of the most striking aspects of the Farrelly Brothers' films is the progression they made in disability representations as their films evolved. They developed new challenges to cultural imagery and film industry practices in incremental, possibly deliberate, steps. This progression has been recognised by some writers as moving to stronger social model understandings of disability, e.g. from 'freak-phobic' to 'freak-centric' (LeBesco, 2004). In so doing, the audience is progressively re-positioned with each film, and encouraged to question ableist conventions of normality (see later sections of this chapter). Whatever the reason was for this evolution, it seems probable that the processes of renegotiation involved in these gradual, but steady, shifts pushed the audience and the industry into confronting conventional attitudes to disability, with boundaries of 'acceptance' and understanding being stretched further with each successive film. Even with their later films audience reviewers on IMDB were surprised at the content, with one reviewer 'ivko' (Review 2, organised in 'helpfulness') entitling their review of *Stuck on You* (2003) as 'Touching comedy', saying:

> I resisted seeing it for a long time because the concept sounded so offensive. But offensiveness is the last word I would use to describe this movie. The conjoined twin never feels like fodder for cheap jokes. Yes, it plays prominently in the plot, but it never feels like you are laughing at them, only with them.
>
> (ivko, 2004, para 1)

Significantly, several reviewers on the same page also spoke of the mismatch between 20th Century Fox's 'offensive' marketing of the film and the content of the film itself, which indicates the industry's reluctance to move beyond the conventionally exploitative imagery of disabled people in case it puts their target audiences – young people, and particularly men – off.[10] Indeed, portrayals such as this may have been perceived as a threat to those who do not want to change wider industry practices. The growing politicisation of these disabled people's stories is likely to be seen as 'risky' (as discussed in previous chapters), especially if the films are seen as thwarting the expectations of their intended audience. This risk may be seen to be worse if one considers the growing acknowledgement of the cultural 'misrecognition' (Fraser, 2000) of disabled people across all conventional portrayals of disability. In addition to the potential impacts on this audience, who tend to be identified with a penchant for political incorrectness (King, 2002), the industry may also fear the ripple effects on wider audiences, who may demand 'better' representations. This is especially significant for those who seek more liberal, even inspirational, messages in films, especially disability-themed drama films, which are often seen as 'Oscar bait' (Rodgers, 2012). Such effects then might necessitate a rethink across the industry.

Ostensibly, the gross-out images of *Little Britain*, *Derek*, and the films of the Farrelly Brothers may look similar, but the small amount of criticism and research in this area suggests there are significant differences in representation and reception which lead to very different forms of understanding and attitudinal reaction, possibly feelings of charity and pity in the former, and an awareness of the need for equality in the latter. Nonetheless, the linking of disabled people with gross-out comedy has obvious dangers in an era where there is an increased tendency to see, and report on, disability in pejorative terms (Briant et al., 2011), where disabled people are often portrayed as undeserving, and as fraudsters and burdens, often linking people with impairments with ideas of the abject (Hughes, 2009), and/or evoking feelings of pity, contempt, and disgust (Soldatic and Pini, 2009). These are ever-present, crucial factors to consider in evaluating the transgressive qualities of gross-out as a genre to re-present disability. To explore the potential of these portrayals, including the positioning of disabled people in communicative structures, and the manifestation of meanings in different contexts, it is first necessary to understand the gross-out genre/mode on its own terms.

It is clear that the Farrelly Brothers are well-known for their success as contributors to gross-out films. It is also apparent that they have received recognition from some within the disabled people's community for challenging conventional representations of impairment and disability (LeBesco, 2004). As briefly discussed, they have created controversies which have been echoed in other films and television programmes, especially regarding the position of disabled protagonists as leading, if deeply flawed, personalities. (This refers to disabled *characters* rather than disabled *performers*, though they have increasingly been played by disabled actors.) They have also received criticism for their direct invocation of common stereotypes. There are clear parallels between this work and the later work in British TV programmes, with *Little Britain, Life is Short, and Derek*, all receiving criticism for the language used and stereotyping. Similarly, the film *Tropic Thunder* caused much debate on its release in 2008, especially for its use of the word 'retard' (see Cox, 2008 for example).

Indeed, the debate about the portrayal of learning difficulties/disabilities, or the intellectually disabled, and the use of the word 'retard' (seventeen times, according to Dolski, 2013), alongside equally offensive/parodic images of white actors 'blacking up' (Robert Downey Junior, in order to play a Black soldier in the production of a film) is perhaps emblematic of the dilemmas, and potential contradictions, of disability and impairment representations, even though these are very different debates which are related to dissimilar forms of oppression and privilege.[11] As a depiction of the making of a film-within-a-film, defenders of *Tropic Thunder* have argued that this type of strategy was used to satirise Hollywood's attitudes to diversity, and to parody their attempts to implement it, highlighting the superficiality of their liberal ideals, and their often shallow performances of equality. This is exemplified in Ben Stiller's character, Tugg Speedman, taking advice on how to play 'Simple Jack' to win awards, parodying the tendency for well-known non-disabled actors to take on disabled character roles as a tried and tested means to win an Oscar. These storylines set the scene for comedic ableist slurs and language in advice such as, e.g. 'Don't go full retard'. But Cieply reported the widespread opposition to the film by many disabled groups, and demands for a boycott (Cieply, 2008). Indeed Dolski said:

> Promotional movie posters for the 'Simple Jack' subplot read, 'Once upon a time ... There was a retard' and 'What he doesn't have in his head, he makes up for in his heart.' [...]. The intent of their over-the-top characterization may be satirical in nature, but they fail to acknowledge

the ramifications of disparaging a group of people. If the intent is to be funny, does that then make it okay?

(2013, 16)

The issue of intent was discussed in earlier chapters, alongside the positioning of the disabled characters within the film – ostensibly there were none here (even though we may regard Stiller to be a disabled actor), as the jokes about playing 'full retard' can be seen to be drawing attention to what is meant by such language and the concepts that go with it.[12] Such reflections possibly add to the audience's self-reflections on the ways in which we rank people according to their intellectual capacities, physical features, and associated forms of self-presentation. The film has a large cast and is quite polyphonic in that we see the personalities, inadequacies, and strengths of most characters, allowing us a number of identifications. As such, it cannot be said to centre one particular point of view on disability, race, or any other issue, even if its cast is predominantly made up of non-disabled white men, who are parodying an industry which has the needs of white, non-disabled men at its core.

For similar reasons to those suggested by Dolski, some have argued that disabled people are portrayed badly in the films of the Farrelly Brothers, as outlined above. In many ways their films, and the gross-out genre in general, are an easy target for criticism if crude measures of 'positive' and 'negative' imagery are used to measure their worth. Typically, such judgements tend to be made on the basis of their fit to common stereotypes, such as those outlined by Barnes (1991) or Norden (1994), or whether they perpetuate dominant tropes, such as the linking of violence to mental health (Byrne, 2000). This can lead to a reductive approach being taken to portrayals; for example, the National Alliance on the Mentally Ill, an American grass-roots support and advocacy organisation, accused the film *Me, Myself and Irene* of misinformation, cruelty, and tastelessness (NAMI.org, 2000), condemning the portrayal of the violent and obscene behaviour of the central (dual) character Charlie/Hank. Academics working in psychiatry were also critical of this film, not least the diagnosis of 'advanced delusionary schizophrenia with involuntary narcissistic rage' given to Charlie in the storyline, deemed to perpetuate the misinformation that schizophrenia involves dual or multiple personalities (Byrne, 2000). Positioning psychiatrists as advocates for people with mental health difficulties, Byrne argues (with no sense of irony) that 'abusing people with schizophrenia is a privilege that psychiatrists have a duty to challenge' (2000, 365).

Similar judgements of the potential damage done by this film have come from other professionals working in medical environments, particularly psychiatric disciplines (e.g. Hocking, quoted in Molitorisz, 2005; and Wedding and Niemiec, 2003), whereas a more multidimensional view of the film's merits has been taken by disability writers from the social sciences, such as LeBesco (2004).

The criticisms of Byrne, NAMI, and others tend to have overlooked many other aspects of the film's diegesis, most significantly, perhaps, the social causes of Charlie's mental distress, and his success at parenting. His putz-like character is likely to generate affection from the audience, as a character type which tends to elicit 'rueful identifications' (Taylor, 2015, 68). Further, such critiques tend to ignore any identifications from other people experiencing similar forms of mental distress, given that most of Hank's rage came from the range of oppressive experiences he suffered due to the actions of others.

The paradoxes involved in, or indeed impossibilities of producing, unequivocally 'good' images of disability and impairment in contemporary cinema are particularly evident in the case of the Farrelly Brothers' films, for several reasons discussed throughout the rest of the chapter. Overall, their body of work has combined critical deconstructions of conventional disability stereotypes with gross-out strategies in ways which have tested the film industry's acceptance of representational change. As the political 'messages' about disability became more explicit, the resistance to it also seemed to have increased, not least through the continued marketing of their films according to sensationalised imagery, regardless of clear changes in authorial intent. Although the brothers' work is perhaps less likely to have been seen in terms of excessive 'risk' in the ways that disabled writers and directors (and often women) tend to experience marginalisation and censorship (see Chapter Three, for example), their increasing centring of disabled people's points of view had become more than apparent by the time they released *Stuck on You*, in 2003, possibly their 'coming out' film in terms of any commitment to the social model of disability. As suggested, the evolution of their films also seems to have presented challenges to their primary gross-out audience, pushing them, with increasing force, to examine their own attitudes to disability. The following comments (the fifth reviewer on IMDB viewer comments, organised in terms of 'helpfulness') demonstrate some of these responses at this key point:

> Aside from the lack of sexual humor, there's a major difference between the style of comedy the Farrellys employ here than in some of their prior films. Whereas many of their previous works have often made fun of the people that suffer from certain 'disorders,' Stuck On You presents us with two friendly, easy-going guys who've grown accustomed to their situation and choose not to see their conjoined lives as a handicap. Rather, the film derives its humor from the way 'outsiders' view their condition.
>
> Li-1 (2004, para 6)

It is clear from these comments that the mimetic strategy leaves little room for misunderstanding their intent. The application of Irigary's (1985) views on mimesis and stereotypes of women (discussed later) are useful here in that we can see that one of the Farrellys' strategies towards disability proceeds from the deliberate re-presentation of stereotypical views of disability in order to call them into question.

Others point to the reluctance of the film industry to move with these shifting conceptions of impairment. As the first viewer review, organised by 'helpfulness', antony-1 stated:

> Fox's marketing treatment of the film is appalling. In the trailer, Matt Damon's character says: 'We're not Siamese, we're American,' and the trailer plays it like he is stupid. Whereas in fact, when watching the film, the context is very different – he's reacting with indignation, and in defence of their conjoined nature. This is indicative of the entire film. Never is their conjoined-nature used for humour in a bad way.
>
> antony-1 (2004, para 3)

It is clear that many viewers were put in a position where they had to face the change of approach in representations of impairments, and how that may affect their enjoyment of a more considered form of humour. Here a viewer writes on this in IMDB reviews – the third review, organised in relation to 'helpfulness':

> Compared to some of directors Bobby and Peter Farrelly's other films, such as *Dumb and Dumber*, *There's Something About Mary*, and *Me, Myself And Irene*, we could say that the humor in *Stuck On You* is much more subtle. That fact may be off-putting to viewers who come to *Stuck On You* primarily as fans of the Farrelly Brothers' previous work. There are still outrageous gags here, but they tend to be funnier if you exercise your intellect a bit, and believe it or not they are more rooted in reality than some other Farrelly Brothers films.
>
> Brandt Sponseller (2005, para 2)

Here is a clear acknowledgement that the audience is being asked to reflect on their own previous understandings and prejudices. Although a number of other reviewers condemned the film as unfunny, sentimental, and guilty of exploring serious subject matter in an inappropriately un-serious genre, Sponseller's thoughts suggest that gross-out is compatible with the processes of meaning-making of an active audience, especially in the light of the potentially new ideas expressed on impairment and disablement. In this case, then, it is likely that those who do not 'work' at interpretation will stop watching their films. This seems to have been the case as the box office shows substantially smaller profits for *Stuck on You* then for previous films, making comparatively marginal profits; while *Kingpin* did less well than the other films which were moving towards an increasingly politicised view of disability, but this film was directed and not written by them, unlike most others discussed in the chapters.[13]

However, the films have been both damned and praised by disabled and non-disabled people alike (as indicated earlier) and there is a clear lack of consensus about their worth. A typical viewer response of the more disdainful type is jharvey-4 (reviewer 11, on IMDb, organised by 'helpfulness'), who, discussing *Stuck on You* complained,

> but like many recent Farrelly releases it's muddled and illustrates a tug of war between the movies the Farrellys want to make the [sic] and movies the Farrelly's fans want them to make.
>
> (2004, Review 11, para 2)[14]

Indeed, their films exemplify the futility of arguments about 'bad' and 'good' disability films, even though most disabled people speaking on these concerns (see earlier chapters) tend to agree that representations of disability, across the cultural landscape, were usually poor, tending to repeat damaging stereotypes of deviance, pathology, and general 'otherness' from presumed norms. It is improbable that ways can be found to depict disabled people which meet with widespread approval, even within the disabled people's community. Nor do I think we should look for such a recipe, a concern I will return to in the final chapter.

Placing the emphasis on 'negative' or stereotyped imagery (see Kriegel, 1987; Barnes, 1992 and Norden, 1994) has also often meant that crude, mainstream, or popular images are often overlooked for their radical potential, as Mallett (2010) has pointed out in relation to *South Park*. As suggested in earlier chapters, it is very clear that we all make meaning, and identifications, according to a wide range of social, cultural, and personal contexts. These multiple interpretations of depictions in general are borne in mind in the following examination of films written or directed by the Farrelly Brothers which feature impairment and disability. Aspects of text/viewer interactions are focussed on the mode of gross-out and impairment, exploring the degree of implication afforded to viewers.

From *Dumb and Dumber* to *Dumb and Dumber To*

Dumb and Dumber

Dumb and Dumber, released in 1994, was the first film directed by the Farrelly Brothers. The trailers and the marketing of this film positioned the viewer to anticipate a protracted cinematic one-liner which went something like: people accredited with 'mild' learning difficulties make stupid, amusing, and humiliating mistakes all the time, and they don't even know when they're making them. The clips which advertised the film were likely to lead the prospective audience to expect a road movie featuring the two central characters, Harry (Jeff Daniels) and Lloyd (Jim Carrey) in a narrative which would be characterised by their involvement in a series of humiliating incidents. Leaving the audience in no doubt about these intentions, another trailer for the film (YouTube, 2013a) structured its clips (often featuring them in a car which had been decorated to resemble a dog) around a series of definitions:

Dumb: a person lacking mental power;
Idiot: an adult mentally inferior to a child of three; and
Stupid: a person below normal intelligence.

After this, the narrator concludes 'if they each had half a brain they'd still only have half a brain' (IMDB.com, 2018a). It is no surprise then, given these trailers, as well as the film's title, that the stories of Harry and Lloyd have been interpreted by some as making a mockery of people with learning difficulties by emphasising their lack of intelligence and using 'hate words' such as retard (see for example, Berger, 2012).

Thus, this film presented itself as a joke solely at the expense of people with learning difficulties, and as a template based on a formulaic recipe to attract film-goers who wanted a laugh at the expense of people who they could view as different to themselves. This formula positioned the potential viewer as superior; wiser, sexier, less naïve, and in possession of more cultural capital. It was certainly marketed as such, with glimpses of Lloyd confusing Austria with Australia, invoking Australian stereotypes, and generally misinterpreting the needs, instructions, and expectations of those around them (YouTube, 2014).

However, as in the case of Ricky Gervais's *Derek* (discussed earlier) the impairment status of the two is unclear. Indeed, they have much in common with early cinema of the 1910s and 1920s, with their names as a clear homage to this era, i.e. the leading actor and film-maker Harold Lloyd. This is also seen in the emphasis placed on naivety and slapstick traditions. Much like their namesake Harold Lloyd, their characters' attempts at social improvement, and romantic relationships, are thwarted; and like him, Harold and Lloyd somehow survive the continuing dramas whilst wrecking their chances of achieving their cherished dreams, especially their goals of attracting beautiful women and keeping a long-term job (King, 2002). Both their problems and their successes seem to be brought about by their own lack of the capacity to understand the significance of the actions of those around them. This includes the trust they give to a kidnapper who they pick up when he is posing as a hitch-hiker, and who they accidentally kill. Their lack of understanding about what is deemed to be normal and abnormal is also tied to gross-out moments when, for example, Harry's parakeet Petey is killed by the kidnapper and Lloyd tapes its head to its body in order to sell it to a 'blind' boy, Billy (Brady Bluhm).

The comedy wrought from their attempts to fool a disabled person though such a ridiculous idea, dependent on both impairments for the comedy (impaired intelligence for them and lack of vision for Billy), also creates a degree of disgust at the dubious use of a decapitated dead animal. The use of Billy's impairment here invokes stereotypes of blindness as a marker for vulnerability, victimhood, and lack of agency (see Norden, 1994). It is unclear whether this is done with any sense of irony, to allow us to question such stereotypes, but LeBesco finds it unequivocal that the audience is being asked to laugh *at* Billy, rather than with him. The use of animals, often dead, is quite common in cinema which aims to elicit disgust (Hanitch, 2011, 24). The gross-out moments invariably feature Harry, including having his tongue stuck to an icy pole, coming down with diarrhoea after Lloyd puts 'Turbo Lax' in his drink, and having fellow diner, Sea Bass (Cam Neely) spitting on his burger meal. These gross-out moments are filmed in close-up, or medium close-up, following a common trend to use close-ups as a device to elicit audience disgust (Hanitch, 2011). As Hanitch demonstrates (following Williams, 1991), the affective states experienced by cinema viewers should not be addressed in a simple fashion, and we need to 'acknowledge the complex tension between different emotions' (2011, 14), likely to be felt by viewers in such moments. In Harry's gross-out moments, both his narrative trajectory and the closeness of the camera work encourage viewers to feel both disgust and sympathy, or even empathy, for his character. Furthermore, the gross-out moments in which he is involved can be characterised in terms of 'anticipatory disgust', as most of the audience will have chosen to watch the film due to their fondness for and identification with the gross-out genre.

Thus, they are likely to be viewed 'positively' (Hanitch, 2011, 17), adding to the likeability of the character. Simply put, Hanitch explains that cinematic disgust can be divided into two main types, sudden and anticipatory. Sudden disgust is theorised to occur against our expectations as a mix of shock and revulsion. This is to be found, most obviously, in horror films and is 'negatively valenced' (ibid., 17). Conversely, he argues that anticipatory disgust is likely to come from signposting to the disgusting incident, often by the camera revealing things to the audience which the characters are unaware of. Whereas the gross-out form tends to set up such expectations in advance of seeing the film, to the target audience, Hanitch explains that anticipatory disgust is where each anticipated disgust-evoking scenario within films involves a suspension of emotion, where the viewer's cognitive and bodily responses prepare them for the disgusting scene, creating anticipation which causes 'increased attention and vigilance' (2011, 16) to the incident, instigating an ambivalence comprised of repulsion and 'sheer attraction and curiosity' (ibid., 17) . It is argued that this culminates in a 'prediction response' which is 'positively valenced' (ibid., 117). Hanitch suggests that such processes are a source of pleasure for the viewer, particularly in making predictions and gaining closure on expectations. This is likely to create more affection for those at the centre of the gross-out comedy and it adds to the benevolent depiction of Harry and Lloyd as people who are seen to operate outside the norms of contemporary society. In turn, this poses challenges to social conventions, including neurotypicality, where wisdom is often found in innocence. This is a familiar trope in films which depict people with learning difficulties, autism, and cognitive impairments; other such portrayals are to be found in *Rain Man, Forrest Gump*, and *Being There*, as discussed briefly in Chapter Four.

Kingpin

The next film directed by the Farrelly Brothers was *Kingpin*, in 1996, written by Barry Fanaro and Morth Nathan. In addition to gross-out, it can also be placed in the sport comedy genre (IMDB.com, 2018b). The central characters are Roy Munson (Woody Harrelson), a talented State Amateur Bowling Champion, and his adversary Ernie McCracken (Bill Murray). Early in the film, Munson's hand is severed due, inadvertently, to the actions of McCracken, when he seeks revenge for losing to Munson at the state bowling championship. From then on he uses a prosthetic hand. Years later Munson befriends, then manages, an Amish man, Ishmail, who also has exceptional skills in bowling, convincing him to turn professional in order to win a lucrative competition.

The gross-out moments in this film went further than *Dumb and Dumber*; whereas the latter had an explosive diarrhoea scene, Kingpin shows Roy vomiting after he has provided sexual services to his landlady (who is portrayed as older and unattractive) as payment in kind for his rent, while she muses, 'What is it about good sex that makes me have to crap?'. Although Roy was far from innocent in the earlier parts of this scene, having set up a fake mugging so he could rescue her to gain her approval and gratitude in order that she would allow him to continue to live there, her expressions of sexual pleasure and his revulsion after sex is portrayed in a way which leads the viewer to a 'disgust-empathy' (Hanitch, 2011, 22) for Roy. This is conceptualised by Hanitch as a viewing position where we have similar knowledge to the character embroiled in the situation and where there is likely to be 'a high degree of congruence between the character and the viewer: both are disgusted' (ibid., 22). Whilst this may be especially true for the target audience of young people, and men in particular, it is less likely to be true for older women, who may find their empathy lies with the landlady from the start, with a disgust for his deceitful behaviour and for his repulsion towards her at the finish of this sequence of events. Again, the camera is used carefully to elicit such disgust, from medium close-ups of her smoking a post-coital cigarette on the bed, to perceptual point of view reaction shots of Roy vomiting into the toilet, taken by looking under her raised knees, on the bed, to Roy and the toilet in the distance.

Once again, a disabled character is central to the story, from Roy's initial (gross-out) hand crushing, early in the film, to the very end, and our empathy with him is encouraged, despite his many flaws. The Farrelly Brothers' drive to challenge the conventional normality/abnormality dichotomy was apparent from the start of the film. The very first scene shows Munson jumping over and wrecking a white picket fence in his eagerness to speak to his father. Not only can this casual destruction of the fence be seen as a sign of the boundaries they wish to cross, and destroy, it also seems to symbolise their direct intention to challenge the normalities embedded within the American Dream; the idea of a suburban middle-class lifestyle, perhaps most notably explored in David Lynch's *Blue Velvet*, in 1986, and much later in the TV show *Desperate Housewives* (running from 2004 to 2014). Young Munson's affection for his father, and his desire to please him, also hints at Farrelly's preoccupation with normative gender roles and 'appropriate' forms of embodiment, themes dominating most of their later films, e.g. *Shallow Hal, Me, Myself and Irene*, and the skits in *Movie 43*.

Right from their first films it seems that the Farrellys' aim for 'narrative equality' (Wilde, 2004b) between disabled and non-disabled characters, especially as the gross-out moments are shared across a number of characters. Disabled characters are usually shown sympathetically, but as flawed human beings who are capable of harm, as is clear from the characters of Lloyd, Harry, and Munson, discussed so far. As Sancho (2003) has pointed out in her review of disability on television, 'likeability' is a key criterion in portrayals of disabled characters which appeal to all audiences, but the virtues of likeable characters are wrought from a combination of human weaknesses with a mix of recognisable traits that many of us might identify with ourselves, often facing dilemmas which resonate with viewers' own experiences. It is also notable that neither of these films aim for narrative resolution in ways which would normalise their disabled characters; in other words, the Farrellys subvert the normative structure which typifies conventional Hollywood films, as postulated by Darke's idea of the normality genre. At this stage the Farrelly Brothers seemed to be heavily reliant on non-disabled, well-known actors, as there was little visible evidence of obviously disabled actors (in roles where the impairment of the actor matches the impairment of the character), although several of their leading actors have been associated with less obvious impairments, including Woody Harrelson and Jim Carrey, both reputed to have ADHD, for example (see fastbraiin.com, 2016, for example).

There's Something about Mary

In 1998, *There's Something about Mary* was released by the Farrelly Brothers; this has been the most profitable of their films (earning $369,884,651 worldwide at the time of writing – February 2018, from an estimated budget of $23,000,000; IMDB, 2018c). It was the most profitable comedy film of that year and it was also the first of their films to feature a character (but not an actor) who had an obvious impairment from the start of the film, posing a very direct challenge to audience prejudices as the film proceeded. At the beginning of the film a character with learning difficulties named Warren (played by W. Earl Brown) is used in a typically 'prosthetic' way (Mitchell and Snyder, 2000) to frame the central romantic narrative of the story. In this case, Ted, the romantic male lead (Ben Stiller), assists Warren to help him escape a bullying incident. Having set Warren up as a figure of fun and humiliation by a group of young men, the bullies proceed to attack him physically. Subsequently, Warren's sister, Mary (Cameron Diaz), the seemingly unattainable object of Ted's desire, thanks him for his help and asks him for a date. A gross-out incident ruins it; Ted is rushed to hospital with a bleeding scrotum after it gets stuck in his trouser zip, in the bathroom.

Thirteen years later, and having lost contact with her, Ted is shown to still be tormented by his continuing love for her, motivating him to employ Pat Healy (Matt Dillon) to find Mary for him. As a gross-out which is combined with romantic comedy (a common hybrid, as shown in King, 2002), this storyline could easily fit the stalking myth scenarios discussed in Chapter Three. Pat finds Mary and attempts to gain her attention by expressing his passion for 'working with retards', perhaps compounding the appeal to the audience's prejudices we first saw when Warren was being bullied in the first scene of the film. Mary is clearly oblivious to the fact that Healy has been employed by Ted, and so is also unaware that he already knows of her deep commitment to her brother. On meeting, and becoming attracted to her, he is shown to be deliberately using this knowledge as a means to seduce her, particularly by attempting to impress her with his claims to have a caring and charitable disposition. This scene echoes the disability-centric 'meet cute' moment between Ted, Mary, and Warren at the beginning of the film, but the audience knows it is fake, perhaps shifting the viewer to consider the rights and wrongs of the men's differing attitudes to disability, and reflections on their own amusement at these scenes.

When she recoils from the word 'retard', he seems unaware of his own prejudice, compounding the initial error by going on to explain how he is 'training' one 'mong' so that he can be let out of his cage and use a leash. As this diatribe continues the focus is repeatedly switched around to illuminate the prejudices of the viewer, first of all through Mary's outrage at his opinion and eventually through the gradual unravelling of his slimy character, including lies about his wealth and career. Furthermore, in the following scenes it soon becomes apparent that disability is a more than a subsidiary theme within the film. Not only was her eventual choice between several prospective boyfriends centred on her brother's views and their relationships with him, there was an interlocking narrative around another potential suitor, a non-disabled man, Tucker (Lee Evans), who fakes an impairment to win her affections.

The film blends the two genres of romantic comedy and gross-out successfully, whilst placing disability, as disablement, at centre stage. Moreover, at this stage, the viewers – likely drawn from gross-out fans and those with tastes for rom-coms – were still an unsuspecting audience, considering the cruder caricatures of low intelligence in *Dumb and Dumber*, and the more marginal place of impairment and disability in *Kingpin*, where there were no obvious messages about impairment, other than the lead protagonist being disabled, and the subsequent negotiation of his life after his accident. Reflecting the appeal made to a diverse range of viewers, the film gained an extremely wide audience for such a low budget film (as one of the best performing films in any genre that year), whilst portraying disabled people in a different manner. It is, of course, a matter of interpretation whether Warren's character can be seen as an improvement on its own terms, especially as he was used as a token of exchange between the men who were competing for a romantic relationship with Mary. He seems to be the 'something' about Mary, which means that he is placed at the centre of events whilst simultaneously being shown as having little more than the status of object for other people; the abnormality from which normality makes itself, as Siebers (2010) has theorised about disability in relation to modern art. Nonetheless, it is anti-discriminatory attitudes towards disability which win in the competition for Mary's heart.

Also, Mary's attitude towards Warren was one framed primarily in terms of protection, a feature of cultural representations and social norms which can result in people with learning difficulties being infantalised and robbed of independence. It is also notable that the considerable amount of gross-out incidents which occur in this film all involved the non-disabled characters (apart from one featuring a dog). In addition to Ted's zipper incident, Mary has one of the most memorable gross-out moments of the film, which is often cited as one of the best scenes in gross-out films *per se*.[15] After Ted masturbates before a date with Mary, to cool his ardour, Mary asks him if the semen hanging from his ear is hair gel, and, in his embarrassment he says yes. She proceeds to transfer it from his ear to her hair, to alarming effect. Her hair sticks straight up from her head, to which she is oblivious, as Ted looks on hesitantly in a bemused but admiring manner. Using reverse angle shots and medium close-ups, we are able to occupy both of their subject positions, which simultaneously encourages us to laugh at them both while feeling disgust-sympathy towards them. Again, our previous knowledge that he had ejaculated just before she came to the door, and couldn't find its whereabouts, led us to anticipatory disgust that she would find it first. It is significant that disabled characters do not have gross-out moments, a useful strategy given that this was the first film which began to highlight ableism and disablism (see below), necessitating a focus on the prejudices of non-disabled characters. The disabled character is also absent in many scenes, yet discourses of disability pervade the film throughout. Although this might raise concerns about the visibility of disabled people, it also demonstrates that the counting of disabled characters, or even in-depth qualitative readings of disabled characters' narratives, are only part of the picture; the discourses of ableism and disablism which almost invisibly pervade our stories of ourselves and others, often structuring the ways we live and the choices we make, are equally important to our cultural outlooks on disability.

Perhaps the most exciting development of the film was the ways in which it played with audience attitudes to disability and impairment, by encouraging aggressive forms of humour against disabled people, then calling these into question. This is likely to pose a dilemma of identification for the audience, who are placed in the position of re/considering attitudes to disability and impairment, whilst continuing to be rewarded with the gross-out moments they had presumably come to see. This type of strategy takes a mimetic approach, as suggested on previous pages, in that it deliberately re-presents stereotypical views of disability in order to challenge them. It is Mary, a conventionally attractive woman with no impairment, who controls the mimetic process through her superior role in relation to the other characters, lending her a kind of moral authority as the loving sister of, and apparent advocate for, her brother with a 'learning disability'. Whilst this begs questions about the agency and recognition of people with learning difficulties, and their right to speak for themselves, the film was a progression from previous depictions. As the sister of a disabled character, her choice between five men leads her to prioritise preferences which are reliant, at the very least, on an authentic form of recognition for him – her final decision is between the two men her brother likes the most, perhaps redeeming his status as the object of others' actions.

So, it is Mary, arguably the leading protagonist, who is simultaneously at the centre of everyone's gaze as the primary focus of the 'model reader' of the rom-com audience, and with Ted, for the gross-out audience. Both Mary and Ted, as the romantic leads, are the ones who will call the audience's views into question. Irigary (1985) argues that the only way that negative views can be challenged successfully is when they are exposed and demystified. Speaking about women, she has argued that mimesis presents a conventionally negative depiction of women, without reducing women to that view, and mocks the portrayal on its own terms so that it must be discarded as a fiction. It is believed this will lead to shifts in conceptions of female subjectivity. Similarly, this strategy seems essential to the denaturalisation of disabling imagery, particularly through transitional phases of representational change, arguably one we are currently in, given challenges to the lack of representational diversity in the current era (see previous chapters). In the much later film, *The Lobster*, we see similar processes at work in the characters who are intent on choosing a partner with the same impairment, ultimately casting doubt on why people with particular impairments are deemed as unsuitable partners. Specifically, Mary's actions in *There's Something about Mary* mock common views of learning disability, especially those which are associated with ridicule, bullying, disempowerment, and dependency. They also challenge the ways she is objectified as a woman by three of her potential partners, who fail to see beyond their physical attraction to her.

Unlike the previous two films, their following film *Outside Providence* (directed by Michael Correnti) was only written and produced by the Farrelly Brothers, based on a novel by Peter Farrelly. It involves two disabled characters, one being Jackie (Tommy Bone), brother of the main protagonist Tim Dunphy (played by Shawn Hatosy), and a dog, Clopsy, with one eye and three legs. The themes of disability were more incidental in this film, subsidiary to a coming-of-age, drug-fuelled story, anchored in the gritty realities of living in a family led by a single-parent father (played by Alec Baldwin). However, in subsequent films directed by the Farrelly brothers, the mimetic process becomes stronger, whereby disabled characters address stereotypes through their own 'voices'. Of considerable note was their next film, *Me,*

138 *The gross-out genre*

Myself and Irene, where a number of impairments and disability concerns were represented, including mental health issues and physical impairments.

Me, Myself and Irene

Images of disabled men, in particular, were subjected to novel new questions of masculinity and subjectivity in *Me, Myself and Irene*.[16] Layla (Traylor Howard), the new wife of the central protagonist Charlie (Jim Carrey, also one of the leads in *Dumb and Dumber*), gets pregnant with triplets who, it is assumed, are the biological children of her black lover Shonté (Tony Cox), a man with restricted growth and the limousine driver who they meet when he drives them at their wedding. She takes Shonté's side in an argument on tipping, which occurs when Shonté accuses Charlie of race discrimination, merely for asking him 'Do you people take cheques?'. One assumes Charlie means the limousine service but Shonté interprets the reference to 'you people' as racism. Arguably this scene plays with our expectations of the diminished sexual and economic power of both disabled and Black people, especially as Shonté appears to be in a lower paid job than Charlie, who is a police officer. Yet, race discrimination is assumed by Shonté before he questions Charlie's potential prejudice against his size – a bi-sociative joke which works on several levels. Shonté's assumption that this is a racial slur rather than a disablist one could be considered funny to those who are focusing on the spectacle of his size. This might force the audience to examine their own assumptions about a hierarchy of difference, prejudice, and oppression, where we might expect mocking on the basis of his height. Further it may lead us to ask questions about intersecting privileges and oppressions.

The argument between them begins an arresting juxtaposition of male, disabled narratives, initiating Charlie's first experience of mental distress, positioning us to ask whose side we are on, and why? We have discovered that Charlie is a kind, loving man, and we now know that Shonté identifies himself primarily as a Black man, with MENSA level intelligence (we are told), which begins to cast some doubt on Charlie's masculine capital, as a self-effacing white man with average intelligence. Any diminishment of confidence is likely to have been compounded by Layla apologising for Charlie's behaviour, immediately after Shonté has beaten Charlie up with his baton (also proving his physical prowess). The camera is used in this scene to position the viewer as witness, going from longer shots of the couple going over the threshold of their home to reverse angle close-ups of Charlie's and Shonté's faces as Shonté shouts and beats him, and Charlie attempts to defend himself; the camera moves back out to a medium shot to maximise our sight of the impact of the blows inflicted on Charlie.

Layla elopes with Shonté a year after her wedding, after her sons are born (one named Shonté Jr, but none named after Charlie), but Charlie goes on to bring up his sons. He is shown to be a caring father and is seemingly oblivious to any questions about parenthood, considering all his sons are Black.

He also continues to do his job as a police officer, despite the contempt and abuse shown to him by some members of his local community. Eventually, in the face of all these difficulties, his masculine capital seems to be eroded on all fronts and he is diagnosed with mental health problems. In the wake of all the stresses in his life, Charlie's former character as a 'nice guy' has changed so that we see him veer between his previously gentle self and a new angrier persona, 'Hank'. Despite the obvious dangers of perpetuating new stereotypes of 'split personalities', the engagement with such mental health stereotypes gains extra strength through the comparisons that can be made between these two sides of his character and the emotional attachments which are easily made with each persona, i.e. Charlie as a kind and loving man, and Hank as a wronged one.

In turn, and in contrast with the readings made by psychiatrists such as Byrne (2000), I am arguing that these depictions pose challenges to conventional stereotypes of mental illness (as straightforwardly evil and violent) by firmly anchoring his character in narratives which exposed oppressive cultural factors and prejudices, questioning notions of competence, rather than buying into performances of 'madness' and portraying violent dispositions that come exclusively from within. Perhaps the most radical aspect for this film was the rare depiction of active, successful parenting, something which was rarely featured in cinematic images of disability and impairment, and is still something of a rarity.[17] The absence of 'disabled parenting' (Wilde and Hoskison-Clark, 2013) simultaneously adds to the assumption of asexual or deviant sexualities so often ascribed to disabled people (Shakespeare, 1996). It also compounds ideas of dependency, distracting us from envisaging interdependent relationships, where disabled people can both give and receive love and help (Wilde and Hoskison-Clark, 2013). In *Me, Myself and Irene*, Charlie is also seen as a successful sexual agent in his pursuit of Irene (Renée Zellweger), whilst the value of interdependent family relationships is also apparent in the love Charlie receives back from his sons.

Later films

Like *Outside Providence*, the next film the Farrellys were involved in broke with the dialogue of the incipient critique of disability stereotypes, when they directed the live action parts of *Osmosis Jones* in 2001. This is an animated film featuring Osmosis Jones, a police officer who is actually a white blood cell fighting a deadly virus. The return to the type of strategies which characterised *Me, Myself and Irene*, and *There's Something about Mary* was apparent when they released (directed and co-wrote) *Shallow Hal*. This was a story which was notable for its absence of explicit impairment and disability themes, and a reduced amount of gross-out moments, but memorable for its focus on superficiality, pain, and self-destruction, drawing clear links between self-sabotage and the heteronormative 'male gaze'. As such, it can be read in a similar way to the previous films; as a story which mimics discriminatory attitudes towards disability by putting the onus on the prejudices of Hal (Jack Black) and his expectations of female beauty. The bulk of the comedy reveals how his expectations of female beauty are offensive to others and damaging to himself, not least in obstructing him from recognising the 'inner beauty' of others, preventing him from realising his heart's desire.

Nevertheless, Fat Studies scholar Katharina Mendoza (2009) questions the radical potential of *Shallow Hal*, demonstrating how the fat incarnation of Rosemary, played by Gwyneth Paltrow as both the slim and fat-suited version of herself, is shown less than the slender one imagined by Hal – who has been hypnotised into seeing the beauty within the real, fat, Rosemary. She argues that Paltrow's body achieves the status of the 'real' in the film, as a possible 'revenge fantasy' for members of the audience who want 'the opportunity to laugh at what is usually desired' (Mendoza, 2009, 282). It would also serve as a revenge fantasy against expectations of the heteronormative male gaze (with or without desire).

It is clear that much of the comedy does rely on 'cheap fat jokes', and it is possible that the

> recuperation of the fat character [in these films] hinges on the presence of their thin personas – on the literal, diegetic, narrative that inside all that fat there is inside a thin person just waiting to get out.
>
> (ibid., 281)

But the film is also open to multiple readings, offering a dominant reading which is critical of the 'shallowness' of Hal, and of the reduction of beauty to fashionable forms of low body weight and slender shape, whilst also providing narrative closure which is entirely dependent on Hal's change in attitude; importantly Rosemary is still fat so there is no slim happy ever after, just the suggestion of one based on a woman who is categorised as fat alongside a man who is far less than the 'ideal man' (on the same basis of impossible body ideals and romantic character).

Since then, the Farrellys have made seven more films which have continued this pattern of releasing 'disability films' in between romantic comedies, before they eventually returned to the more slapstick-orientated comedies of *The Three Stooges* in 2012, and *Dumb and Dumber To* in 2014.

Stuck on You

Their next, and most explicitly political film, was *Stuck on You*, in 2003, a film which deals directly, and firmly, with the discrimination faced by its lead protagonists, Bob (Matt Damon) and Walt (Greg Kinnear) Tenor, twins who are conjoined at the waist and share a liver. This is one of the few times that the casting of non-disabled actors in disabled roles can be seen in a positive light. With a probable number of twelve conjoined twins in the world, of any age, at the time (Wallis, 2013), it would be a difficult task to find actors who were conjoined, especially ones who might want to take part in a gross-out comedy; the majority of those who might be appropriate in terms of age are also women (although this film could just as easily have been made about women).[18]

In some ways the film is an exemplar of how to deal with issues of disabled sexuality. Questions about the sex life of conjoined twins have been an object of fascination for many years (Dreger, 2012). Despite the knowledge that Chang and Eng Bunker, brothers from Thailand who became known as the 'Siamese twins', had active sex lives with their wives, having had twenty-two children between both families, their sex lives have been treated as a source of moral concern and 'discomfort' (Dreger, 2012). Although they were living in the mid-nineteenth century, their lives were still deemed worthy of a news story in 2014 (Leonard, 2014). This sensationalised tabloid newspaper coverage invited the readers into their story through a direct appeal to gross-out, most obviously seen in the headline's emphasis on the need for a reinforced bed, suggesting a voyeuristic interest in their shared activities, particularly on the intricacies of how they had sex as a 'foursome'. This was also reflected in a large amount of reader comments which imagined sexual scenarios. Dreger (2012) has also shown this enthrallment with the sex lives of conjoined twins to be evident elsewhere. Her examination of contemporary television audiences' curiosity with the sexual and romantic plans of Abigail and Brittany Hensel, who share a single body, is one example of this. Similarly, I have found a great interest in the sexual lives of Violet and Daisy Hilton amongst young audiences who had watched the film *Freaks* (1932), expressing great surprise that one of them was shown to have a boyfriend.

As a film which is all about conjoined twins, *Stuck on You* has great capacities for addressing the objectification of disabled people in general. In particular, these attitudes towards sex and non-normative bodily functions epitomise the ways in which the ableist/disablist gaze renders the body as abject, and often non-sexual/asexual, although it is also a 'damaging myth' to associate sexuality with 'normality', or asexuality with abnormality, as Kim (2011) has argued. *Stuck on You* confronts the audience directly with assumptions about disabled people's sexuality, playing with its status as taboo, or as an unwanted topic (see Sancho, 2003, and Shakespeare et al., 1996, for more on this subject). However, this was not the first time that conjoined twins were used in comedy, or romance. When Daisy and Violet Hilton's characters (who have their real names) negotiated their romantic liaisons with respective partners in *Freaks*, we hear a Violet's boyfriend complaining that she always uses her sister 'as an excuse, for an alibi' (suggesting she is attracted to Daisy's boyfriend).[19] But *Stuck on You* takes this fascination with intimate relationships much further, most obviously in scenes which portray one of them having sex.

Further, the features of the gross-out comedy, and the much more accessible style of the Farrelly Brothers' film-making, facilitate direct engagement with ideas of the abject. In many ways *Stuck on You* epitomises the cinematic deconstruction of the idea of disability and abjection. Van Alphen outlines the theoretical positions of Kristeva (1982b) to show that,

> abjection can be traced back to the first rejection, that is, to the separation from the mother helping her baby to establish him/herself in the symbolic order.
>
> (2016, 120)

He goes on to say that:

> Abjection preserves some of that pre-objectal relationship and some of the ambivalence that is experienced by the subject when it becomes an independent body separated from the mother.
>
> (ibid., 121)

In the case of Bob and Walt, and other conjoined twins, the ambivalence which may occur for most individuals is likely to be complicated when separation from the parent is achieved, but complete separation from another human being is not. As Savulescu and Persson have argued, the philosophical and psychological study of conjoined twins 'raise philosophical questions about our nature and identity' (2016, 43). At best then, perhaps we can see the fascination shown towards conjoined twins to be linked to questions about our own identities and 'independent' existence, including the connections and separations of our own bodies and minds, selves and mothers, and self from others. Putting two characters who have such an unusual relationship to primary processes of physical and emotional separation – taken for granted as the norm, invariably rendering conjoined twins unambiguously different, in philosophical, psychological and emotional terms – is a risky strategy as a platform on which to portray disability, particularly in the gross-out genre which concerns itself primarily with the abject. However, on these terms, conjoined twins can be seen as one of the clearest examples for illustrating wider cultural mechanisms of disablement, and their foundations in ideas of abnormality and practices of abjection. Van Alphen's explanation of the cultural deployment of abjection is valuable here:

> Abjection, no longer referring to an ambiguous object but to a process or activity, refers to cultural mechanisms that exclude certain groups of people or individuals by stigmatising them with loathing. Xenophobia is usually fuelled by abjection. But not only foreigners, also other marginalised groups within a society are often considered to be ugly, dirty or frightening, which evoke aversive responses in the rest of that society. Homophobia, racism, sexism and ageism are also structured by the mechanism of abjection. Subjects react to the abject with repulsion and loathing in order to restore the border separating self and other. The other is 'abjected' from the self, because the abject is seen as not

respecting borders, rules and positions of a society. These abject others are not only abjected by means of exclusionary mechanisms but they are simultaneously needed and produced by societies. This is so because subjects are formed by the exclusion of what they are not.

(2016, 120–121)

These understandings of abjection are key to the Farrelly Brother's presentation of disablement in the film, confronting cultural fascinations with sexuality, separation, and independence throughout. This is underwritten by characterisations of their personalities which show them to be very different people; Walt as outgoing, confident, and sexually attractive to more women, Bob being almost the opposite, shy, athletic, and less ambitious. Again, these differences generate much of the comedy as they are often in conflict and in competition to meet their own needs at the expense of the other. The use of gross-out often plays with common fascinations, including sexual liaisons, and the management of different skills and career choices. There are also amusing choreographed scenes featuring inventive solutions to work tasks, which draw our attention to the barriers of disabling work practices based on expectations of single bodies. We also see and hear Bob's pain as a bus door closes with him hanging on the outside and Walt on the inside, again showing an environment which is premised on the mobility of individual bodies – perhaps not deemed quite as funny or 'gross' if this was to happen to a wheelchair user, given the hierarchy of impairments in the public imaginary (see Wilde, 2018a). We also witness the everyday brutality inflicted by people who regard them as nothing more than spectacle, shouting comments such as 'Freaks!' and 'Hey, you're stuck together!'. We also see that they manage such 'micro-aggressions' in very different ways, neither of which lead the viewer into individualising this as a problem of disabled people's attitudes.[20] Throughout there are unflinching confrontations with their experiences of joint embodiment, often filmed in medium-shots so we can see the awkwardness of situations they have to navigate, focussing on the use of their bodies, whilst we are also close enough to see their emotional responses to their situation.

As LeBesco has demonstrated, the emphasis placed on impairment and disability extends beyond the protagonists in *Stuck on You*, with disabled actors much more visible in this film (some appeared in earlier films, such as *There's Something about Mary*, but were less in both number and visibility). These actors included people with learning difficulties and add to the increasingly political content. LeBesco explained:

> Here, developmentally disabled actor Ray 'Rocket' Valliere plays a waiter in the restaurant owned by Walt and Bob, and when a rude customer admonishes Rocket for spilling a soda and complains to Walt and Bob about hiring 'Jerry's Kids,' Walt and Bob display their own freak status and kick out the rude, normate customer.
>
> (2004, para 5)

As such we can see a switch here to disabled people being the arbiters of moral judgements, a considerable shift from the ableist-centric positioning of the earlier films. Although I find myself in some disagreement, as I have discussed in previous sections, LeBesco said that the films up to *Me, Myself, and Irene* had tended to 'use "normals" treatment of disabled people as the barometers by which they can be morally evaluated' (2004, para 9). Although we see Bob and Walt electing for separation in order to live their lives in ways more appropriate to their needs, we are left in no doubt about their evaluations of normality, when they return to run the restaurant they worked in together, Velcro-ing themselves together, whilst living their independent lives. Right to the end, the exposition of disabled bodies was central to the telling of disabled character's lives, and our engagement with them.

Writers such as Thomson (1997; 1999) and Quayson (2007), have shown that tropes of vulnerability, wounded-ness, monstrousness, and ideas of the abject are ubiquitous in the misrecognition of disabled people, as other to the norm, to the 'we-world' which is watching and judging their difference as extraordinary. *Stuck on You* has enabled the Farrelly Brothers to examine these tropes and to re-present the fascination with the disabled body in ways that afford more opportunities for their deconstruction than other forms of comedy or drama might; thus, viewers are more likely to see disabled people as more like themselves, enabling the recognition of the adversity wrought from disablement. In a similar way, Lars von Trier confronts the curiosity about sex with disabled bodies in *The Idiots,* and locates them in wider issues about how we consider 'the real' (again with non-disabled actors 'performing' disability). If we do not consider genre it is also easy to read this as disablist, as non-disabled people humiliating disabled people, but this is a satire of cultural attitudes to disabled people; Walters, for example, has insisted that this film needs to be read as 'only really comprehensible when viewed in light of its counter-hegemonic aspirations' (2004, 40). It offers a critique of normalcy, ableism, and disablism, most obviously in the ways in which it explores 'those behaviors that are made to seem mandatory by a society whose aim is to maintain the structures that ensure conservative sameness' (ibid., 41).

Similarly, if we read *Stuck on You* as a deconstruction and critique of disablist attitudes it can be seen to 'recover the sacred' (Arya, 2014) of abject bodies, allowing us to question divisions of abnormality and normality, not least because it is unlikely that we can watch Bob and Walt (as likeable personalities) without identifying with them in some way, from sexual failures to barriers in employment. Whereas the abject dimensions of *Stuck on You* may be seen as threatening to many viewers as a double dose of 'a constant threat to the unity and hence identity of the subject' (Arya, 2014, 113), this cannot be said of the niche audience who seek out gross-out films. Indeed, the correspondence between topic and genre seems a perfect fit for this audience, given their attitudes towards disabled people.[21] If gross-out films are regarded as 'abject art', this drive to the 'body being undone and taken apart [...] conveyed by flesh, in particular viscera, bodily fluids and wounds', the representations of Bob and Walt can be seen as a valuable way to evoke 'feelings of vulnerability' which 'remind us of our animal nature' (Arya, 2014, 85). Addressing such feelings of vulnerability may well be fundamental to changing cultural representations and understandings of disability, which appear to lie at the core of perceived risks of offending the non-disabled 'model reader' of most media (e.g. see Shakespeare, 1994). It may also be the reason why the Farrelly Brothers' films were declining in popularity at this point (see footnote 12 .

Returning to rom-coms and sports films, the Farrellys directed two more films, *Fever Pitch* and *The Heartbreak Kid* (which they also wrote), but they also produced another disability film, *The Ringer,* which was significant in its contribution to representations of disability on film; it employed over 150 people with 'intellectual disabilities', in 'small parts and supporting roles' (spinalcordinjuryzone.com, 2005). Peter Farrelly said:

> My whole point in making this movie is to make people with mental disabilities accessible, make people know who they are and feel comfortable with them.
>
> (cited in Bauer, 2005, para 6)

This, suggests an ongoing commitment to breaking down audience resistances to new, more challenging portrayals of disability, on the basis of finding 'just like us' identifications for the non-disabled model reader, as he indicates in the following statement:

> If you don't know someone who's mentally challenged, and you meet them, you're afraid of them because you don't know what to expect... It's not bad. It's just normal. But if you do know them, you're very comfortable.
>
> (ibid., para 7)

It is notable that 20th Century Fox's decision to fund the film depended upon the agreement and involvement of the Special Olympics organisation, an organisation run *for,* rather than *by,* people with intellectual disabilities, perpetuating a range of attitudes and practices which have been seen as detrimental to the rights of those with intellectual disabilities (see Storey, 2005, for example), even if debates about the rights and wrongs of a segregated Olympics are disregarded. Thus, it is unsurprising that the Special Olympics representative imposed changes such as the removal of a scene in a strip club, and use of language such as 'retard', given the tendency to protect people with learning difficulties as if they were small children. Indeed, the protection of people with learning difficulties from sexual activities and other influences, on the basis of 'vulnerability', has become increasingly recognised as a significant form of oppression, especially in the face of restrictions to independent living and considerable barriers to social inclusion (see Hollomotz and The Speakup Committee, 2008, for example). Such scenes and use of language were common occurrences in earlier films, adding to their gross-out traits. Although the film was eventually made, the condition of funding, and the consequent safeguarding of content, resulted in a film which was more conservative in its use of gross-out than would have been the case in conditions of fuller creative freedom.

Dumb and Dumber To

Dumb and Dumber To was a long-anticipated sequel to *Dumb and Dumber* (after the prequel *Dumb and Dumberer* (2003), made with neither the original cast nor any input from the Farrellys), but it was largely received in terms of disappointment by critics and also 'diehard fans' of the original (IMDB.com 2018d). Whilst some observed that it followed a similar format which was true to the personalities of Harry and Lloyd in the first film, most described poor audience experiences, with few laughs and content which was largely filled with 'flat jokes' (ibid.). A number of people who claimed themselves to be big fans of the first film commented that Harry and Lloyd were 'meaner' in this film and several said it was both painful and disappointing to watch. It could be argued that the formula used in *Dumb and Dumber To* was no longer radical twenty years after the first film, a period which saw great changes in anti-discrimination legislation, although some said they expected more than a repetition of the old jokes. Describing it as the 'worst movie of all time', rrmin347 (reviewer 10, for this film on IMDb, in the reviews put in order of 'helpfulness') seemed to speak for the majority when they said:

> I wanted this to be a good movie so badly, because I am such a big fan of the original… But it is NOT a good movie at all. It's terrible.
> This was the worst sequel of all time… All it did was try to rehash moments from the original movie, and it failed miserably.
> (rrmin347, 2014, para 1)

Fans of the Farrelly brothers would also have come to expect gross-out moments and the valorisation of people with learning difficulties (if we are still assuming that the characters have them). However, although the gross-out moments and kind-heartedness were as evident in *Dumb and Dumber To* as they had been in the previous two, their pranks and mean-ness played a bigger part, meaning narrative inequalities were greater.

One example of the disparities in characterisations, and the increased tendency to 'punch down' happens when they break into a nursing home to steal some hearing aids, and the old woman they intend to rob tells Lloyd that she has 'diamonds under her blanket', whereupon he was directed to put his hand in her 'grandgina'. Like *Kingpin*, this results in her gratitude, whereupon she parts with her hearing aids for free. Unlike *Kingpin*, the joke is firmly fixed on the grossness of her repulsive sexual identity as an old woman, a message of contempt which is heavily driven home with the image of a disgusted-looking Lloyd blowing dust from his fingers.

Comedy such as this has understandably been interpreted as misogynistic (McNab, 2014). Such criticisms demonstrate the importance of both narrative equality within films, and the need for comedy to innovate and critique rather than to rely on previously successful formulae.[22] Further, such scenes as the one just outlined would suggest that narrative equalities have *decreased* in the work of the Farrelly Brothers in the making of this film, with old stereotypes being re-iterated, often as the core of the joke.

When LeBesco was writing of the Farrelly Brothers' work in 2004, she said that her analysis

> charts the discrepancies in political motive between their early films, in which disability functioned as little more than a punch line, and their most recent, in which disabled people are the heroic embodiment of all things good.
>
> (2004, para 2)

This seems to have been true of all their 'disability films' right up to *The Ringer* in 2005. From this point they released two rom-coms, *The Heartbreak Kid* and *Hall Pass*, then *The Three Stooges* (perhaps one of the main influences for *Dumb and Dumber*, alongside Harold Lloyd). *Dumb and Dumber To* is a return to the former positioning of disabled characters, even beyond it, to a position which punches down. Downey, who describes herself as a 'die-hard fan' of the original, compared the two (without reference to disability politics), arguing that *Dumb and Dumber To* is contrived, with 'big set-up gags' which emulate the scenarios of the first but fall flat. Despite using similar elements as the first film, she demonstrates the shift in perspective through the examples of the depictions of the older female characters, from the previous depiction of an old woman who Lloyd admires because she has taught him her worth, regardless of her age, to the cruel, derogatory use of the old lady's 'grangina' joke of *Dumb and Dumber To*. This lack of parity between the way gross-out comedy is used with ostensibly similar characters, is one example of why she perceives that they have become 'obnoxious bullies' in the latter film.

Although the box office returns show substantial profits for *Dumb and Dumber To*, which might suggest a preference for this less political type of gross-out, it is equally likely, given user reviews, that many people went to see it as fans of *Dumb and Dumber*.[23] Nonetheless, the evolution of the Farrelly Brothers' films, the vast differences in profits between films, their appeal to a distinct target group with marked dispositions for discriminatory attitudes, and their return to a less political formula, alerts us to some of the biggest challenges to the cultural representation of disabled people, not least the profit motives of the film industry, spurious perceptions of risk, and the drive for maximising profits.

The Farrelly Brothers: to be continued…?

The films written and directed by the Farrelly Brothers have provided a rare opportunity to examine what happens when film-makers discard the usual trope of disability and attempt to re-present disabled people as central to their own lives. In a number of ways, they can be seen to have presented ideas which challenge stereotypes and ideas of difference without encouraging new stereotypes. Aimed at an unlikely and potentially resistant audience, it is possible that this has contributed to the forging of a cultural recognition based on a '*non-identitarian* politics that can remedy misrecognition without encouraging displacement and reification' (Fraser, 2000,120, *author's emphasis*), a challenge I will return to in the conclusion.

For film-makers who have done so much to improve representations of disability, and have been fêted for so doing, one of Downey's (2014) most scathing comments about *Dumb and Dumber To* needs to be borne in mind:

> The sequel feels like the Farrelly brothers sat in a room and analyzed the original 'Dumb and Dumber' to reduce it to a series of elements, then tried incorporating as many of them as possible to guarantee success.
>
> (2014, para 27)

Can, and should, we do this for all disability films, to guarantee box office profits, successful comedy, cinematic enjoyment, or more 'politically correct' outcomes? These are some of the concerns I will now address in the concluding chapter.

Notes

1 The word disgust is being used here in a theoretical sense to mean 'the offence taken to noxious objects or ideas that evoke a nausea response' (Nabi, 2002, 695) rather than a lay/colloquial understanding of usage of the word to denote such emotions as anger.
2 See: http://www.silentera.com/PSFL/data/N/NellsEugenicWedding1914.html.
3 (Radio Times, 2016); he has also been accused of a misogynistic variant of gross-out dialogue, e.g Landreth (2014, 6).
4 Derek, marketed by Channel Four as a comedy about a 'tender, innocent man' (Deans, 2012). We are encouraged by the authors to read the portrayal as a benign, even empathetic and loving, portrait of its central character, Derek, a nursing home care assistant (Dean, 2014). Which might be seen to immunise Gervais from guilt and attack, as there were also allegations of his 'baiting of the disabled' and criticisms of the gross-out portrayal of old women as 'physically repellent' (Landreth, 2014, para 4), inviting the audience to laugh at the misogyny/ageism rather than the ignorance behind the attitudes.
5 Other characters with ambiguous impairments include Little Britain's Andy Pipkin, a wheelchair using character who often leaves it to walk around when his friend/'carer' is absent.
6 The Farrelly's first feature film was *Dumb and Dumber* in 1994, whereas Gervais first delivered 'politically incorrect' material on Channel Four's *11 O'clock Show* between 1998 and 2000, and *Little Britain* was first broadcast on the radio in 2000, and on BBC Three (TV) in 2003.
7 A notable exception is Richardson (2016) who covers both of these areas in his book about transgressive bodies. This chapter draws on some of that work, having different interpretations of particular representations, but has different emphases bringing the two together more closely to examine the constructions of disability.

The gross-out genre 149

8   See, for example, reviewer comments on IMDB for *There's Something About Mary*, and Mills (2010) and Akass (2010) on *Little Britain*.
9   This is true in the UK and the USA, in the Disability Discrimination Act 1995, and the Americans with the Disabilities Act (1990).
10 This included sensationalist stickers posted on public toilet doors in the UK (in bars), and trailers for the film which emphasise flirtations and sex with (often) bikini-clad women, alongside other hegemonically masculine pursuits such as sport. See for example, https://www.youtube.com/watch?v=At-LrR-vqUk (accessed 30 January 2018).
11 Depending on preferred terminology, which differs widely.
12 There are some sources which have claimed that Ben Stiller has bipolar disorder, and that his parents had mental health concerns, e.g. https://www.elementsbehavioralhealth.com/mental-health/celebrities-bipolar-disorder/ (accessed 3 February 2018).
13 Figures on IMDB show a Box Office figure of $65,784,503, against an (estimated budget of $55,000,000 [date assessed unknown] – see http://www.imdb.com/title/tt0338466/ [accessed 9 February 2018]. This is a big reduction from the previous films they both wrote and directed. *Shallow Hal* had an estimated budget of $40,000,000 and worldwide Box Office of $141,069,860 on 21 September 2012, http://www.imdb.com/title/tt0256380/). Before that, *Me, Myself and Irene* made $149,270,999 from an estimated budget of $51,000,000. In-between these films there were also other films which they had been involved in, which fared poorly e.g. *Say It Isn'tSso* (they were producers), and *Osmosis Jones* (directing only the live action scenes) and both films lost money (see http://www.imdb.com/title/tt0181739/, and http://www.imdb.com/title/tt0239949 all accessed 9 February, 2018). *Kingpin* made a slight loss; see http://www.imdb.com/title/tt0239949/, though it has been assessed as underrated by some since – see Film Comment (2000).
14 Like the other viewer responders, the identity of this commentator – as disabled or non-disabled – is unclear as nothing is said.
15 For example, it is listed as number 2 on 'Top ten hilarious gross out movie scenes', at https://www.youtube.com/watch?v=OYxlE4ox3n0 (accessed 9 February 2018).
16 Most of the disabled characters in all their films are men, even if masculinity is not a particular focus.
17 This has been taken on by broadcast industries over recent years with several characters in British soap operas being involved in parenting storylines, e.g. the character of Izzy Armstrong in *Coronation Street,* who uses a surrogate to have her own child, Jake. Indeed, there seem to have been more films which have disabled parents in them after this film, including *Snowcake*, featuring an autistic mother who loses her child (see Wilde, 2009b), and more recently *Baby Driver* had a Deaf father for the protagonist (see Wilde, 2017a). Before this period there seemed to be an emphasis in parental stories placed on the 'problems' of hearing children of Deaf parents, and on the issues that children with learning disabilities/difficulties might face after their parents experience a decline in health, or die. As such, all reflect an individualist bias towards disabled families, with the major plots framing issues in terms of family and individual resources rather than social support and forms of disablement. Films before *Me, Myself and Irene*, would include *Best Boy* (1979, about a boy with learning disabilities), *Beyond Silence* in 1996, with a theme of a musical daughter of Deaf parents, re-iterated in a more recent film (2014), *La Famille Bellier,* with the biggest change being a gift for singing rather than the clarinet talents of the first.
18 About 70 per cent of conjoined twins are women according to edition.com (2017).
19 *Freaks* was not made as a comedy, but there are comedic moments in it, such as these.
20 Walt tends to use such attention as an opportunity for social interaction which Bob tends to ignore – see the trailer for example (YouTube, 2013b).

150 *The gross-out genre*

21 As discussed earlier, this cannot be presumed to be true for all audience members.
22 Even though this would clearly not be possible in films with large casts, with most films needing central protagonists to drive the story, this could be possible across more limited supporting characters, such as this one, avoiding a crudely simplistic, one-dimensional representation such as this.
23 From a budget of $25,000,000 it made $169,837,010 by 5 March 2015: http://www.imdb.com/title/tt2096672/ (accessed 10 February 2018).

7 Conclusion, or when is an ending not an ending?

As Nikulin says about comedy, and of his own book on comedy and philosophy, the conclusion should work towards 'the realization of a good ending' (2014, 135) but it is 'never final'. In similar terms, my aim is to bring the themes I have discussed together to make contributions to ongoing discussions of disability, film, and comedy in ways which contribute to debates on, and ideas for, representational change. In so doing, I will raise more questions than I find answers. I believe such agendas to be 'unfinalisable', especially if we want to promote dialogue and inclusion. This means that I will suggest areas for attention but these will remain open-ended.

Further, I have suggested that the tendency to monologism has created many of the problems of disability representation. Here I am using Gardiner's definition of monologism as a

> [s]ituation wherein the matrix of values, signifying practices, and creative impulses that constitute the living reality of language and socio-cultural life are sub-ordinated to the dictates of a single, unified consciousness or perspective.
>
> (Gardiner, 1998, 65)

Monologism takes a number of forms, and I have already suggested a number of contributing factors to the prevalence of monologism within the comedy films I have discussed. Chapter Three, for example, outlined the lack of diversity in casting, looking solely at the romantic comedy genre, showing that white, non-disabled, and younger people, with a narrow range of body types, are placed at the centre of most of the action, usually telling of heterosexual love between white non-disabled people who have cisgender identities. Indeed, complaints about diversity in portrayals of disability and people with impairments, across all of cinema, have often centred on the issues of what might be called, for want of better term, disability drag (see Woodburn and Ruderman, 2016, for example), where non-disabled people play disabled characters (often with the hope of Oscars, BAFTAs, or other awards). Occasionally, films are criticised on these terms alone, such as *Breathe*, with Andrew Garfield playing a disabled campaigner, Robin Cavendish (see

Donaldson, 2017 for an example of such criticisms). Indeed, complaints about using non-disabled actors are quite common for the biopic genre, including criticisms of the casting of Daniel Day Lewis as Christy Brown in *My Left Foot*, and Eddie Redmayne as Stephen Hawking in *The Theory of Everything* (e.g. Harris, 2014; Ryan, 2015, respectively).

Such criticisms are often linked to content; Novic has criticised Guillermo del Toro's *The Shape of Water* both for its content and its use of a 'non-disabled' actor, Sally Hawkins, despite her having dyslexia and lupus (2017). Here, he has woven issues of casting and content together to criticise her poor use of sign language, as indicative of the problems of casting those who don't identify as disabled people. I do not agree with this analysis, especially as the character is identified as 'mute', which could easily suggest a character's poor or non-use of sign language as a preference for limited communication. Additionally, questions are raised about disabled identities in this case, and potentially others, where those who do not 'identify as disabled' are cast in roles as characters with impairment. This is especially so when there is no match between the character and the actor's impairments. Just because Sally Hawkins does not identify as disabled does not mean she should be considered as a non-disabled person, a position taken by both Wanshel and Spiegel in their criticisms of her casting (Wanshel, 2018; Spiegel, 2018). This would fly in the face of most variants of the social model, as her lack of identification would do nothing to diminish the social, cultural, and communicative barriers which she would encounter, including resistance from the industry, and any fears of discrimination. Indeed, as someone who is playing a non-verbal character, Hawkin's dyslexia would fall into the category of communication impairments.

Certainly, the under-employment of disabled actors is an important concern, but it cannot be linked so simply with representational issues, as the example above suggests. Given 97.6 per cent of roles are for characters who are *not* designated as disabled characters (Smith et al. 2016, 2), a call for impairment matching provides counter arguments for those in power against employing disabled actors in one of the vast majority of roles that are presumed to be non-disabled; currently, there is no particular need to avoid casting disabled or Black actors in generic roles even though white non-disabled people dominate in these roles. The number of disabled actors who are employed is difficult to ascertain, with figures only available for the disabled people in the whole sector. There is even mixed evidence on this at the time of writing; estimates would not exceed 5 per cent of the workforce, given the data in the British Film Institute's audit of screen industry workers (Carey et al. 2017, i), but Randle and Hardy (2017) provided a much smaller estimate of between 0.8 and 2 per cent, and Creative Skillset's research found that only 0.3 per cent identified as disabled (Creative Skillset, 2012, 33). These latter figures are likely to be more accurate given the methodologies used, e.g. sampling of specific groups of workers rather than across the screen industries. These low figures also reflect Raynor and Hayward's study of the type of work disabled actors tend to do, showing they received less work in film (28 per cent of their acting jobs) than they gained in television (32 per cent) (2005, 3). Bhavnani (2007, 46) has reported that there were 3 per cent of disabled people working in the film industry, a higher figure which was explained mainly by people reporting they had a learning 'disability' (2007, 48). Although Smith et al.'s report (2016) on 800 popular films found only 2.4 per cent of those who were identified as disabled characters in speaking roles or identified by name, this report does not provide data on disabled actors in roles which are not coded as 'disabled'.[1]

There is another significant concern in these debates about disabled actors; there is a clear reluctance, for most people with impairments, to claim any disabled identities they may have (see Randle et al., 2007), due to realistic fear of discrimination (ibid., see pages 20, 54, and 116). The under-reporting of impairments, or of the claiming of disabled identities, tends to exacerbate the tendency of reducing the category of disabled actors to those with more obvious impairments. It is unlikely that many disabled actors with less obvious impairments will identify as a disabled person, particularly as this is likely to perpetuate discrimination, and heighten fears of it. There is also evidence that disabled actors do not develop 'sequential careers', suggesting an industry perception that disabled actors are always at 'entry level', minimising chances for disabled people to become film stars (Randle and Hardy, 2017, 454). Conversely, actors such as Sally Hawkins risk opprobrium for playing disabled characters when they have not 'come out' as disabled, adding to the potential burden of discrimination inherent to such an ableist industry.

Such is the Gordian knot of disability in the world of film, with representational and employment concerns deeply interwoven in the fabric of the film industry's ideologies, practices, and processes. At a time when representational and inclusion concerns are on potential agendas for change, there are dangers that we may thwart our own goals by a masquerade of disability. As Siebers has argued:

> Many representations of people with disabilities [...] use narrative structures that masquerade disability for the benefit of the able-bodied public.
> (2004, 13)

As a diverse group of people who are all affected by ableist hegemony, in its many forms, there is a need to think critically about the politics of disability performance that do not rely on ableist expectations.

So, as important as it is to have more disabled actors in cinema and broadcast media, as an appallingly under-represented group of actors (notwithstanding the caveats discussed), the presence of non-disabled actors does *not* map neatly onto monologism in signifying practices; it is common to find disabled actors cast in roles which stigmatise disabled people further, as was seen in the discussion of depictions of people with restricted growth in Chapter Three. Whilst the statistic of 2.4 per cent disabled *characters* (rather than actors) found by Smith et al. (2016) may also be indicative of the presence of disabled people in the film industry, caution should be exercised in the interpretation of how disability is being defined, particularly as their methods of coding disability could be regarded as subjective estimations of impairment severity and extent of disablement (see footnote 1). Indeed, it is likely that many impairments may be neglected in the schemes of measurement for diversity. This is especially so when impairment storylines are subtle, or not an obvious feature of the plot; *The Lobster* would probably not be coded for disability despite its thorough-going satire of ableist norms.

Another instance of impairment subtlety can be found in the film *Baby Driver*. As I have suggested elsewhere, the central character of Baby (Ansel Elghort) may be interpreted as autistic, signified by his habit of wearing headphones all the time. Several writers discussed the film in relation to the depiction of tinnitus (e.g. Phillips 2017) and we are also made aware that he had an early childhood trauma – it is suggested that these connect him with his late mother, a former singer. However, I have argued that any assumptions about Baby's lack of speech, or a failure to listen to people, that we may assume early in the story are demonstrated to be 'profoundly wrong' by the end of the film. Furthermore, the ways in which the film plays with audience assumptions about impairment challenges 'common, and potentially ableist, assumptions about communication and social life', though in a subtle manner, adding to characterisations and musical and 'visual thrills' which make this film so enjoyable (Wilde, 2017a, para 7).

It is likely that the audience would presume the disability content of the story relates primarily to the character of Joseph, Baby's foster father, who uses a wheelchair and communicates using sign language. Although the actor CJ Jones is Deaf, one could question the use of a wheelchair as part of his characterisation if we were to use principles of impairment matching. Conversely, he was creatively cast as the Black parent of Baby (a white young man) with no specific reason to do so. Hence, we have a disabled character (Baby) who is played by a (presumably) non-disabled actor, and a Black actor (CJ Jones) cast when the narrative does not demand it, performing one impairment he does have and another which he doesn't. In a non-discriminatory culture this is perhaps an ideal; depictions of disablement as part of the narrative and the inclusion of impairment traits which have little or nothing to do with the story, alongside a cast which is 'racially' diverse, with white and Black characters capable of good and evil (see Wilde, 2017a).

In sharp contrast, another action-genre film featuring disability was released in 2017, *Kills on Wheels*, which received far more attention for being a 'disability film', a film which employed two disabled people in central roles; Zoltán Fenyvesi as Zoli and Ádám Fekete as Barba – though they were not professional actors. This was also about a hitman, the third and central character Rupaszov, a wheelchair-using character but played by a (presumably) non-disabled actor, Szabolcs Thuróczy. Described as a 'plucky' film in Leslie Felperin's (2017) review, this was a rather laboured in its attempts to challenge conventional tropes of disability within its imagining of what life as a disabled hit-man would look like (Wilde, 2017b). This was a frame story, where the action drama of the film was an extension of Zoli and Barba's 'real' story, invented by Zoli in his efforts to make a decision about whether he should have a major operation to improve his life (and impairment). This centring of impairment and the character's decision-making about 'cure' perhaps serves to perpetuate individualistic interpretations of disability as deficit. This is particularly significant when we consider that the framing shows their own lives as far less fascinating than their roles helping the fictional hit man, especially when we factor in any knowledge that we have that they are both disabled and the central 'action hero' actor is not.

The placing of the two disabled actors in comedic scenarios, such as a catheter emptying in the street, was possibly used to demonstrate that disabled people can laugh at themselves, reflecting the writer/director's desire to change people's attitudes towards disabled people. Moreover, this and other comedy moments in the film can be interpreted as anticipating non-disabled viewer's prejudices, much like the selfwork Stronach and Allan (1999) theorised. These characters seem to have been written *with* the non-disabled viewers' experiences and projected dispositions towards disabled people in mind. One example is when they exhibit a self-deprecating response to being invited to dance at a party; they slowly rise from the sofa, saying 'sure, we are (Barba)…but it may take a while' (Rupaszov). Here it is the non-disabled actor who delivers the self-deprecating punchline as is often the case in the film. Further, as a disabled member of the audience I often felt that the film was 'smashing you over the head with a message' (Gavin, 2001, 85), ticking off 'issues' such as disabled men are sexual beings, disabled men can make jokes about themselves, and disabled men can be active and villainous, doing things you wouldn't expect. So, the film seemed to be something of a treatise on disabled masculinity, even repeating the conventional Oedipal scenario in Zoli's pride-based decision on whether or not to take money from his father for his operation (see Wilde, 2004c, for deeper discussion of this common trope). Indeed, the primary function of the women in the film (as marginal characters) was to 'to be there to fix the difficulties experienced by the male characters, and to act as a signifier for their sexual "normality"' (Wilde, 2017b, para 11). At the same time as 'raising issues', the catheter-emptying scene, for example, was rather gratuitous and was played for laughs without any links being made to the lack of disabled toilets – situations which many disabled people are likely to face. The misjudging of such comedy resembles arguments made in earlier chapters about the speculation of non-disabled writers and directors who set out to represent disability and change people's attitudes – this missionary impulse is evident here in Atilla Till's writing and direction of the film, said to be 'inspired by his volunteer work with the disabled (sic)' (Simon, 2016).

Previous chapters have demonstrated that the perspectives of writers and directors are a crucial dimension of the monologism found in most disability films, but this is an area which has received little, if any, critical attention in film studies, disability studies, or auteur theory. Like other disability films which attempt to raise issues, *Kills on Wheels* has clear 'hybrid functions' as both 'pedagogical text and commercial commodity', much like those operating in AIDS television texts (Gavin, 2001, 85). In this case, the viewer who chooses to watch films featuring disabled people often expects them to be 'about disability', or more accurately to be 'about having an impairment'.[2] Gavin argues that 'shared assumptions about genre, in this case relating to the issue, discursively constrain the available interpretive options' (ibid., 85) and are likely to result in failures of engagement with the disability 'issues' coded as such in the text. He suggested that, in such cases, 'the received message may therefore be far more simplistic and contextually thinner than otherwise intended' (ibid., 93).

Carpenter's (2011) theorising on disability-as-genre is valuable here. Just as Deleyto reminded us to conceptualise genre as an 'open shelf' (2009, 16), Carpenter also asks us to think of both disability and genre as 'dynamic sites of action' (Carpenter, 2011, para 5). Further, drawing on the work of Carter (2007), Carpenter encourages us to think of disability as 'metagenre'. Carter argues:

> Representing a 'higher category,' metagenre is 'a genre of genres,' an expansive notion that points to 'similar *kinds* of typified responses to related recurrent situations.'
>
> (2007, 393; emphasis in original)

Thus, he argues that disability is one such metagenre which circulates in and between 'activity systems' (ibid., 10) such as those within the film industry; this ableist metagenre of 'abnormality' and 'difference' is thus capable of a range of 'typified responses', falling into themes such as pity, charity, exceptionality, and victimhood, or the construction of 'stupid', suicidal and evil personalities. These themes and characters are often tied to particular genres, resulting, for instance, in disabled people often being cast as evil characters in action films, and as the butt of the joke in comedies. As suggested, this 'disability metagenre' is often invoked by non-disabled writers and directors, such as Atilla Till, to share the awareness they have gained in working with disabled people, a disposition which has similarities to the empathic speculative mediations on the impacts of particular impairments (e.g. in *Wonder* and *Me before You*). In all three of these examples the writers and directors were non-disabled, and used the films to highlight 'issues', not least those that pertain to those who are close to the disabled person. These three films also featured male disabled characters, as 81 per cent of films featuring disabled characters do (Smith et al., 2016, 2), perhaps reflecting the preoccupations of the writers and directors.[3] Thus, the disability genre echoes previous arguments about the white male as a universal figure for the 'plenitude of human diversity' (Dyer, 1988, 47) to an alarming degree. Although only 19 per cent of disabled characters are women, all women continue to be under-represented in films, with an overall figure of 31.4 per cent of female characters, also begging further questions about the employment of female writers and directors in the film industry.[4]

Although disabled or non-disabled identities cannot be mapped unproblematically onto attitudes towards disability or impairment narratives, the dominance of curiosity-based, potentially voyeuristic, portrayals can be seen to be a dominant feature of many stories written and directed by non-disabled people. This may be less true of disabled writers and directors. I am suggesting that approaches to story-making and storytelling from an (albeit less critical and under-informed) external observer's point of view tend to contribute to the individualist bias of most cinematic portrayals of disability. Carpenter (2011) argues that these individualist points of view dominate cultural representations of disability, founded on ableist assumptions, taking them to be the norm, thus perpetuating the neglect of 'social and cultural oppression' within stories of disability (ibid., para 9).

However, the Farrelly Brothers' films have demonstrated that such positioning towards disabled people is not coterminous with disability status, given that neither of them identify as disabled (even though *Dumb and Dumber To* demonstrates their capacity to adopt different, more discriminatory, approaches). Their intent to see and show things 'differently', in order to (according to Peter Farrelly) 'break the mold' of disability imagery (Allen 2018, para 7), and the advice received from Peter Farrelly's close (disabled) friend Danny Murphy were probably the most significant factors in the evolution of disability representations within their work (Ramisetti, 2014; Allen, 2018), and their subsequent popularity amongst disabled audiences (Allen, 2018). Indeed, they are a good reminder that:

> Texts and discourses are defined by what they *do* and how they are *used* rather than by what they *are*. Or perhaps more accurately, what they are *is* what they do.
>
> (Carpenter, 2011, para 8, author's emphasis)

There is certainly a need to pay far more attention to the role of writers and directors in representing disability, raising questions about what they allow the text to do to disabled characters, examining how people are used to portray disability and impairments, and exploring how disabled characters and disabled actors are used. It is imperative to continue investigations into how disability themes are addressed, in addition to exploring the positions of disabled actors and crew within their productions. Although I am highlighting the roles of writers and directors here, the key roles that cinematographers, production designers, costume designers, sound mixers, music writers, and many others play in creating meaning should not be forgotten (as explorations of films in the book have illustrated), although further discussion on auteurship and the collaborative production of meaning is beyond the scope of my discussion here.

158 *Conclusion*

Chapters throughout the book have shown that comedy films (and other comedy media) can easily work against valuing disabled people's lives. This is especially true of the conventional romantic comedy genre where the narrative often adopts a monologic structure. Despite the presence of other discourses within *Me Before You*, including motifs which uphold hegemonic ideals of meritocracy, analysis of visual and narrative elements of the film demonstrated a firm focus on Lou's life, aided to a large extent by the 'tragedy' of Will's disablement and suicide decision; the unified perspective was Lou's, combining to reinforce our beliefs and expectations of the 'productive, useful, unified citizen's body' (Hadley, 2014, 6). The current forms which romantic comedy takes seem to have provided few shifts towards more polyphonic stories. Even though *The Big Sick* worked to parody conventional attitudes to 'race' within its structure, and included a number of differing perspectives, such as the opinions of Kumail's girlfriend's (Emily) parents, Emily's role was understandably marginal, since for much of the film she was in a coma (true to the real-life story it was based on). As we might expect, *The Lobster*, as a satire of contemporary culture and our ideals about bodies and romance, created a much more polyphonic structure (whilst also parodying the romantic comedy genre), potentially shifting our expectations of the genre and of normative bodies. Like *The Lobster*, the Farrelly Brothers films (with varying degree of polyphony over times, as discussed) might have been expected to appeal to a very niche audience, risking insufficient box office returns. And their decision to risk losses further by deliberately seeking representational change for disabled people (Allen, 2018) is likely to have been viewed as a dangerous strategy by a film industry which is invested in disability genres as part of an ableist disability metagenre, possibly necessitating the return to the *Dumb and Dumber* territory, for which Danny Murphy had first criticised them (Ramisetti, 2014).

Further, comedy films might be considered as particularly resistant to change when Palmer's three variables of offensiveness (1994, 164) and Gavin's arguments about resistances to issue-based messages are considered (2001). While disability is regarded as 'a weakness' by media industries, as Peter Farrelly argues (Allen, 2018, para 6), writing and direction which challenge conventional ideas of 'the world external to the joke' (Palmer, 1994) (and the misrecognised positions of disabled people within it), may be avoided as too risky as it is not in keeping with stereotypic views. Although one might surmise that the screen industries would avoid comedies which position disabled people as 'the butt of the joke', given the dominance of discourses of charity, exceptionality, benevolence, and pity, which have dominated in Oscar-winning disability films (Cox, 2012), the rise of the multiply-offending 'tolerant subject' on the wave of anti-PC sentiments suggests that decisions on which comedy films get made and released will depend to a large extent on their conformity to the disabled metagenre. The idea of the non-disabled, white, male tolerant subject can be seen as ideal for an industry which is struggling to come to terms with its deep inequalities and the potential anxieties these may produce; as yet there has been little recognition that the centralising of this figure is part of the problem. Previous discussions have suggested that spurious ideas of risk curtail opportunities for 'others', and disproportionately favour white, non-disabled, middle class (cis) men, perhaps drawing on ideas of universality, plenitude, and auteurship to justify such a bias. The idea that profit might be based on a predictable 'for anyone as someone structure', which is in turn based on genres which are known to have mass audience appeal is likely to strengthen perceptions of risk, and resistance to representational change. The appeal to the disability metagenre in most films which feature impairment 'saves' the audience from 'having to truly encounter' disabled people, who continue to be subjected to 'the violence of recognition, categorisation and comprehension' which results in the 'partial negation' of disabled people's being (Hadley, 2014, 7, following Lévinas).

Orson Welles is reputed to have said to André Bazin:

> I believe that a work is good to the degree that it expresses the man who created it.
>
> (Callow, 2015, xiii)

He may well have meant these words as they were written (see Rich, 2003 for brief discussion of his attitudes to women for example) but they have taken on particular significance in the current era, reflected in some of the concerns of the #MeToo, #TimesUp, #AskMoreOfHim movements, in relation to the effects of male power in the film industry. Lauzen (2012) has shown that much of the marginalisation of women is related to perceptions of risk, and a bias towards films which will appeal to people such as themselves – a group disproportionately comprised of white, non-disabled men. The evidence examined in this book suggests that concerns about risk are weighted in favour of white, non-disabled, middle- or upper-class males, and the idea that the perspectives of 'others' are too niche continues to predominate. It also seems to be true across comedic genres, even though satire and parody can provide a way out of some of the genre-bound impasses. However, the charting of the Farrelly Brothers films suggest limited conditions of possibility for representational change, given their return to a less political mode. Nonetheless, it is clear that comedy has played a leading role in the debates about political correctness and should be regarded as a valuable tool in the telling of disabled people's lives.

To come to some kind of a conclusion, the demands of 'others' for opportunities to express their experiences and create alternative cinematic and comedic encounters has been overwhelming over recent years. It's time to say something new, with an expanded sense of the many social worlds we exist in. In so doing, cinema may become less monologic in its telling of disabled lives.

Darla K. Anderson, speaking at the 2018 Oscar ceremony said, art can change and connect the world. And this can only be done when we have a place for everyone and anyone who feels like 'an other' to be heard.

(Marcos, 2018)

The cinema of the future will be much richer if it becomes more dialogic, expressing the lives of us all, and enhancing dialogue between us.

Notes

1 This is a statistic from Smith et al.'s report (2016), *Inequality in 800 Popular Films*. Whilst it is indicative of the presence of disabled people in the film industry caution should be exercised in the interpretation of how disability is being defined. Smith et al. draw up a list of rules for what is and what isn't 'coded' as disability in the investigation, exceptions including gods and zombies, type and 'severity of facial scars, and so on...
2 This reflects differences in US and UK terminology, but both uses here refer to disablement.
3 The figure of 81 per cent comes from a sample of characters counted according to whether they speak, or are named in the cast, thus excluding extras..
4 Again the figure of 31.4 per cent counts only those who speak or are named.

Bibliography

Abberley, P. (1987). The Concept of Oppression and the Development of a Social Theory of Disability. *Disability, Handicap and Society*, 2(1), pp. 5–19.

Abbot, S. and Jermyn, S. (2009). Introduction – A Lot Like Love: The Romantic Comedy in Contemporary Cinema. In: S. Abbott and D. Jermyn eds. *Falling in Love Again: Romantic Comedy in Contemporary Cinema*. London: L.B. Tauris and Co Ltd, pp. 1–8.

Akass, K. (2010). Postscript: Little Britain USA. In: S. Lockyer, ed., *Reading Little Britain*, London: I.B. Tauris, pp. 209–214.

Aiden, H. and McCarthy, A. (2014). *Current Attitudes Towards Disabled People*. London: Scope.

Albrecht, G. (1999). Disability Humor: What's in a Joke? *Body & Society*, 5(4), pp. 67–74.

Allan, K. and Burridge, A. (2006). *Forbidden Words: Taboo and the Censoring of Language*. Cambridge: Cambridge University Press.

Allen, H. (2018). Farrelly Brothers. [online] *Ability Magazine*. Available at: https://abilitymagazine.com/farrelly-brothers.html [Accessed 10 March 2018].

Altman, R. (1999). *Film/genre*. London: British Film Institute.

Andrew, D. (1988). Breathless: Old as New. In: D. Andrew ed., *Breathless: Jean Luc Godard, Director*. New Brunswick: Rutgers University Press. pp. 3–20.

Angerstein, J. (2015). *500 Days of Summer: A Deconstruction of the Manic Pixie Dreamgirl?* [online]. Jack Eats Films. Available at: http://jackeatsfilms.blogspot.co.uk/ [Accessed 5 January 2018].

antony-1 (2004). *A Wonderful Film – What Cinema is Made For. But Badly Mis-marketed.* [online]. Available at: http://www.imdb.com/title/tt0338466/reviews?ref_=tt_urv [Accessed 9 February 2018].

Appadurai, A. (2015). Mediants, Materiality, Normativity. *Public Culture*, 27(2), pp. 221–237.

Arnot, C. (2007). Making Sense of Humour – Chris Arnot Discovers What a Gay Academic Finds To Enjoy and Admire About a Homophobic Northern Comic. *The Guardian*. [online] Available at: https://www.theguardian.com/education/2007/nov/06/highereducationprofile.academicexperts [Accessed 16 August 2017].

Arya, R. (2014). *Abjection and Representation*. Basingstoke: Palgrave MacMillan.

Asp, J. (2015). Stockholm: Visionary Award Winner Lanthimos Rocks Lobster. *Variety*. [online] November 16. Available at: http://variety.com/2015/film/festivals/stockholm-visionary-award-winner-lanthimos-rocks-lobster-1201642216/ [Accessed 3 March 2018].

Bibliography

Backstrom, L. (2012). From the Freakshow to the Living Room: Cultural Representations of Dwarfism and Obesity. *Sociological Forum*, 27(3), pp. 682–707.

Bahuguna, A. (2015). *51 Best Romantic Comedy Movies Every Bollywood Viewer Must Watch*. [online] Available at: mensxp.com, https://www.mensxp.com/entertainment/top-10s/27972-51-best-romantic-comedies-every-bollywood-lover-must-watch.html [Accessed 21 December 2017].

Balducci, F. (2011). A different shade of pink: Literary thresholds and cultural intersections in Italian chick lit. PhD thesis, Victoria University of Wellington. Available at: http://researcharchive.vuw.ac.nz/bitstream/handle/10063/1929/thesis.pdf?sequence=1 [Accessed 28 January 2018].

Bakhtin M. (1984). *Rabelais and His World*. Translated by Hélène Iswolsky. Bloomington: Indian University Press.

Barajas, J. (2017). *Maya Angelou Knew How a Laugh Could be a Survival Tool*. [online] PBS Newshour. 21 February, Available at: https://www.pbs.org/newshour/arts/maya-angelou-knew-laugh-survival-tool [Accessed 3 March 2018].

Baril, A. (2015) How Dare You Pretend to be Disabled? The Discounting of Transabled People and Their Claims in Disability Movements and Studies. *Disability and Society*, 30(5), 689–703.

Barnard, T. (2010). 'The Whole Art of a Wooden Leg': King Vidor's Picturization of Laurence Stalling's 'Great Story'. In: S. Chivers and N. Markotic eds., *The Problem Body: Projecting Disability on Film*. Columbus: The Ohio State University Press, pp. 23–42.

Barnes, C. (1991). *Disabled People in Britain and Discrimination: A Case for Anti-Discrimination Legislation*. London: Hurst and BCODP.

Barnes, C. (1992). *Disabling Imagery and The Media: An Exploration of the Principles for Media Representations of Disabled People*. Halifax: Ryburn.

Barnes, C. (1997). A Legacy of Oppression: A History of Disability in Western culture. In: L. Barton and M. Oliver eds., *Disability Studies: Past, Present and Future*, pp. 3–24.

Barnes, C. and Mercer, G. (1996). *Exploring the divide: Illness and disability*. Leeds: The Disability Press.

Barnes, C. and Mercer, G. (2005). Disability, Work and Welfare: Challenging the Exclusion of Disabled People. *Work, Employment and Society*, 19(3), pp. 527–545.

Barnes, H. (2015). Yorgos Lanthimos: Reality TV Flavoured The Lobster. *The Guardian*. [online] Available at: https://www.theguardian.com/film/2015/may/15/yorgos-lanthimos-cannes-palme-dor-contender-colin-farrell-lobster [Accessed 15 May 2018].

Barnes, H. (2016). Me Before You Defends Film Against Disability Campaigners. *The Guardian*. [online] Available at: https://www.theguardian.com/film/2016/jun/06/me-before-you-director-thea-sharrock-disability-campaigners [Accessed 8 March 2018].

Barrett, G. (1989). *Archetypes in Japanese Film: The Socio-Political and Religious Significance of The Principal Heroes and Heroines*. Cranbury, NJ: Associated University Presses.

Bauer, P.E. (2005). What's So Funny About Disability? Well…, *New York Times*. [online] Available at: http://www.nytimes.com/2005/12/11/movies/whats-so-funny-about-disability-well.html [Accessed 8 February 2018].

Baughan, N. (2016). *The Invisible Woman: Film's Gender Bias Laid Bare*. [online] BFI. Comment. Available at: http://www.bfi.org.uk/news-opinion/sight-sound-magazine/comment/invisible-woman-film-gender-bias-laid-bare [Accessed 19 February 2018].

Bauman, Z. (1993). *Modernity and Ambivalence*. Cambridge: Polity Press.
Bauman, Z. (2000). *Liquid Modernity*. Cambridge: Polity Press.
Bawarshi, A. (2000). The Genre Function. *College English*, 62(3), pp. 335–360.
BBC (2012). C4 Drop I'm Spazticus Sketch After Police Called. [online] BBC News. 12 April, Available at: http://www.bbc.co.uk/news/entertainment-arts-17689141 [Accessed 7 August 2017].
Beasley, C., Holmes, M., and Brook, H. (2015). Heterodoxy: Challenging Orthodoxies about Heterosexuality. *Sexualities*, 18(5/6), pp. 681–697.
Beaver, F.E. (2007). *A Dictionary of Film Terms: The Aesthetic Companion to Film Art*. New York: Peter Lang.
Beck, U. (1992). *Risk Society: Towards a New Modernity*. Translated by M. Ritter. London: Sage.
Beck, U. (2007). *World at Risk*. Cambridge: Polity Press.
Beck, U. and Beck-Gernsheim, E. (1995). *The Normal Chaos of Love*. Oxford: Polity Press.
Beckman, F. (2012). Hearing Voices: Schizoanalysis and the Voice as Image in the Cinema of David Lynch, in J. Jagodzinski, *Psychoanalysing Cinema: A Productive Encounter with Lacan, Deleuze, and Žižek*. New York: Palgrave MacmiIllan, pp. 71–88.
Begley, S. (2015). How the Romantic Comedy for Senior Citizens Became Film's Hippest Genre. *Time*. [online] Available at: March 12, http://time.com/3734380/romantic-comedies-senior-citizens/ [Accessed 21 December 2017].
Belam, M. and Levin, S. (2018). Woman Behind 'Inclusion Rider' Explains Frances McDormand's Oscar Speech. *The Guardian*. [online] Available at: https://www.theguardian.com/film/2018/mar/05/what-is-an-inclusion-rider-frances-mcdormand-oscars-2018 [Accessed 8 March 2018].
Bell (Jr), D.A. (1980). Brown v Board of Education and the Interest Convergence Dilemma. *Harvard Law Review*, 93(3), pp. 518–533.
Bell, E., Haas, L., and Sells, L. (1995). *From Mouse to Mermaid: The Politics of Film, Gender and Culture*. Bloomington: Indiana University Press.
Benedictus, L. (2010). Little Britain: What is Life Like as a Small Person? *The Guardian*. [online] Available at: https://www.theguardian.com/lifeandstyle/2010/jun/14/small-world-people-of-restricted-growth [Accessed 20 September 2017].
Bennett, T., Savage, M., Silva, E.B., Warde, A., Gayo-Cal, M., and Wright, D. (2009). *Class, Culture, Class, Distinction*. London: Routledge.
Berger, P. and Pullberg, S. (1966). Reification and the Sociological Critique Of Consciousness, *New Left Review*, 1(35), pp. 56–71.
Bergson, H. (2011). (trans. C. Brereton and F. Rothwell). *Laughter: An Essay on the Meaning of the Comic*. London: Macmillan.
Berger, R. J. (2012). What's So Funny About Disability? [online] *The Society Pages*. Available at: https://thesocietypages.org/specials/whats-so-funny-about-disability/ [Accessed 9 February 2018].
Bhavnani, R. (2007). *Barriers to Diversity in Film: A Research Review*. Report commissioned by the UK Film Council, London: City University.
Birmingham Post (2008). Birmingham Film-Maker Justin Edgar Hits Out at Hollywood Treatment of Disabled. *Birmingham Post*. [online] Available at: http://www.birminghampost.co.uk/whats-on/film-tv/birmingham-film-maker-justin-edgar-hits-3953525 [Accessed 11 January 2017].
Birrell, I. (2016). Where Are the Disabled Actors? *The Independent – Voices*. [online] http://www.independent.co.uk/voices/where-are-the-disabled-actors-a6831001.html [Accessed 3 July 2017].

Blackpool Gazette (2011). Nothing Sacred. [online] Available at: http://www.blackpoolgazette.co.uk/whats-on/nothing-sacred-1-3989818 [Accessed 26 August 2017].

Blomley, N.K. (1994). Editorial: Activism and the Academy. In: *Environment and Planning D: Society and Space*, 12, pp. 383–383.

Bolt, B. (2004). *Art Beyond Representation: The Performative Power of the Image*. London: Tauris.

Bolt, B. (2006). *Materializing Pedagogies. Working Papers in Art and Design 4*. [online] Available at: http://sitem.herts.ac.uk/artdes_research/papers/wpades/ vol4/bbfull.html [Accessed 10 July 2017].

Bolt, D. (2013). *The Metanarrative of Blindness: A Re-reading of Twentieth Century Anglophone Writing*. Michigan: University of Michigan.

Bordwell, D. and Carrol, N. (1996). *Post-theory: Reconstructing Film Studies*. Madison: The University of Wisconsin Press.

Bourdieu, P. (1986). Forms of Capital. In: J.E. Richardson ed., *Handbook of Theory of Research for the Sociology of Education*. Translated by R. Nice. Westport: Greenwood Press.

Bowdre, K. (2009). Romantic Bodies and the Raced Body. In: S. Abbott and D. Jermyn eds., *Falling in Love Again: Romantic Comedy in Contemporary Cinema*. London: L.B. Tauris and Co Ltd, pp. 105–116.

Box Office Mojo (2018). All films listed in references, Available at: http://www.boxofficemojo.com/movies/[Accessed 28 January 2018].

Brabazon, T. (2005). What Have You Ever Done on the Telly? The Office, Post Reality Television and Post Work. *International Journal of Cultural Studies*, 8(1), pp. 101–117.

Branney, P. (2008). Subjectivity, Not Personality: Combining Psychoanalysis and Discourse Analysis. *Social and Personality Psychology Compass*, 2(2), pp. 574–590.

Brassett, J. (2009). British Irony, Global Justice: A Pragmatic Reading of Chris Brown, Banksy, and Ricky Gervais. *Review of International Studies*, 35, pp. 219–245.

Briant, E., Watson, N. and Philo, G. (2011). Bad News for Disabled People: How The Newspapers are Reporting Disability. Project Report, Strathclyde Centre for Disability Research and Glasgow Media Unit, University of Glasgow, Glasgow, UK.

Brooks, D. (2000). *Bobos in Paradise: The New Upper Class and How They Got There*. New York: Simon and Schuster.

Brown, R.S. (1994). *Overtones and Undertones: Reading Film Music*. Berkeley: University of California Press.

Brown, R.C. (2006). *Common as Muck: The Autobiography of Roy 'Chubby' Brown*. Royston Vasey: Hachette Digital.

Brown, M. (2017). Researchers Find a 'Culture of Nepotism' in the British Film Industry. *The Guardian*. [online] Available at: https://www.theguardian.com/film/2017/jun/28/ researchers-find-culture-of-nepotism-in-british-film-industry [Accessed 18 January 2018].

Brylla, C. and Hughes, H. (2017). *Documentary and Disability*. London: Palgrave Macmillan.

Bucaria, C. and Barra, L. (2016). Taboo Comedy on Television: Issues and themes. In: C. Bucaria and L. Barra eds., *Taboo Comedy: Television and Controversial Humour*. London: Palgrave MacMillan, pp. 1–18.

Burt, M.R. (1980). Cultural Myths and Supports for Rape. *Journal of Personality and Social Psychology*, 38, pp. 217–230.

Bury, M. (1982). Chronic Illness as Biographical Disruption. *Sociology of Health and Illness*, 4(2) pp. 167–182.

Butler, J. (1993) *Bodies That Matter: On the Discursive Limits of Sex*, Oxon: Routledge.
Butler, C. (2018). Three Billboards and the New Philistinism. [online] Spiked. Available at: http://www.spiked-online.com/newsite/article/three-billboards-and-the-new-philistinism/20782#.Wl9we6hl-Ul [Accessed 17 January 2018].
Byrne, P. (2000). Schizophrenia in the Cinema. *Psychiatric Bulletin*, 42, pp. 364–365.
Byrne, P. (2009). Screening Madness: A Century of Negative Movie Stereotypes of Mental Illness, Time to Change, Available at: https://www.bl.uk/collection-items/screening-madness-a-century-of-negative-movie-stereotypes-of-mental-illness [Accessed 1 February 2018].
Cadwallader, J. R. (2012). Like a Horse and Carriage: Non-normativity in Hollywood Romance. *Journal of Media and Culture*, 15(6). Available at: http://journal.media-culture.org.au/index.php/mcjournal/article/view/583 [Accessed 19 December 2017].
Callow, S. (2015) *One Man Band*. London: Vintage.
Campsie, A. (2016). Five of Scotland's Most Beautiful Privately Owned Castles. *The Scotsman*. [online] Available at: https://www.scotsman.com/news/five-of-scotland-s-most-beautiful-privately-owned-castles-1-4101786 [Accessed 14 January 2018].
Carey, H., Crowley, L., Dudley, C., and Sheldon, H., and Giles, L. (2017). *A Skill Audit of the UK Film and Screen Industries: Report for the British Film Institute*- Lancaster: Work Foundation.
Campbell, F.A.Kumari (2009). *Contours of Ableism: The Production of Disability and Abledness*. Basingstoke: Palgrave Macmillan.
Campbell, F. K. (2017a). Queer Antisociality and Disability Unbecoming: An Ableist Relations Project? In: O. Sircar and D. Jain. eds., *New Intimacies/Old Desires: Law, Culture and Queer Politics in Neoliberal Times*, New Delhi: Zubaan Books, pp. 280–316.
Campbell, F.K. (2017b). *Answering Our Detractors – Argument in Support of Studies in Ableism as an Approach to Negotiating Human Differences and Tackling Social Exclusion*. [online]. Conference on Studies in Ableism University of Manchester, 19 June 2017, Available at: https://www.academia.edu/33586090/ [Accessed 21 June 2017].
Capehart, J. (2017). The Real Reason Working-class Whites Continue to Support Trump, *The Washington Post*. [online] Available at: https://www.washingtonpost.com/blogs/post-partisan/wp/2017/06/06/the-real-reason-working-class-whites-continue-to-support-trump/?utm_term=.1abe5431612a [Accessed 1 September 2017].
Cardona, A. (2017). The Polite Canadian Stereotype? You Can Thank WWII and America for it. *HuffPost*. [online] Available at: http://www.huffingtonpost.ca/2017/06/13/canadian-stereotypes-overly-polite_n_17071742.html [Accessed 12 September 2017].
Carroll, N. (1996). Prospects for Film Theory: A Personal Assessment. In: D. Bordwell and N. Carrol, *Post-theory: Reconstructing Film Studies*. Madison: The University of Winsconsin Press, pp. 37–70.
Carlson, M. (2017). The Life of a Disabled Child, From Taunts to Hate Crimes. *The New York Times -The Opinion Pages*. [online]. Available at: https://www.nytimes.com/2017/01/06/opinion/the-life-of-a-disabled-child-from-taunts-to-hate-crimes.html [Accessed 19 August 2017].
Carpenter, R. (2011). Disability as Socio-rhetorical Action: Towards a Genre-based Approach. *Disability Studies Quarterly* [online] 32(3), Available at: http://dsq-sds.org/article/view/1666/1605 [Accessed 10 March 2018].

166 Bibliography

Carter, M. (2007). Ways of Knowing, Doing, and Writing in the Disciplines. *College Composition and Communication*, 58(3), pp. 385–418.

Caulfield, D. (2011). Channel 4's Seven Dwarves. *Disability Arts Online* [online]. Available at: http://www.disabilityartsonline.org.uk/channel4-seven-dwarves [Accessed 20 September 2017].

Chamarette, J. (2012). *Phenomenology and the Future of Film: Rethinking Subjectivity beyond French Cinema*. Basingstoke: Palgrave Macmillan.

Channel 4.com (2018). *Three Billboards Outside Ebbing, Missouri*. [online] Film 4/ Channel4. Available at: http://www.channel4.com/programmes/film4/videos/all/three-billboards-outside-ebbing-missouri-interview-special/5701054332001 [Accessed 23 January 2018].

Chemaly, S. (2016). Why All Male Minions Really Do Matter For Children. *Huffpost*. [online] Available at: http://www.huffingtonpost.com/soraya-chemaly/why-allmale-minions-reall_b_7804296.html [Accessed 17 September 2017].

Cheyne, R. (2012). Introduction: Popular genres and Disability Representation. *Journal of Literary and Cultural Disability Studies*, 6(2), pp. 117–123.

Child, B. (2012). Kiera Knightley Dealt with Dyslexia by Reading Sense And Sensibility Script. *The Guardian*. [online] Available at: https://www.theguardian.com/film/2012/jan/31/keira-knightley-dyslexia-sense-sensibility [Accessed 3 July 2017].

Chivers, S. and Markotić, N. eds. (2010). *The Problem Body: Projecting Disability on Film*. Columbus: The Ohio State University Press.

Chortle (2016). Alternative Comedy was Driven by Hatred of the Working Class. [online] *Chortle*. Available at: http://www.chortle.co.uk/news/2016/01/14/23954/alternative_comedy_was_driven_by_hatred_of_the_working_class [Accessed 15 August 2017].

Cieply, M. (2008). Nationwide 'Thunder' Boycott in the Works. *New York Times* [online]. Available at: http://www.nytimes.com/2008/08/11/movies/11thun.html [Accessed 3 February 2018].

Clark, L. (2003). Disabling Comedy: 'Only When We Laugh', Paper given at the Finding the Spotlight Conference, Liverpool Institute for the Performing Arts, 30 May. Available at: http://disability-studies.leeds.ac.uk/files/library/Clark-Laurence-clarke-on-comedy.pdf [Accessed 21 February 2018].

Classic.fm (2018). Mozart's Music in the Movies. [online] Classic.fm.com. Available at: http://www.classicfm.com/composers/mozart/pictures/mozarts-music-movies/mozart-music-movie-trading-place/ [Accessed 29 January 2018].

Clay, A.D. (2014). *The Filthy Truth*. New York: Touchstone.

Cockburn, P.F. (2012). You've Got to laugh: Disability Comedy. *Access Magazine*. [online]. Available at: http://www.accessmagazine.co.uk/disability-comedy/ [Accessed 17 September 2017].

Cohen, P. M. (2010). What Have Clothes Got To Do With It? Romantic Comedy and the Female Gaze. *Southwest Review*, 9(1–2), pp. 78–88.

Coleman-Fountain, E. and McLaughlin, J. (2013). The Interactions of Disability and Impairment. *Social Theory & Health*, 11(2), pp. 133–150.

Connell, R.W. (2005) *Masculinities*. Cambridge: Polity Press.

Coogan, T. and Mallett, R. (2013). Introduction – Disability, Humour and Comedy . *Journal of Literary and Cultural Disability Studies*, 7(2), pp. 247–253.

Cooper, C. (2014) Tough Austerity Measures in Greece Leave Nearly a Million People with No Access to Healthcare, Leading to Soaring Infant Mortality, HIV Infection and Suicide. In *Independent*, 21 February, https://www.independent.co.uk/news/

world/europe/tough-austerity-measures-in-greece-leave-nearly-a-million-people-with-no-access-to-healthcare-9142274.html [Accessed 27 May, 2018].

Corker, M. (1999). The Conspiracy of Normality. *Body and Society*, 5(4), pp. 75–83.

Cooper, S. (2016). Narcissus and the Lobster (Yorge Lanthimos 2015). *Studies in European Cinema*, 13(2), pp. 163–176.

Cox, D. (2008). The Imbecilic Truth about the Tropic Thunder Retard Debate. *The Guardian*. [online] Available at: https://www.theguardian.com/film/filmblog/2008/sep/22/tropicthunder.benstiller [Accessed 8 March 2018].

Cox, D. (2012). Disability in Film: Is Disability Finally Moving with the Times, in *The Guardian*, 12 November, https://www.theguardian.com/film/filmblog/2012/nov/12/disability-in-film-untouchable [Accessed 28 May 2018].

Cox, J. (2017). Privately Owned Public Spaces. *Greenspace Information for Greater London CIC Newsletter*. [online] Available at: http://www.gigl.org.uk/privately-owned-public-spaces/ [Accessed 16 January 2018].

Craig, C. (1991). Rooms Without a View. *Sight and Sound*, June, pp. 10–13.

Creative Diversity Network (2017). *Diamond: The First Cut*. [online] Available at: https://creativediversitynetwork.com/diamond/the-first-cut/. [Accessed 10 January 2018].

Creative Skillset (2012). *Employment Census of the Creative Media Industries*. London: Creative Skillset.

Crenshaw, K. (1991). Mapping the Margins: Intersectionality, Identity Politics, and Violence Against Women of Color, in *Stanford Law Review*, 43(6), pp. 1241–1299.

Cromb, B. (2008). Gorno, Violence, Shock and Comedy. *Cinephile*, 4 [online], pp. 18–24, http://cinephile.ca/archives/volume-4-post-genre/gorno-violence-shock-and-comedy/ [Accessed 1 February 2018].

Culler, J. (1982). *On Deconstruction*. New York: Cornell University Press.

Cumberbatch, G. and Negrine, R. (1992). *Images of Disability on Television*. London: Routledge.

Darke, P. (1995) 'Link': An evaluation. Unpublished consultation paper for Yorkshire Television, October, https://disability-studies.leeds.ac.uk/wp-content/uploads/sites/40/library/Dark-Link-an-evaluation.pdf [Accessed 20 May 2018].

Darke, P. (1998). Understanding Cinematic Representations of Disability. In: T. Shakespeare, ed., *The Disability Reader: Social Science Perspectives* London: Cassell.

Darke, P.A. (1999). The Cinematic Construction of Physical Disability as Identified Through the Application of the Social Model to Six Indicative Films Made Since 1970. PhD thesis, University of Warwick.

Darke, P.A. (2003). Now I Know Why Disability Art is Drowning in the River Lethe (With Thanks to Pierre Bourdieu). In: S. Riddell and N. Watson, eds., *Disability, Culture and Identity*. London: Pearson, pp. 131–142.

Darke, P. (2010). No Lie Anyway; Pathologising Disability on Film. In: S. Chivers and N. Markotic, eds., *The Problem Body: Projecting Disability on Film*. Columbus: The Ohio State University Press, pp.97–107.

Davis, L.S. (2003). Serious Fun: Galapagos Takes its Alternative Comedy Revue Rather Seriously. *Brooklyn Paper*. [online] Available at: https://www.brooklynpaper.com/stories/26/45/26_45piehole.html [Accessed 8 March 2018].

Day, E., Hoggard, L. and Bromwich, K. (2015). 99% of Women Working in the Film and TV Industries have Experienced Sexism. *The Guardian*. [online] Available at: https://www.theguardian.com/film/2015/sep/27/sexism-film-industry-stories [Accessed 29 January 2017].

Bibliography

Dean, W. (2014). Derek TV Review: It's Time to See the Funny Side of Ricky Gervais' Kind Character. *The Independent*. [online] Available at: http://www. independent.co.uk/arts- entertainment/tv/reviews/derek-tv-review-its-time-to-see-the-funny-side-of-ricky-gervais- [Accessed 8 February 2018].

De Lange, D.E. (2011). *Cliques and Capitalism: A Modern Networked Theory of the Firm*. New York: Palgrave Macmillan.

Delaney, B. (2017). Our Social Lives Have Become Echo Chambers. Time to Get Uncomfortable. *The Guardian*. [online] 29 December. Available at: https://www.theguardian.com/commentisfree/2017/dec/29/our-social-lives-have-become-echo-chambers-time-to-get-uncomfortable [Accessed 3 March 2018].

Deleuze, G. (1986). *Cinema I – The Movement-Image*. Minneapolis: University of Minnesota Press.

Deleuze, G. (1989). *Cinema II – The Time-Image*. London: The Athlone Press.

Deleuze, G. (2013). *Cinema I – The Movement-Image*. London: The Athlone Press.

Deleuze, G. and Guatarri, F. (2003). *A Thousand Plateaus: Capitalism and Schizophrenia*. London: Continuum.

Deleuze, G. and Guattari, F. (2004). A Thousand Plateaus. In: J. Rivkin and M. Ryan eds., *Literary Theory: An Anthology*. Oxford: Blackwell Publishing Ltd.

Deleyto, C. (2009). *The Secret Life of Romantic Comedy*. Manchester: Manchester University Press.

Delgado, R. (2015). Why Obama? An Interest Convergence Explanation of the Nation's First Black President. *Law and Inequality: A Journal of Theory and Practice*, 33(2), pp. 345–369.

Dickey, J. (2014). Everyone is Altered: The Secret Hollywood Procedure That Has Fooled Us for Years. [online] Mashable. Available at: http://mashable.com/2014/12/01/hollywood-secret-beauty-procedure/#eDMjkLMh2mqH [Accessed 30 December 2017].

Douglas, M. (1966). *Purity and Danger: An Analysis of the Concepts of Pollution and Taboo*. London: Routledge and Kegan Paul.

Duncker, K. (1945). On Problem-Solving (Translated by L. S. Lees). *Psychological Monographs*, 58(5), pp. 1–113.

Dolski, E.A. (2013). The Pitiful Bellringer: The Implications of Representations of Disability in Media and Literature. *Education and Development Masters Theses*, [online] 184, Spring, pp. 5–17, Available at: https://digitalcommons.brockport.edu/cgi/viewcontent.cgi?article=1189&context=ehd_theses [Accessed 3 February 2018].

Donaldson, K. (2017). It's Time to Stop Disability Drag. *Pajiba*, [online] 20 September, Available at: http://www.pajiba.com/film_reviews/its-time-to-stop-disability-drag.php [Accessed 5 March 2018].

Douglas, M. (1966). *Purity and Danger: An Analysis of the Concepts of Pollution and Taboo*London: Routledge.

Downey, S.A. (2014). 7 Reasons Why 'Dumb and Dumber To' was Horrible, from a Die-hard Fan. [online] *Medium*. Available at: https://medium.com/@sarahadowney/7-reasons-why-dumb-and-dumber-to-was-horrible-from-a-die-hard-fan-6437a71fca9d [Accessed 4 March 2018].

Dreger, A. (2012). The Sex Life of Conjoined Twins. *The Atlantic*. [online] [Accessed 9 February 2017].

Dyer, R. (1988). White. *Screen*, 29(3), pp. 44–62.

Dyer, R. (1990). *Now You See It*. London: Routledge

Dyer, R. (1997). *White*. Abingdon: Routledge.

Edition.cnn.com (2017). Conjoined Twins Fast Facts. [online] CNN. Available at: https://edition.cnn.com/2013/07/11/world/conjoined-twins-fast-facts/index.html [Accessed 7t February 2018].

Eitzen, D. (1999). The Emotional Basis of Film Comedy. In: C. Plantinga and G.M. Smith, eds., *Passionate Views: Film, Cognition and Emotion*. Baltimore: John Hopkins University Press, pp. 84–99.

Ellingson, T. (2001). *The Myth of the Noble Savage*. Berkeley and Los Angeles: University of California Press.

Ellis, K. and Goggin, G. (2015). *Disability and the Media*. London: Palgrave.

Emerson, J. (2012). Andrew Sarris, Auteurism and His Take on His Own Legacy. [online] RogerEbert.com. Available at: https://www.rogerebert.com/scanners/andrew-sarris-auteurism-and-his-take-on-his-own-legacy [Accessed 23 February 2018].

Enns, A. and Smit, C.R. eds. (2001). *Screening Disability: Essays on Cinema and Disability*. Lanham, MD: University Press of America, Inc.

Erbland, K. (2017). The Highest Grossing Indies in 2017 (Final List). *Indiewire*, [online] 6 June, Available at: http://www.indiewire.com/2017/06/highest-grossing-indie-films-2017-1201764229/ [Accessed 6 January 2017].

Ettinger, B.L. (2006). Matrixical Trans-subjectivity. *Theory, Culture and Society*, 23(2), pp. 182–122.

Evans, E. (2015). How a Joke Can Help Us Unlock the Meaning of Mystery in Language. [online] *The Conversation*. Available at: https://theconversation.com/how-a-joke-can-help-us-unlock-the-mystery-of-meaning-in-language-51365 [Accessed 8 March 2018].

Evans, J. and Hall, S. (1999). *Visual Culture: The Reader*. London: Sage.

Evans, J. (1999). Feeble Monsters: Making Up Disabled People. In: S. Hall and J. Evans eds., *Visual Culture*. London: Sage, pp. 274–288.

Everett, W. (2007). (ed.) *Questions of Colour in Cinema: From Paintbrush to Pixel*, Bern: Peter Lang.

Faludi, S. (1991). *Backlash: The Undeclared War Against Women*. London: Vintage.

Fastbraiin.com (2016). 21 Celebrities Who Thrive with ADHD, Available at: https://www.healthcentral.com/article/celebrities-with-adhd [Accessed 6 February 2018].

Felperin, L. (2017). Kills on Wheels Review: Hitman in a Wheelchair Fires up Plucky Comedy Drama. *The Guardian*. [online]. Available at: https://www.theguardian.com/film/2017/sep/15/kills-on-wheels-review-hitman-wheelchair-representation-disability [Accessed 9 March 2018].

Fenichel, O. (1999). The Scoptophilic Instinct and Identification. In: S. Hall and J. Evans eds., *Visual Culture*. London: Sage, pp. 327–339.

Ferriss, S. and Young, M. (2008). Introduction: Chick flicks and Chick Culture. In: S. Ferriss, and M. Young eds. *Chick Flicks: Contemporary Women at the Movies*. Oxon: Routledge, pp. 1–25.

Film Comment (2000). Film Comment's Best of the Nineties Poll: Part Two. [online] filmcomment.com, Available at: https://www.filmcomment.com/article/film-comments-best-of-the-90s-poll-part-two/ [Accessed 9 February 2018].

Follows, S. (2016). How Does the Average of Actors Differ Between Genres? in StephenFollows.com, 21 November, https://stephenfollows.com/age-of-actors/ [Accessed 26 May 2018].

Foster, A. and Furst, S. (1996). *Radio Comedy, 1938–1968: A Guide to 30 Years of Wonderful Wireless*. London: Virgin Books.

Bibliography

Frank, A. W. (1995). *The Wounded Storyteller: Body, Illness and Ethics.* Chicago, IL: University of Chicago Press.

Fraser, N. (2000). Rethinking Recognition. *New Left Review*, 3, May–June, Available at: https://newleftreview.org/II/3/nancy-fraser-rethinking-recognition [Accessed 17 September 2017]. pp. 107–118.

Fraser, B. (2016). *Cultures of Representation: Disability in World Cinema.* New York: Wallflower Press.

Freund, P. (2001). Bodies, Disability and Spaces: The Social Model and Disabling Spatial Organisations, *Disability and Society*, 16(5), pp. 689–706.

Friedman, S. (2014). *Comedy and Distinction – The Cultural Currency of a 'Good' Sense of Humour.* Oxon: Routledge.

Frye, N. (2002). The Argument of Comedy. In: B. Richardson ed., *Narrative Dynamics: Essays on Time, Plot, Closure and Frames.* Columbus: Ohio State University, pp. 102–109.

Gage, J. (1999). *Colour and Meaning: Art, Science and Symbolism.* Berkeley: University of California Press.

Gardiner, M. (1998). Bakhtin and the Metaphorics of Perception. In: I. Heywood and B. Sandywell eds., *Interpreting Visual Culture: Explorations in the Hermeneutics of the Visual*London: Routledge pp. 57–73.

Gartner, A. and Joe, T. (1987). *Images of the Disabled, Disabling Images.* London: Praeger.

Gavin, J. (2001). Television Teen Drama and HIV/AIDS: The Role of Genre in Audience Understandings of Safe Sex. *Continuum*, 15(1), pp. 77–96

Gehring, W.D. (2008). *Romantic versus Screwball Comedy: Charting the Difference.* Plymouth: The Scarecrow Press Inc.

Gentleman, A. (2009). Inside the Dignitas House, in *The Guardian*. [online] 18 November, https://www.theguardian.com/society/2009/nov/18/assisted-suicide-dignitas-house [Accessed 17 May 2018]

Geraghty, G. (2008). *Now a Major Motion Picture: Film Adaptations of Literature and Drama.* Plymouth: Rowan and Littlefield.

Gilbey, R. (2016). 'I'm Not a Thing to be Pitied': The Disability Backlash Against Me Before You. *The Guardian*. [online] 2 June, Available at: https://www.theguardian.com/film/2016/jun/02/me-before-you-disabled-backlash-not-pitied [Accessed 1 March 2018].

Gilliard, C. and Higgs, P. (2014). *Ageing, Corporeality and Embodiment.* London: Anthem.

Giddens, A. (1991). *Modernity and Self-identity: Self and Society in the Late Modern Age*Cambridge: Polity Press.

Girard, R. (2013). *Violence and the Sacred.* Trans. Patrick Gregory. New York: Bloomsbury.

Goodley, D. (2011). *Disability Studies: An Interdisciplinary Introduction.* London: Sage.

Goodley, D. (2012). Jacques Lacan + Paul Hunt = Psychoanalytic Disability Studies. In: D. Goodley, B., Hughes, and L. Davis eds., *Disability and Social Theory.* London: Palgrave Macmillan.

Goodley, D. (2014). *Dis/ability Studies; Theorising Ableism and Disablism.* Abingdon, Oxon: Routledge.

Goldman, S. (2009). 'Joan Rivers.' Jewish Women: A Comprehensive Historical Encyclopedia. 20 March, *Jewish Women's Archive*, 2017, https://jwa.org/encyclopedia/article/rivers-joan [Accessed on 26 August 2017].

Bibliography 171

Graeber, D. (2015). Radical Alterity is Just Another Way of Saying 'Reality': A Reply to Eduardo Viveiros. *Journal of Ethnographic Theory*, 5(2), pp. 1–41.

Grant, B.K. (2007). *Film Genre: From Iconography to Ideology*. London: Wallflower Press.

Greco, P. (2012). Zoe Kazan on Writing Ruby Sparks, and Why You Should Never Call Her a 'Manic Pixie Dream Girl'. *Vulture*. [online]. Available at: http://www.vulture.com/2012/07/zoe-kazan-ruby-sparks-interview.html [Accessed 5 January 2017].

Green, M. (1991). The Mouth of Texas. *People*. [online] Available at: http://people.com/archive/the-mouth-of-texas-vol-36-no-22/ [Accessed 8 March 2018].

Green, M.C., and Brock, T. C. (2000). The Role of Transportation in the Persuasiveness of Public Narratives. *Journal of Personality and Social Psychology*, 79, pp. 701–721.

Greyser, N. and Weiss, M. (2012). Left Intellectuals and the Neoliberal University. *American Quarterly*, 64(4), pp. 787–793.

Grindon, L. (2011) *The Hollywood Romantic Comedy: Conventions, History, Controversies*. Chichester: John Wiley.

Gross, D.A (2016). When You Listen to Music You're Never Alone. Online. *Nautilus*. Available at: http://nautil.us/issue/34/adaptation/when-you-listen-to-music-your e-never-alone [Accessed 9 January 2018].

Grue, J. (2016). The Problem with Inspiration Porn: A Tentative Definition and a Provisional Critique. *Disability and Society*, 31(5), pp. 838–849.

Hadley, B. (2014). *Disability, Public Space, Performance and Spectatorship*. Basingstoke: Palgrave MacMillan.

Hall, J.L. (2006). Opposites Attract: Politics and Romance in 'The Way We Were' and 'Speechless'. *Quarterly Review of Film and Video*, 23(3), pp. 155–169.

Hall, R. (2012). Film and Television Industry 'Discriminates Against Women, Ethnic Minorities, and the Working Class'. *The Independent*. [online] Available at: http://www.independent.co.uk/arts-entertainment/films/news/film-and-television-indus try-discriminates-against-women-ethnic-minorities-and-the-working-class-7630929.html [Accessed 6 September 2017].

Hall, S. (1980). Encoding/decoding. In: S. Hall, D. Hobson, A. Lowe, and P. Willis, eds. *Culture, Media, Language: Working Papers in Cultural Studies, 1972–79*. London: Hutchinson and CCCS: University of Birmingham, pp. 117–127.

Hall, S. (1996). Who Needs Identity? In: S. Hall and P. du Gay, eds., *Questions of Cultural Identity*, London: Sage, pp. 1–17.

Haller, B. (2003). Guest Editor's Introduction to DSQ Symposium on Disability and Humor. *Disability Studies Quarterly*, 23(3–4), http://dsq-sds.org/article/view/430/607 [Accessed 21 February 2018].

Hanitch, J. (2011). Towards a Poetics of Cinematic Disgust. *Film-Philosophy*, 15(2), pp. 11–35.

Harrington, R. (1997). Revenge of the Gross-Out King! John Waters 'Pink Flamingos' Enjoys a 25th Year Revival. *Washington Post*. [online] Available at: http://www.washingtonpost.com/wp-srv/style/longterm/movies/review97/fpinkflamingos.htm [Accessed 8 February 2018].

Harris, S.J. (2014). Abled-bodied Actors and Disability Drag: Why Disabled Roles Are Only For Disabled Performers, in *Balder & Dash*, at Rogerebert.com, https://www.rogerebert.com/balder-and-dash/disabled-roles-disabled-performers [Accessed 28 May 2018].

Harris, M. (2015). The New York Film Festival Grapples with the Death of an Icon. *Grantland* [online] http://grantland.com/hollywood-prospectus/the-new-york-film-festival-grapples-with-the-death-of-an-icon/ [Accessed 3 January 2017].

Harvey, D. (2000). The Godfather of Gross-Out. *Film Comment*, 36(4), pp. 34–36.

Hayhoe, S. (2008). *God, Money and Politics*. Charlotte, North Carolina: Information Age Publishing.

Hawkins, C. (2014). 11 Female Film Pioneers Who Paved the Way to Hollywood. *Mic.com*. [online] Available at: https://mic.com/articles/84569/11-female-film-pioneers-who-paved-the-road-to-hollywood#.QM39TCIZA [Accessed 28 January 2017].

Hayek, S. (2017). Harvey Weinstein is My Monster Too. *New York Times*. [online] 12 December, Available at: https://www.nytimes.com/interactive/2017/12/13/opinion/contributors/salma-hayek-harvey-weinstein.html [Accessed 31 December 2017].

Heaney, S. (2016). Taboo Infringement and Layered Comedy: A Linguistic Analysis of Convolution in Gervais and Merchant's Life's Too Short. *Comedy Studies*, 7, pp. 152–168.

Higgie, R. (2017). Public Engagement, Propaganda or Both? Attitudes Towards Politicians on Political Satire and Political Programs. *International Journal of Communication*, 11, pp. 930–948.

Hobbs, A. (2013). Romancing the Crone: Hollywood's Recent Mature Love Stories. *Journal of American Culture*, 36(1), pp. 42–51.

Hoeksema, T. B. and C. R. Smit (2001). The Fusion of Film Studies and Disability Studies. In: C. R. Smit and A. Enns eds. *Screening Disability: Essays on Cinema*. Lanham, MD: University Press.

Hollomotz, A. and The Speakup Committee. (2008). 'May We Please Have Sex Tonight?'– People with Learning Difficulties Pursuing Privacy in Residential Group Settings. *British Journal of Learning Disabilities*, 37(2), pp. 91–97.

Hughes, B. (2009). Wounded/Monstrous/Abject: A Critique of the Disabled Boy in the Sociological Imaginary. *Disability and Society*, 24(4), pp. 399–410.

Hughes, B. and Paterson, K. (1999). Disability Studies and Phenomenology: The Carnal Politics of Everyday Life. *Disability and Society*, 14(5), pp. 597–610.

Hughes, B. (2012). Fear, Pity and Disgust: Emotions and the Non-Disabled Imaginary. In: N. Watson, A. Roulstone, and C. Thomas, *Routledge Handbook of Disability Studies*, London: Routledge.

Hupperetz, L. (2016). The Pursuit of Love in the 21st Century: The Lobster as a Critique on our Online Dating Society. Academic Research Writing, Amsterdam University College, 15 May. Available at: https://www.academia.edu/25704036/The_Pursuit_Of_Love_In_The_21st_Century_The_Lobster_as_A_Critique_On_Our_Online_Dating_Society [Accessed 3 January 2017].

Ignatieff, M. (1995). Nationalism and the Narcissism of Minor Differences. *Queens' Quarterly*, Spring, 102(1), pp. 13–25.

Ilić, V. (2017). Dystopia-En-Abyme: Analysis of The Lobster's Narrative. *Etnoantropoloski problemi*, 12(2), pp. 467–487.

Imrie, R., and Edwards, C. (2007). The Geographies of Disability: Reflections on the Development of a Sub-Discipline. *Geography Compass*, 1(30), pp. 623–640.

Inahara, M. (2009). This Body Which Is Not One: The Body, Femininity, and Disability. *Body and Society*, 15(1), pp. 47–62.

Institute of Contemporary Arts (2017). *Yorgos Lanthimos Focus*. [online] Institute of Contemporary Arts, Available at: https://www.ica.art/whats-on/season/yorgos-lanthimos-focus [Accessed 31 December 2017].

IMDB.com (2018a). *Dumb and Dumber* – Taglines. [online] Available at: http://www.imdb.com/title/tt0109686/taglines [Accessed 9 February 2018].

IMDB.com (2018b). *Kingpin*. [online] Available at: http://www.imdb.com/title/tt0116778/ [Accessed 6 February 2018].

IMDB.com (2018c). *There's Something About Mary*. [online], Available at: http://www.imdb.com/title/tt0129387/ [Accessed 9 February 2018].

IMDB.com (2018d). *Dumb and Dumber To* [online] Available at: https://www.imdb.com/title/tt2096672/ [Accessed 29 January 2018]

Irigary, L. (1985). *This Sex Which is Not One*. Ithaca and New York: Cornell University Press.

Irwin, W. and Gracia, J.J.E. (2007). *Philosophy and the Interpretation of Pop Culture*. Plymouth: Rowan and Littlefield.

ivko (2004). *Touching Comedy*, in IMDB Stuck on You User Reviews, 3 May, [online] Available at: http://www.imdb.com/title/tt0338466/reviews?ref_=tt_urv [Accessed 8 February2018].

Jagodzinski, J. (2012). *Psychoanalysing Cinema: A Productive Encounter with Lacan, Deleuze, and Žižek*. New York: Palgrave MacmiIllan.

Jeffers McDonald, T. (2007). *Romantic Comedy: Boy Meets Girl Meets Genre*. London: Wallflower Press.

Jenkins, E.S. (2013). Animation, Affect and Ideology. *Critical Inquiry*, 39(3), pp. 575–591.

Jermyn, D. (2011). Unlikely Heroines? Women of a Certain Age and 'Romantic Comedy'. *Cineaction*, 84, pp. 25–33.

Jermyn, D. (2014). The How and Why of Romantic Comedy Research. Paper given at Gender and Genre, Couples and Culture, at The Cinema Museum, London, 22 November.

Jessen, L. (2016). Disability Advocates React to 'Me before you': 'Our Suicides' are 'Tragedies'. *The Daily Signal*. [online] Available at: http://dailysignal.com/2016/06/03/disability-advocates-react-to-me-before-you-our-suicides-are-tragedies/ [Accessed 21 February 2018].

Jharvey (2004). Farrelly Brothers Deeply Conflicted…, 2 April, [online] Available at: http://www.imdb.com/title/tt0338466/reviews?ref_=tt_urv [Accessed 18 February 2018].

Johnson, K.R. and Holmes, B.M. (2009). Contradictory Messages: A Content Analysis of Hollywood-Produced Romantic Comedy Films. *Communication Quarterly*, 57(3), July–September, pp. 352–373.

Jones, D. O. (2007). The Soul that Thinks: Essays on Philosophy, Narrative and Symbol in the Cinema and Thought of Andrei Tarkovsky, [online] PhD thesis of College of Fine Arts of Ohio University. Available at: https://etd.ohiolink.edu/rws_etd/document/get/ohiou1194999476/inline [Accessed 29 January 2018].

Kent, D. (1987). Disabled Women: Portraits in Fiction and Drama. In: A. Gartner and T. Joe, eds., *Images of the Disabled, Disabling Images*, New York: Praeger, pp. 47–63.

Kermode, M. (2016). 'The Lobster' Review: Surreal Satire and Black-humour laughs. *The Guardian*. [online] Available at: https://www.theguardian.com/film/2015/oct/18/the-lobster-review-colin-farrell-rachel-weisz-mark-kermode [Accessed 21 February 2018].

Kettle, J. (2011). Jerry Sadowitz: His Dark Materials. *The Guardian*. [online] 9 November. Available at: https://www.theguardian.com/stage/2011/nov/09/jerry-sadowitz-interview [Accessed 26 August 2017].

Kharach, B. (2006). Dana Gould, Writer and Comedian. *Gothamist*. [online] Available at: http://gothamist.com/2006/12/27/dana_gould_writ.php [Accessed 10 September 2017].

Kift, D. (1996). *The Victorian Music Hall: Culture, Class and Conflict*. Cambridge: Cambridge University Press.

Klobas, L.E. (1988). *Disability Drama in Television and Film*. Jefferson, NC: McFarland and Co. Inc.

King, G. (2002). *Film Comedy*. London: Wallflower Press.

Kim, E. (2011). Asexuality in Disability Narratives. *Sexualities*, 14(4), pp. 479–493.

Knauss, K. (2012). Romance Unveiled: Romance at the Opera in 'Moonstruck' (1987), 'Pretty Woman' (1990), and' Little Women' (1994). *Musicological Annual*. [online] Available at: https://revije.ff.uni-lj.si/MuzikoloskiZbornik/article/viewFile/2496/2182 [Accessed 29 January 2018]

Koller, M.R. (1988). *Humor and Society: Explorations in the Sociology of Humor*. Houston: Cap and Gown Press Inc.

Koutsourakis, A. (2012). Cinema of the Body: Politics of performativity in Lars von Trier's Dogville and Yorgos Lanthimo's Dogtooth. *Cinema: Journal of Philosophy and the Moving Image*, 3, pp. 84–108.

Kriegel, L. (1987). The Cripple in Literature. In: A. Gartner and T. Joe, eds. *Images of the disabled, disabling images*. New York: Praeger, pp. 31–46.

Kristeva, J. (1982a). *Approaching Abjection, Powers of Horror*. New York: Columbia University Press.

Kristeva, J. (1982b). *Powers of Horror. An Essay on Abjection*. Translated by L. S. Roudiez. New York: Columbia University Press.

Kruse, I. I. R. J. (2003). Narrating Intersections of Gender and Dwarfism in Everyday Spaces. *Canadian Geographer / Le Géographe canadien*, 47(4), 494–508.

Krutnik, F. (2002). Conforming Passions? Contemporary Romantic Comedy. In: S. Neale, ed., *Genre and Contemporary Hollywood*. London: BFI, pp. 130–147.

Kuipers, G. (2006). Television and Taste Hierarchy: The Case of Dutch Television Comedy. *Media, Culture and Society*, 28(3), pp. 359–378.

Lacob, J. (2012). Game of Thrones and Life's Too Short: Two different TV dwarfs. [online] *Daily Beast*. Available at: http://www.thedailybeast.com/game-of-thrones-and-lifes-too-short-two-different-tv-dwarfs [Accessed 17 September 2017].

Landreth, J. (2014). Fresh from Baiting the Disabled, Ricky Gervais's Derek Takes Aim at the Elderly. *New Statesman*, 28 April, Available at: https://www.newstatesman.com/culture/2014/04/fresh-baiting-disabled-ricky-gervais-s-derek-takes-aim- elderly [Accessed 30 January 2018].

Lang, B. (2015). Study Finds Few Lead Roles for Women in Hollywood. *Variety*. [online] 19 February, Available at: http://variety.com/2015/film/news/women-lead-roles-in-movies-study-hunger-games-gone-girl-1201429016/ [Accessed 29 January 2017].

Latif, N. and Latif, L. (2016). How to Fix Hollywood's Race Problem. *The Guardian*. [online] Available at: https://www.theguardian.com/film/2016/jan/18/hollywoods-race-problem-film-industry-actors-of-colour [Accessed 16 December 2017].

Lauzen, M. M. (2012). Where Are the Film Directors Who Happen to Be Women? *Quarterly Review of Film and Video*, 29(4), pp. 310–319.

Lauzen, M. (2015). Studios Need to Address Diversity in a Changing World, in *Variety*, 26 February, Available at: http://variety.com/2015/voices/opinion/studios-need-to-address-diversity-in-a-changing-world-1201441701/ [Accessed 29 January 2017].

Lawson, M. (2013). Derek: Cruel, or Just Unusual? *The Guardian* [online]. Available at: https://www.theguardian.com/culture/2013/jan/31/ricky-gervais-derek-cruel-unusual[Accessed20 January 2018].

Lee, B. (2017). Stronger Review – Jake Gyllenghaal is Oscar-worthy in Moving Boston Marathon Drama. *The Guardian.* [online] Available at: https://www.theguardian.com/film/2017/sep/08/stronger-review-jake-gyllenhaal-boston-marathon [Accessed 7 January 2018].

Lee, S. (2007). Political Correctness Gone Mad. [online] Available at: http://www.stewartlee.co.uk/written-for-money/political-correctness-gone-mad/ [Accessed 24 August 2017].

LeBesco, K. (2004). There's Something About Disabled People: The Contradictions of Freakery in the Films of The Farrelly Brothers. *Disability Studies Quarterly*, [online] 24(4). Available at: http://www.dsq-sds.org/article/view/895/1070 [Accessed 8 February 2018].

Leonard, T. (2014). How the Original Siamese Twins had 21 Children by Two Sisters…While Sharing One (Reinforced) Bed. *Mail Online.* [online] Available at: http://www.dailymail.co.uk/news/article-2825888/How-original-Siamese-t wins-21-children-two-sisters-sharing-one-reinforced-bed.html [Accessed 9 February 2018].

Linton, S. (1998). *Claiming Disability: Knowledge and Identity.* New York: University Press.

Lippman, J. R. (2015). I Did It Because I Never Stopped Loving You: The Effects of Media Portrayals of Persistent Pursuit on Beliefs About Stalking. *Communication Research*, 45(3), pp. 394–421.

Littlewood, J. and Pickering, M. (1998). 'Heard the One about the White Middle-Class Heterosexual Father-In-Law?': Gender, Ethnicity and Political Correctness in Comedy. In: S. Wagg, ed., *Because I Tell a Tale or Two: Comedy, Politics and Social Difference.* London: Routledge, pp. 291–312.

Liverpool University Press (2017). *Journal of Literary and Cultural Disability Studies,* http://online.liverpooluniversitypress.co.uk/loi/jlcds [Accessed 17 September 2017].

Li-1 (2004). The Farrelly's Best Since There's Something about Mary. [online] IMDB User Reviews, 16 May. Available at: http://www.imdb.com/title/tt0338466/reviews?ref_=tt_urv [Accessed 9 February 2018].

Livingstone, S. and Bovill, M. (1999). *Young People, New Media: Report of the Research Project Children Young People and the Changing Media Environment.* London, UK: Media@LSE.

Lockyer, S. (2010a). *Reading Little Britain: Comedy Matters on British Television.* London: I.B. Tauris and Co. Ltd.

Lockyer, S. (2010b). Introduction. In: S. Lockyer, *Reading Little Britain.* London: I.B Tauris and Co. Ltd, pp. 1–16.

Lockyer, S. (2015). From Comedy Targets to Comedy-Makers: Disability and Comedy in Live Performance. *Disability and Society*, 30(9), pp. 1397–1412.

Lodderhouse, D. (2016). Yorgos Lanthimos: I Just Think it's Interesting to Start a Dialogue. British Film Institute, Interviews. [online] Available at: http://www.bfi.org.uk/news-opinion/news-bfi/interviews/yorgos-lanthimos-i-just-think-interesting-to-sta rt-dialogue [Accessed 7 January 2017].

Logan, B. (2017). David Chappelle, Ricky Gervais, and Comedy's Ironic Bigotry Problem. *The Guardian.* [online] 3 April. Available at: https://www.theguardian.com/stage/2017/apr/03/dave-chappelle-ricky-gervais-standup-comedy-transgender [Accessed 2 December 2017].

Longmore, P. (1987). Screening Stereotypes: Images of Disabled People in Television and Motion Pictures. In: A. Gartner, and T. Joe eds., *Images of the Disabled, Disabling images* New York: Praeger, pp. 65–78.

Lorenzo, A. (2016). The Film Industry is Steeped in Racism Whether You Want to Accept it or Not. *Huck Magazine*. [online] 25 April 2016. Available at: http://www.huckmagazine.com/perspectives/need-talk-race-film-industry/ [Accessed 3 July 2017].

Luzzi, J. (2016). *A Cinema of Poetry: Aesthetics of the Italian Art Film*. Baltimore, Maryland: John Hopkins University Press.

MacDonald, S. (2012). Gervais in the Clear Over Rant at Susan Boyle. *The Sun*. [online] Available at: https://www.thesun.co.uk/archives/news/324305/gervais-in-the-clear-over-rant-at-susan-boyle/ [Accessed 8 March 2018].

Manoharan, K. and Jones, R.S. (2015). Unravelling the Minion Genome. *Journal of Interdisciplinary Science*, 4, pp. 41–43.

Margulies, I. (1996). *Nothing Happens: Chantal Akerman's Hyperrealist* Everyday. Durham: Duke University Press.

Marine, J. (2015). Colour in Storytelling (Video), in How Color Has Become Such an Important Storytelling Tool in Cinema, Available at: https://nofilmschool.com/2015/08/history-importance-color-cinema-storytelling-film-lewis-bond [Accessed 28 January 2018].

Marotta, V. (2002). Zygmunt Bauman: Order, Strangerhood and Freedom. *Thesis 11*. August.

Marshall, K. (2009). Somethings Gotta Give and the Classic Screwball Comedy. *Journal of Popular Television*, 37(1), pp. 9–15.

Martin, A. (2013). In the Mood for (Something Like) Love: The Situation of the Rom Com Today. *Cineaste*, Winter, 39(1), pp. 16–20.

Magowan, M. (2015). 'Minions' Most Sexist Movie of the Year, Voted Triple S for Worst Movie of the Year, in Reel Girl: Imagining Gender Equality in the Fantasy World. Available at: http://reelgirl.com/2015/07/minions-most-sexist-kids-movie-of-the-year-rated-triple-s-for-gender-stereotyping/ [Accessed 17 September 2017].

Malcolm, D. (2004). The Station Agent. *The Guardian*. [online] Available at: https://www.theguardian.com/film/2004/mar/26/dvdreviews.shopping4 [Accessed 17 March 2017].

Mallett, R. (2009). Choosing 'Stereotypes': Debating the Efficacy of (British) Disability Criticism. *Journal of Research in Special Educational Needs*, 9(1), pp. 4–11.

Mallett, R. (2010). Claiming Comedic Immunity, or What You Get When You Cross Contemporary British Comedy with Disability *Review of Disability Studies*, 6(3), pp. 5–14.

Mansfield, N. (2000). *Subjectivity: Theories of the Self from Freud to Haraway*. Allen and Unwin: St Leonards NSW.

Markotić, N. (2016). *Disability in Film and Literature*. Jefferson: MacFarland & Co.

Marcos (2018). SDSU Alumni win big at Academy Awards with 'Coco'. [online] Available at: The California State University- Alumni, at: https://www2.calstate.edu/csu-system/news/Pages/SDSU-Alumni-Win-Big-at-Academy-Awards-with-Coco.aspx [Accessed 10 March 2018].

McIlvenny, P. (2003). Disabling Men: Masculinity and disability in Al Davison's graphic autobiography, The Spiral Cage'. In: S. Ervø, and T. Johansson, *Bending bodies, Moulding Masculinities*. Aldershot: Ashgate, pp. 238–256.

McKenna, T. (2015). From Tragedy to Farce: The Comedy of Ricky Gervais as Capitalist Critique. In: T. McKenna, *Art Literature and Culture from a Marxist Perspective*, pp. 197–209.

McKinstry, L. (2017). A–Z of Political Correct Madness: The Left's 'Thought Police' Continues to Censor Language as 'Manfully' is Labelled Sexist, on *Mail Online*, 18 November, http://www.dailymail.co.uk/news/article-5094791/A-Z-politically-correct-madness.html [Accessed 20 May 2018].

McLean, C. (2016). Ricky Gervais: 'David Brent is All About White Middle-Class Male Angst'. *The Telegraph*. [online] 20 August, Available at: https://www.telegraph.co.uk/films/2016/08/20/ricky-gervais-interview-david-brent-is-all-about-white-middle-cl/ [Accessed 8 March 2018].

McNab, G. (2014). Dumb and Dumber To, Movie Review: This Revolting and Misogynistic Film Will Put You Off Your Popcorn. *Independent* [online]. Available at: http://www.independent.co.uk/arts-entertainment/films/reviews/dumb-and-dumber-to-movie-review-this-revolting-and-misogynistic-film-will-put-you-off-your-popcorn-9931102.html [Accessed 9 February 2018].

McRuer, R. (2006). *Crip Theory: Cultural Signs of Queerness and Disability*. New York: New York University Press.

Medhurst, A. (2007). *A National Joke: Popular comedy and English Cultural Identities*. Oxon: Routledge.

Media (2014). A Fond Farewell. *The Guardian*. [online]. Available at: https://www.theguardian.com/media/2004/jan/29/broadcasting.tvandradio [Accessed 28 January 2018].

Meekosha, H., and R. Shuttleworth. (2009). What's So 'Critical' about Critical Disability Studies. *Australian Journal of Human Rights* 15(1), pp. 47–75.

Menard, D.G. (2003). A Deleuzian Analysis of Tarkovsky's Theory of Time-Pressure, Part 1 'Cone-Physics'. *Off Screen*. [online] 7(8). Available at: http://offscreen.com/view/tarkovsky1 [Accessed 4 September 2017].

Mendoza, K. R. (2009). Seeing Through the layers: Fat Suits and Thin Bodies in The Nutty Professor and Shallow Hal, in E. Rothblum and S. Solovay (eds), *The Fat Studies Reader*. New York: New York University Press.

Mihailovic, A. (1997). *Corporeal Words: Mikhail Bakhtin's Theology of Discourse*. Evanston, Ilinois: Northwestern University Press.

Miller, J.R. (2012). Crossdressing Cinema: An Analysis of Transgender Representation in Film. PhD Thesis. Texas A&M University. Available from: http://hdl.handle.net/1969.1/ETD-TAMU-2012-08-11672 [Accessed 29 May 2018].

Mills, B. (2010). 'I'm Anti-Little Britain, and I'm Worried I Might Start Laughing': Audience Responses to Little Britain. In: S. Lockyer, *Reading Little Britain*, London: I.B. Tauris, pp. 147–170.

Mills, B. (2011). A Special Freedom: Regulating Comedy Offence. In: C. Bucaria and L. Barra eds., *Taboo Comedy: Television and Controversial Humour*. London: Palgrave MacMillan.

Mills, J. (2017). Friends Hung Man with Learning Difficulties and Beat Him to Death. *Metro*. [online], 19 February 2017. Available at: http://metro.co.uk/2017/02/19/friends-hung-man-with-learning-difficulties-from-tree-and-beat-him-to-death-6457997/ [Accessed 19 August 2017].

Mitchell, D. and Snyder, S. (2000). *Narrative Prosthesis: The Dependencies of Discourse*. Ann Arbor: University of Michigan Press.

Mitchell, D. and Snyder, S. (2006). *Cultural Locations of Disability*. Chicago: University of Chicago Press.

Misek, R. (2010). *Chromatic Cinema: A History of Screen Color*. Chichester: John Wiley.

Molitorisz, S. (2005). Tales of Ordinary Madness. *Sydney Morning Herald*. [online] Available at: http://www.smh.com.au/news/film/tales-of-ordinary-madness/2005/11/24/1132703305730.html [Accessed 8 February 2018].

Monbiot, G (2017). Neoliberalism is Creating Loneliness. That's What's Wrenching Society Apart. *The Guardian*. [online]. Available at: https://www.theguardian.com/commentisfree/2016/oct/12/neoliberalism-creating-loneliness-wrenching-society-apart [Accessed 9 January 2018].

Monk, C. (2015). The British Heritage-film Debate Revisited. In: C. Monk and A. Sergeant, eds., *British Historical Cinema: The History, Heritage and Costume Film*, Oxon: Routledge, pp. 176–196.

Montgomerie, M. (2015). *Screen Fictions and Discourses of Disability: Dodgy Discourse and the Moral Low Ground*. London: Continuum.

Moran, C. C. (2003). Beyond Content: Does Using Humour Help Coping? *Disability Studies Quarterly*, [online] 23(3/4). Available at: http://dsq-sds.org/article/view/434/611. [Accessed 9 January 2018].

Morris, W. (2018). Does 'Three Billboards' Say Anything about America? Well… *New York Times*. [online] Available at: https://www.nytimes.com/2018/01/18/movies/three-billboards-outside-ebbing-missouri.html [Accessed 22 January 2018].

Mortimer, C. (2010). *Romantic Comedy*. Oxon: Routledge.

Mostert, M.P. (2002). Useless Eaters: Disability as Genocidal Marker in Nazi Germany. *The Journal of Special Education*, 36(3), pp. 155–168.

Moyes, J. (2012). *Me Before You*. London: Penguin.

Mulvey, L. (1975). Visual Pleasure and Narrative Cinema. *Screen*, 16(3), pp. 6–18.

Munnery, S. (2016). Is Alternative Comedy Over? Well, Yes, and No…, *The Guardian*. [online] Available at: https://www.theguardian.com/stage/2016/aug/08/edinburgh-standup-simon-munnery-on-alternative-comedy [Accessed 26 August 2017].

Murray, J. (2016). The Lobster. *Cineaste*, 41(4), Fall, pp. 44–46.

Murray, R. (2013). 'The Epidermis of Reality': Artaud, the Material Body and Dreyer's The Passion of Joan of Arc . *Film-Philosophy*, North America [online], 17(1), Available at: http://www.film=philosophy.com/index.php/f-p/article/view/981/883 [Accessed 6 September 2017].

Murray, S. (2008). *Representing Autism: Culture, Narrative, Fascination*. Liverpool: Liverpool University Press.

Mumford, G. (2017). The Keg Party's Over: Why Gross-Out Comedies are Going Down the Pan. *The Guardian*. [online] 20 July, Available at: https://www.theguardian.com/film/2017/jul/20/comedy-movies-the-big-sick-will-ferrell-seth-rogen-the-house [Accessed 19 February 2018].

Nabi, R. L. (2002). The Theoretical versus the Lay Meaning of Disgust: Implications for Emotion Research. *Cognition & Emotion*, 16, pp. 695–703.

NAMI (2000). NAMI protests "Me, Myself & Irene" at National Alliance on Mental Illness [online] Available at: https://www.nami.org/Press-Media/Press-Releases/2000/NAMI-Protests-Me,-Myself-Irene [Accessed 9 February 2018].

National Public Radio Staff (2013). How One Unkind Moment Gave Way to 'Wonder'. [online] 12 September, https://www.npr.org/2013/09/12/221005752/how-one-unkind-moment-gave-way-to-wonder [Accessed 6 January 2018].

Neale, S. (1992). The Big Romance or Something Wild? Romantic Comedy Today. *Screen* 33(3), Autumn, pp. 284–299.

Neale, S. (2000). *Genre and Hollywood*. London: Routledge.

Nesteroff, K. (2016) *The Comedians: Drunks, Thieves, Scoundrels and the History of American Comedy*. New York: Grove Press.

Nicholson, R. (2016). 'Poor Little Snowflake' The Defining Insult of 2016. *The Guardian*. [online] Available at: https://www.theguardian.com/science/2016/nov/28/snowflake-insult-disdain-young-people [Accessed 8 March 2018].

Nicolaou, A. (2016). Slow Motion in Lanthimos' The Lobster. *Medium*. [online] 10 June. Available at: https://medium.com/@silver_argyro/slow-motion-in-yorgos-lanthimos-the-lobster-4bea88519300 [Accessed 7 January 2017].

Norden, M.E (1994). *The Cinema of Isolation*. New Brunswick, N.J: Rutgers University Press.

Novic, S. (2017). When it Comes to Depicting Disability, Hollywood Keeps 'Cripping Up'. [online] Edition.cnn, 1 March, Available at: https://edition.cnn.com/2018/03/01/opinions/hollywood-disability-new-normal-opinion-novic/index.html [Accessed 5 March 2018].

Nikulin, D. (2014). *Comedy, Seriously*. New York: Palgrave Macmillan.

Nunn, G. (2012). Language, Laughter and the Paralympics. *The Guardian*. [online] Available at: https://www.theguardian.com/media/mind-your-language/2012/sep/06/language-laughter-paralympics [Accessed 7 August 2017].

Oatley, K. (1995). A Taxonomy and Theory of the Emotions of Literary Response and a Theory of Identification Found in Fictional Narrative. *Poetics*, 23(1–2), pp. 53–74.

O'Connor, J. (2016). On location: 'Me Before You'. *Financial Times*. [online] Available at: https://www.ft.com/content/c64662b6-272f-11e6-8ba3-cdd781d02d89 [Accessed 24 January 2018].

O'Hara, H. (2016). 34 Women Who Changed Cinema. *The Telegraph* [online]. Available at: http://www.telegraph.co.uk/films/0/women-changed-history-cinema-pictures/ [Accessed 13 January 2017].

Oliver, M. (1990). *The Politics of Disablement*. Basingstoke: Macmillan.

Onion, R. (2014). The Awful Emptiness of Relatable. *Slate*. [online] Available at: http://www.slate.com/blogs/lexicon_valley/2014/04/11/relatable_the_adjective_is_everywhere_in_high_scchool_and_college_discussions.html [Accessed 19 December 2017].

Otieno, P.A. (2009). Biblical and Theological Perspectives on Disability: Implications on the rights of persons with disability in Kenya. *Disability Studies Quarterly*, [online] 29(4). Available at: http://dsq-sds.org/article/view/988/1164 [Accessed 3 March 2018].

Palmer, J. (1994). *Taking Humour Seriously*. London: Routledge.

Pareene, A. (2013). The Rich Summed Up: Nepotism, Cronyism, Narcissism. *Time Magazine* [online]. Available at: https://www.salon.com/2013/08/21/the_rich_summed_up_nepotism_cronyism_narcissism/ [Accessed 2 March 2018].

Parks, T. (2014). Molloy by Samuel Beckett, Book of a Lifetime: A Mad Hilarious Gripping Episode. *The Independent*. [online] Available at: http://www.independent.co.uk/arts-entertainment/books/reviews/molloy-by-samuel-beckett-book-of-a-lifetime-a-mad-hilarious-strangely-gripping-episode-9549057.html [Accessed 23 August 2017].

Paul, W. (1994). *Laughing, Screaming: Modern Hollywood Comedy and Horror*. New York: Columbia University Press.

Pembroke-castle.co.uk (2018). *History Timeline*. [online] Available at: http://pembroke-castle.co.uk/historic_events [Accessed 14 January 2018].

Perlman, M. (2015). Black and White: Why Capitalisation Matters. *Columbia Journalism Review*, 23 June, https://www.cjr.org/analysis/language_corner_1.php [Accessed 26 May 2018].

Phillips, L. (2017). *Baby Driver and the Terrifying Truths of Tinnitus*. [online] *Consequence of Sound*. Available at: https://consequenceofsound.net/2017/07/baby-driver-and-the-terrifying-truths-about-tinnitus/ [Accessed 9 March 2017].

Piggford, G. (2016). Slavoj Žižek's Passion (for the Real) and Flannery O'Connor's Hermaphrodite. *International Journal of Žižek Studies*, [online]10(3). Available at: http://zizekstudies.org/index.php/IJZS/issue/view/51[Accessed 29 May 2018].

Pointon, A. and Davies, C. (1997). *Framed: a Disability Media Reader*. London: BFI Publications.

Presence, S. (2012). An Investigation of Affect in the Cinema: Spectacle and Melodramatic Rhetoric. *Nil by Mouth. Frames Cinema Journal*, [online] 2. Available at: http://framescinemajournal.com/article/an-investigation-of-affect-in-the-cinema-spectacle-and-the-melodramatic-rhetoric-in-nil-by-mouth/ [Accessed 19 February 2018].

Prose, F. (2015). Totalitarian Love. *New York Review of Books*. [online] http://www.nybooks.com/daily/2015/10/06/totalitarian-love-lobster-yorgos-lanthimos/ [Accessed 3 January 2017].

Quayson, A. (2007) *Aesthetic Nervousness: Disability and the Crisis of Representation*. New York: Columbia University Press.

Quinn, R.J. (2016) Deciding for Myself on Me Before You, *HuffPost*, [online] 7 January, https://www.huffingtonpost.com/rob-j-quinn/deciding-for-myself-on-me_b_10629612.html [Accessed 16 May 2018].

Rabin, N. (2017). *Dream Girls: (500) Days of Summer*. [online] Nathan Rabin's Happy Place. Available at: https://www.nathanrabin.com/happy-place/2017/6/22/dream-girls-500-days-of-summer [Accessed 5 January 2018].

Radio Times (2016). Ricky Gervais Criticises 'Homogenised' Gross-Out Movies that are 'Focus Grouped to Death'. *Radio Times*. [online] Available at: http://www.radiotimes.com/news/2016-04-11/ricky-gervais-criticises-homogenised-gross-out-movies-that-are-focus-grouped-to-death/ [Accessed 10 February].

Ragland, E. (2004). *The Logic of Sexuation from Aristotle to Lacan*. Albany: State of New York Press.

Ramisetti, K. (2014). Peter Farrelly Remembers the Late Danny Murphy, Quadriplegic Actor in 'There's Something About Mary': He Was the Bravest Guy I Ever Knew. *NY Daily News*. [online] Available at: http://www.nydailynews.com/entertainment/danny-murphy-quadriplegic-actor-dies-age-58-article-1.1896955[Accessed 20 February].

Ralphthemoviemaker (2017). *The Lobster Film Analysis*. [online video] Available at: https://www.youtube.com/watch?v=6Ynqsc9fS5Q [Accessed 7 January 2018].

Rand, A. (2007, 1999). *Atlas Shrugged*. London: Penguin Books.

Randle, K. and Hardy, K. (2017). Macho, Mobile and Resilient? How Workers with Impairments are Doubly Disabled in Project-based Film and Television Work. *Work, Employment and Society*, 31(3), pp. 447–464.

Randle, K., Wing-Faie, L. and Kurian, J. (2007). *Creating Difference: Overcoming Barriers to Diversity in UK Film and Television Employment*, Hatfield: University of Hertfordshire.

Raynor, O. and Hayward, K. (2005). *The Employment of Actors with Disabilities in the Entertainment Industry: Executive Report*. Los Angeles: Screen Actors Guild.

Revolvy (2017). *Jerry Sadowitz*. [online] Revolvy.com. Available at: https://www.revolvy.com/main/index.php?s=Jerry%20Sadowitz [Accessed 26 February 2018].

Rich, B. (2003). Get Your Dirty Hands Off Us. *The Guardian*. [online] Available at: https://www.theguardian.com/film/2003/aug/29/1 [Accessed 10 March 2018].

Richardson, N. (2016). *Trangressive Bodies: Representations in Film and Popular Culture*. Oxon: Routledge.

Rice, K. (2016). Jojo Moyes Up Front: An Interview with the Me Before You Author. [online] *Signature*. Available at: http://www.signature-reads.com/2016/05/jojo-moyes-up-front-an-interview-with-the-me-before-you-author/ [Accessed 6 January 2018].

Richardson, N. (2016). *Transgressive Bodies: Representations in Film and Popular Culture*. Abingdon: Routledge.

Ritchie, C. (2010). Against Comedy. *Comedy Studies*, 1(2), pp. 159–168.

Robillard, A.B. (1999). Wild Phenomena and Disability Jokes. *Body and Society*, 5(5) pp. 61–65.

Robson, D. (2013). There Really Are 50 Eskimo Words for Snow. *Washington Post*. [online] Available at: https://www.washingtonpost.com/national/health-science/there-really-are-50-eskimo-words-for-snow/2013/01/14/e0e3f4e0-59a0-11e2-beee-6e38f5215402_story.html?utm_term=.b852132b2324 [Accessed 17 September 2017].

Rodgers, L. (2012). How to Win an Oscar. [online] BBC news.co.uk, Available at: http://www.bbc.co.uk/news/entertainment-arts-16932374 [Accessed 24 August 2017].

Rose, D. (2011). The Dwarf Actor Dilemmas [online] BBC News. Available at: http://www.bbc.co.uk/news/magazine-15673041 [Accessed 8 March 2018].

Rottentomatoes.com (2016). 50 Best Romantic Comedies of All Time. [online] Available at: https://editorial.rottentomatoes.com/guide/best-romantic-comedies-of-all-time/ [Accessed 28 February 2018].

Rose, C. (2011). Attenberg, Dogtooth, and the Weird Wave of Greek Cinema. *The Guardian*. [online] Available at: https://www.theguardian.com/film/2011/aug/27/attenberg-dogtooth-greece-cinema [Accessed 31 December 2017].

Rosenbaum, J. (2017). A Cinema of Uncertainty. [online] jonathanrosenbaum,net Available at: https://www.jonathanrosenbaum.net/2017/12/a-cinema-of-uncertainty/ [Accessed 3 March 2018].

rrmin347 (2014). Who Writes the Good Reviews? This Movie was the Worst of All Time… [online] Available at: http://www.imdb.com/title/tt2096672/reviews?ref_=tt_urv [Accessed 9 February 2018].

Ryan, F. (2015). We Wouldn't Accept Actors Blacking Up So Why Applaud 'Cripping Up'?. *The Guardian.*, 13 January, [online] https://www.theguardian.com/commentisfree/2015/jan/13/eddie-redmayne-golden-globe-stephen-hawking-disabled-actors-characters [Accessed 28 May 2018].

Ryan, F. (2016). Are You Pulling My Leg? C4 Strikes Gold by Seeing Paralympics Funny Side. *The Guardian*, [online] Available at: https://www.theguardian.com/tv-and-radio/2016/sep/17/how-the-last-leg-had-last-laugh-paralympic-games [Accessed 17 December 2017].

Saffer, J. (2018). How Changes to Disability Benefits Harm Claimants' Well-being and Sense of Self-identity. [online] The Conversation. https://theconversation.com/how-changes-to-disability-benefits-harm-claimants-well-being-and-sense-of-identity-91951 [Accessed 3 March 2018].

Safran, S.P. (1998). The First Century of Disability Portrayal in Film: An Analysis of the Literature. *The Journal of Special Education*, 31(4), pp. 467–479.

Bibliography

Samaha, A.M. (2007). What Good is the Social Model of Disability? University of Chicago Public Law & Legal Theory Working Paper No.166, Available at: https://chicagounbound.uchicago.edu/cgi/viewcontent.cgi?referer=https://www.google.co.uk/&httpsredir=1&article=1377&context=public_law_and_legal_theory [Accessed 3 March 2018].

Sancho, J. (2003). *Disabling Prejudice, Attitudes Towards Disability and its Portrayal on Television*. British Broadcasting Corporation, Broadcasting Standards Commission and Independent Television Commission. (n.p)

Savulescu, J. and Persson, I. (2016). Conjoined Twins: Philosophical Problems and Ethical Challenges. *The Journal of Medicine and Philosophy*. 41(1), pp. 41–55.

Sandell, R., Dodd, J., and Garland-Thomson, R. (2010). *Re-presenting Disability: Activism and Agency in the Museum*. Abingdon: Routledge.

Scannell, P. (2000). For-Anyone-as-Someone Structures. *Media, Culture and Society*, 22(1), pp. 5–24.

Scotney, J.H. (2010). *Culture Smart: Scotland*. London: Kupergard.

Scott and Champniss (2009) In the Interests of Serving Ricky Gervais..., ...*Some of the Corpses are Amusing*, 3 November, http://sotcaa.org/comment/assisting-ricky-gervais.html [Accessed 20 May 2018].

Seitz, M. Z. (2010). The Offensive Movie Cliché That Won't Die. [online] Salon. Available at: https://www.salon.com/2010/09/14/magical_negro_trope/ [Accessed 6 January 2018].

Senft, N., Chentsova-Dutton, Y., Patten, G.A. (2016). All Smiles Perceived Equally: Facial Expressions Trump Target Characteristics in Impression Formation. *Motivation and Emotion*, 40, pp. 577–587.

Shakespeare, T. (1994). Cultural Representation of Disabled People: Dustbins for Disavowal? *Disability and Society*, 9(3), pp. 283–299.

Shakespeare, T., Gillespie-Sells, K. and Davies, D. (1996). *The Sexual Politics of Disability*. London: Cassell.

Shakespeare, T., (1999a). Art and Lies? Representations of Disability on Film. M. Corker and S. French eds. *Disability Discourse*. Buckingham: Open University Press.

Shakespeare, T. (1999b). Joking Apart. *Body and Society*, 5(4), pp. 47–52, May.

Shakespeare, T. (1999c). The Sexual Politics of Disabled Masculinity. *Journal of Sexuality and Disability*, 17(1), pp. 53–64.

Shakespeare, T. (2010). No Laughing Matter: Medical and Social Experiences of Restricted Growth. *Scandinavian Journal of Disability Research*, 12(1), 19–31, March.

Sherry, M. (2016). The Sociology of Impairment. *Disability and Society*, 31(6), pp. 729–744.

Shiress, T. (2013). Disability and the Media: Free Speech is Everything. [online] Disability Horizons. Available at: http://disabilityhorizons.com/2013/02/disability-and-the-media-free-speech-is-everything/ [Accessed 11 November 2017].

Shumway, David R. (2003). *Modern Love: Romance, Intimacy, and the Marriage Crisis*. New York: New York University Press.

Siebers, T. (2004). Disability as Masquerade, in *Literature and Medicine*, 23(1), Spring, 1–22.

Siebers, T. (2010). *Disability Aesthetics*. Ann Arbor: University of Michigan Press.

Simon, A. (2016). Film Review: Kills on Wheels. *Variety* [online] Available at: http://variety.com/2016/film/festivals/kills-on-wheels-review-1201808320/ [Accessed 9 March 2018].

Sinclair, H. C. (2006). Stalking myth-conceptions: Consequences of myth endorsement for the perception of stalking cases. Paper presented at the meeting of the American Psychology-Law Society, St. Petersburg, FL: March.
Smit, C. R. and Enns, A. (2001) Introduction: the State of Cinema and Disability Studies in A. Enns and C.R. Smit (eds), *2001 Screening Disability: Essays on Cinema*. Lanham, MD: University Press.
Smith, M. (1995). *Engaging Characters. Fiction, Emotion and the Cinema*. Oxford: Clarendon Press.
Smith, M. (2017). Friday Essay: Transgender in Film and Literature. *The Conversation*. [online] 26 January. Available at: https://theconversation.com/friday-essay-transgenderism-in-film-and-literature-71809 [Accessed 18 February 2018].
Smith, N.M. (2016). Oscar Nominees Weigh In on Lack of Diversity: 'There's an Elephant in the Room'. *The Guardian*, [online] 9 February 2016, Available at: http://www.theguardian.com/film/2016/feb/08/oscars-so-white-diversity-issues-protests-sylvester-stallone-creed [Accessed 8 March 2016].
Smith, S.L., Choueiti, M., and Pieper, K. (2016). *Inequality in 800 Popular Films: Examining Portrayals of Gender, Race/Ethnicity, LGBT and Disability from 2007–2015*. The Media, Diversity and Social Change Initiative, Annenburg Foundation and USC Annenburg.
Smith, S.L, Choueiti, M. and Pieper, K. (2017). *Inequality in 900 Popular Films: Examining Portrayals of Gender, Race/Ethnicity, LGBT, and Disability from 2007 to 2016*. The Media, Diversity and Social Change Initiative, Annenburg Foundation and USC Annenburg.
Smith, S.L., Choueiti, M., Pieper, K. (2018). *Inclusion in the Director's Chair?* Annenberg Inclusion Initiative, with Annenberg Foundation, and USC Annenberg.
Sontag, S. (1972). The Double Standard of Ageing. *The Saturday Review*, 23 September, 29–38.
Spiegel, C. (2018). Disability, Race, and the 'The Shape of Water'. [online] *Medium*. Available at: https://medium.com/@charlie.spiegel/disability-race-and-the-shape-of-water-108381ac0019, [Accessed 6 March 2018].
Soldatic, K. and Pini, B. (2011). The Three Ds of Welfare Reform; Disability, Disgust and Deservingness. *Australian Journal of Human Rights*, 15(1) pp. 77–96.
Spinalcordinjuryzone.com (2005). Support 'The Ringer' on Opening Weekend, Dec 23–25. [online] *Spinal Cord Injury Zone*. Available at: https://spinalcordinjuryzone.com/news/2982/support-the-ringer-on-opening-weekend-dec-23-25 [Accessed 10 February 2018].
Sponseller (2005). Under-appreciated Farrelly Brothers Film, [online] http://www.unz.org/Pub/SaturdayRev-1972sep23-00029 21 January, Available at: http://www.imdb.com/title/tt0338466/reviews?ref_=tt_urv [Accessed 9 February 2018].
Startin (2017). Facebook personal communication.
Stronach, I. and Allan, J. (1999). Joking with Disability? What's the Difference Between the Comic and the Tragic in Disability Discourses? *Body and Society*, 5(4), pp. 31–45.
Sutherland, A. (1981). *Disabled We Stand*. London: Souvenir Press.
Stevens, C. (2014). Comedy Great? Gervais is Just a Sniggering Playground Bully: Christopher Steven Reviews Last Night's TV. *Mail Online*. [online] 24 April. Available at: http://www.dailymail.co.uk/tvshowbiz/article-2611762/Comedy-great-Gervais-just-sniggering-playground-bully-christopher-stevens-reviews-nights-TV.html [Accessed 25 February 2018].

Stone, K. (1975). Things Walt Disney Never Told Us. *The Journal of American Folklore*. 88(347), pp. 42–50, Jan–March.

Storey, K. (2005). The Case Against the Special Olympics. *Journal of Disability Policy Studies*, 15(1), pp. 35–42.

Svalavitz, M. (2013). Wealth Selfies: How Being Rich Increases Narcissism, in *Time*, 20 August, http://healthland.time.com/2013/08/20/wealthy-selfies-how-being-rich-increases-narcissism/ [Accessed 27 May 2018].

Tan, E.S. (2011). *Emotion and the Structure of Narrative Film*. New York: Routledge.

Taylor, S. (2015). Arrested Development: Can Funny Female Characters Survive Script Development Processes? *Philament*, 20, pp. 61–77.

Thomas, C. (2007). *Sociologies of Health and Illness*. Basingstoke: Palgrave MacMillan.

Thomas, K. (1977). The Place of Laughter in Tudor and Stuart England. *Times Literary Supplement*, 21 January, pp. 77–81.

Thomson, R.G (1997). *Extraordinary Bodies – Figuring Physical Disability in American Culture and Literature*. New York: Columbia University Press.

Thomson, R.G. (1999). Integrating Disability, Transforming Feminist Theory. *NSWA Journal*, 14(3). pp. 1–26.

Thomas, C. (1999). *Female Forms: Experiencing and Understanding Disability*. Buckingham: Open University Press.

Totoro, D. (2000). Art for All 'Time'. *Film-Philosophy*, [online] 2(4) February, Available at: http://film-philosophy.com/index.php/f-p/article/view/553/466 [Accessed 6 August 2017].

Tvtropes.org (2017a). *Manic Pixie Dream Girl*. [online]. Available at: http://tvtropes.org/pmwiki/pmwiki.php/Main/ManicPixieDreamGirl [Accessed 5 January 2018].

Tvtropes.org (2017b). *Blithe Spirit*. [online] http://tvtropes.org/pmwiki/pmwiki.php/Main/BlitheSpirit [Accessed 7 January 2018].

Tyneside Cinema (2013). Report: The Kids are Alright? Conference Report, Tyneside cinema, 12 December. [online] Available at: http://cargocollective.com/cinemanotes/Report-The-Kids-are-Alright-Conference-Tyneside-Cinema-Thu-12-Dec-2013 [Accessed 8 February 2018].

Van Alphen, E. (2016). Skin, Body, Self: The Questions of the Abject on the Work of Francis Bacon. In: R. Arya and N. Chare, *Abject visions: Powers of Horror in Art and Visual Culture*. Manchester: Manchester University Press.

Vehmas, S. and Watson, N. (2014). Moral Wrongs, Disadvantages, and Disability: A Critique of Critical Disability Studies. *Disability and Society*, 29(4), pp. 638–650.

Vertovec, S., and Wessendorf, S. (eds) (2010) *The Multiculturalism Backlash: European Discourses and Practices*. London: Routledge.

Vitale, C. (2011a). *Guide to Reading Deleuze's 'The Movement-Image', Part I: The Deleuzian Notion of the Image, Or Worldslicing as Cinema Beyond the Human*. [online] Available at: https://networkologies.wordpress.com/2011/04/04/the-deleuzian-notion-of-the-image-a-slice-of-the-world-or-cinema-beyond-the-human/ [Accessed 4 July 2017].

Vitale, C. (2011b). *Guide to Reading Deleuze's 'The Movement-Image', Part II: From the Affect-Image to the Relation-Image*. [online]. Available at: https://networkologies.wordpress.com/2011/04/13/more-on-reading-deleuzes-the-movement-image-from-the-affect-image-to-the-relation-image/ [Accessed 6 August 2017].

Vogue.com (2017). *The 51 Best Romantic Comedies of All Time*. [online] https://www.vogue.com/article/best-romantic-comedies-of-all-time [Accessed 30 December].

Walker, P. (2011). Fiona Pilkington Case: Police Face Misconduct Proceedings. *The Guardian*. [online] 24 May. Available at: https://www.theguardian.com/uk/2011/may/24/fiona-pilkington-police-misconduct-proceedings [Accessed 19 August 2017].

Walker, H. (2012). A Class Act: Unironic Posh Chic is Here. *The Independent*. [online] 25 February, Available at: http://www.independent.co.uk/life-style/fashion/features/a-class-act-unironic-posh-chic-is-here-7299185.html [Accessed 29 January 2018].

Wanshel, E. (2018). How 'The Shape of Water' Makes Disabled People Feel Less Human. *Huffington Post*. [online] Available at: http://www.huffingtonpost.co.uk/entry/shape-of-water-offensive-to-people-with-disabilities_us_5a8b798de4b0a1d0e12c48fc [Accessed 5 March 2018].

Watson, C. (2015). *Comedy and Social Sciences: Towards a Methodology of Funny*. London: Routledge.

Wallis, L. (2013). *Living a Conjoined Life*. [online] BBC News. Available at: http://www.bbc.co.uk/news/magazine-22181528 [Accessed 9 February 2018].

Walters, T. (2004). Reconsidering The Idiots: Dogme95, Lars von Trier and the Cinema of Subversion? *The Velvet Light Trap*, 53, pp. 40–54.

Wedding, D. and Niemiec, R.M. (2003). The Clinical Use of Films in Psychotherapy. *Journal of Clinical Psychotherapy*, 59(2), pp. 207–215.

Wetherbee, B. (2015). The Cinematic Topos of Disability and the Example of Avatar: A Rhetorical Critique. *Ethos: A Digital Review of Arts, Humanities, and Public Ethics*. [online] 2(2). Available at: http://www.ethosreview.org. [Accessed 6 December 2017].

Wheatley, E. (2010). *Stumbling Blocks before the Blind: Medieval Constructions of a Disability*. Ann Arbor: University of Michigan Press.

White, A. (1993). The Dismal Sacred Word: Academic Language and the Social Reproduction of Seriousness. In: A. White ed., *Carnival, Hysteria and Writing: Collected Essays and Autobiography*, Oxford: Clarendon Press.

Wilde, A. (2004a). Performing Disability – Impairment and Disability in Soap Opera Viewing. In: M. King and K. Watson, eds., *Representing Health: Discourses of Health and Illness in the Media*. Basingstoke: Palgrave MacMillan, pp. 66–88.

Wilde, A. (2004b). Disability fictions: the production of gendered impairments and disability in soap opera discourses, unpublished PhD thesis, University of Leeds.

Wilde, A. (2004c). Disabling Masculinity: The Isolation of a Captive Audience. *Disability and Society*, 19(4), pp. 355–370.

Wilde, A. (2009a). Disabling Femininity: The Captivation of an Isolated Audience? *Critical Studies in Television*, 4(2), pp. 4–23.

Wilde, A. (2009b). Alison Wilde Takes a Look at Snowcake. [online] *Disability Arts Online*. Available at: https://www.disabilityartsonline.org.uk/film-and-tv-review?item=497 [Accessed 6 February 2018].

Wilde, A. (2010a). Spectacle, Performance, and the Re-Presentation of Disability and Impairment. *Review of Disability Studies: An International Journal*, 6(3), pp. 34–43.

Wilde, A. (2010b). Alison Wilde Questions Definitions of Disability in Her Review of Dogtooth, [online] *Disability Arts Online*, Available at: http://www.disabilityartsonline.org/film-and-tv-review?item=618 [Accessed 31 December 2017].

Wilde, A. (2014). Disability Culture: The story so far. In: J. Swain, S. French, C. Barnes, and C. Thomas eds., *Disabling Barriers – Enabling Environments*. London: SAGE Publications Limited.

Wilde, A. (2016). Thea Sharrock's Film, Me Before You. [online] *Disability Arts Online*. Available at: http://disabilityarts.online/magazine/opinion/film-directed-thea-sharrock/ [Accessed 26 January 2018].

Wilde, A. (2017a). Baby Driver: A Head on Collision with Disablism. [online] *Disability Arts Online*. Available at: http://disabilityarts.online/magazine/opinion/baby-driver-head-collision-disablism/ [Accessed 6 February 2018].

Wilde, A. (2017b). Kills on Wheels – A Dark Comedy that Tackles Assumptions about Disability. [online] *Disability Arts Online*. Available at: http://disabilityarts.online/magazine/opinion/kills-wheels-dark-comedy-tackles-assumptions-disability/ [Accessed 9 March 2018].

Wilde, A. (2017c). *Reviews/Posts on Four Films Released in 2017*. [online] Available at: http://disabilityarts.online/author/alison-wilde/ [Accessed 1 March 2018].

Wilde, A. (2018a). Troubling Images? The Re-presentation of Disabled Womanhood: Britain's Missing Top Model. *Journal of Popular Television*.6 (1), pp.41–58.

Wilde, A. (2018b) [Forthcoming] Mental Distress, Romance and Gender in Contemporary Films – Greenberg and Silver Linings Playbook. In: G. Goggin, B. Haller and K. Ellis eds., *Routledge Companion to Disability and Media*. London: Routledge.

Wilde, A. and Hoskison-Clark, A. (2013). Families. In: C. Cameron, ed., *Disability Studies*. London: Sage Publications Limited.

Williams, F. (1998). Suits and Sequins: Lesbian Comedians in Britain and the US in the 1990s. In: S. Wagg, ed., *Because I Tell a Tale or Two: Comedy, Politics and Social Difference*. London: Routledge, pp. 146–164.

Williams, L. (1991). Film bodies: Gender, Genre and Excess. *Film Quarterly*, 44(4), pp. 2–13.

Willis, L-P. (2016). 'Hey! What Did You Do to the World?': Conceptualizing the Real with Baudrillard and Žižek. *International Journal of Žižek Studies*, [online] 10(1). Available at: http://zizekstudies.org/index.php/IJZS/issue/view/49. [Accessed 5 September 2018].

Winch, J. (2012). Channel 4 Criticised as Show Asks if it is OK to Hit Disabled People. *The Telegraph*. [online] 3 September, Available at: http://www.telegraph.co.uk/news/9517441/Channel-4-criticised-as-show-asks-if-it-is-OK-to-hit-disabled-people.html [Accessed 10 December 2017].

Wittgenstein, L. (1963). *Philosophical Investigations*. Oxford: Blackwell.

Woodburn, D. and Kopić, K. (2016). *The Ruderman White Paper: On Employment of Actors with Disabilities in Television*. Ruderman Family Foundation, July. (n.p.)

Woodburn, D. and Ruderman, J. (2016). Why are we Okay with Disability Drag in Hollywood? *Los Angeles Times*, [online] 11 July, Available at: http://www.latimes.com/opinion/op-ed/la-oe-woodburn-ruderman-disability-stats-tv-20160711-snap-story.html [Accessed 5 March 2018].

Yates, C.S (2006). A Phenomenological Analysis of Cinematic Worlds. *Contemporary Aesthetics*, [online] 4. Available at: http://www.contempaesthetics.org/newvolume/pages/article.php?articleID=394 [Accessed 30 June 2017].

YoungS. (2014). *I'm Not Your Inspiration Thank You Very Much*. [online] TED.Com, Available at: https://www.ted.com/talks/stella_young_i_m_not_your_inspiration_thank_you_very_much [Accessed 21 February 2018].

YouTube (2011). *Life's Too Short – Johnny Depp*, [online video] Available at: https://www.youtube.com/watch?v=uV3MQtpYikM [Accessed 10 December 2017].

YouTube (2013a). *Dumb and Dumber (1994)*. Official trailer, [online video] Available at: https://www.youtube.com/watch?v=Knzdsr4OsXA [Accessed 9 February 2018].

YouTube (2013b). *Stuck on You (1993)*. Trailer. [online video] Available at: https://www.youtube.com/watch?v=At-LrR-vqUk [Accessed 10 February 2018].

YouTube (2014). *Dumb and Dumber (1994). Official Trailer – Jim Carrey, Jeff Daniels Comedy HD*, [online video] Available at: https://www.youtube.com/watch?v=l13yPhimE3o [Accessed February 8 2018].
Žižek, S. (1997). *Desire: Drive + Truth: Knowledge.* [online] Originally in Umbr(a). Available at: http://www.lacan.com/zizek-desire.htm [Accessed 9 January 2018].
Žižek, S. (2001). *The Fright of Real Tears – Krzysztof Kieslowski between Theory and Post-Theory.* London: BFI publishing.
Žižek, S. (2002). Welcome to the Desert of the Real! *The South Atlantic Quarterly*, 101 (2), pp. 385–389.
Žižek, S. (2006). *The Pervert's Guide to Cinema: Intro.* [Online video] Available at: https://www.youtube.com/watch?v=JoPTbSfB-aw [Accessed 9 July 2017].
Žižek, S. (2009). *First as Tragedy, Then as Farce.* [online] RSA Animate. Available at: https://www.thersa.org/globalassets/pdfs/videos/2010/08/rsa-animate—first-as-tragedy-then-as-farce-/rsa-lecture-slavoj-Žižek-transcript.pdf [Accessed 14 March 2016].

Filmography

10 Things I Hate About You, 1999 [film]. Directed by Gil JUNGER. USA: Buena Vista Pictures.
500 Days of Summer, 2009 [film]. Directed by Marx WEBB. USA: Fox Searchlight Pictures.
A Bout de Souffle, 1960 [film]. Directed by Jean-Luc GODARD. France: StudioCanal.
Appropriate Behaviour, 2014 [film]. Directed by Desiree AKHAVAN. UK: Peccadillo Pictures.
Avatar, 2009 [film]. Directed by James CAMERON. USA: Twentieth Century Fox.
Before Sunset, 2004 [film]. Directed by Richard LINKLATER. USA: Warner Independent Pictures.
Being There, 1979 [film]. Directed by Hal ASHBY. USA: United Artists.
Best Boy, 1979 [film]. Directed by Ira WOHL. USA: International Film Exchange.
Beyond Silence, 1996 [film]. Directed by Caroline LINK. USA: Miramax.
Blue Velvet, 1986 [film]. Directed by David LYNCH. USA: De Laurentiis Entertainment Group.
Breaking the Waves, 1996 [film]. Directed by Lars von TRIER. Netherlands: Argus Film Produktie.
Chasing Amy, 1997 [film]. Directed by Kevin SMITH. USA: Miramax Films.
Children of a Lesser God, 1986 [film]. Directed by Randa HAINES. USA: Paramount Pictures.
City Lights, 1931 [film]. Directed by Charlie CHAPLIN. USA: United Artists.
Death at a Funeral, 2007 [film]. Directed by Frank OZ. UK: Verve Pictures.
Death at a Funeral, 2010 [film]. Directed by Neil LABUTE. USA: Screen Gems.
Des Hommes et de Dieux, 2010 [film]. Directed by Xavier BEAUVOIS. France: Mars Distibution.
Despicable Me, 2010 [film]. Directed by Pierre COFFIN & Chris RENAUD. USA: Universal Pictures.
Dogtooth, 2010 [film]. Directed by Yorgos LANTHIMOS. UK: Feelgood Entertainment.
Dumb and Dumber To, 2014 [film]. Directed by Peter FARRELLY & Bobby FARRELLY. USA: Universal Pictures.

Bibliography

Dumb and Dumber, 1994 [film]. Directed by Peter FARRELLY & Bobby FARRELLY (uncredited). USA: New Line Cinema.
Dumb and Dumberer: When Harry Met Lloyd, 2003 [film]. Directed by Troy MILLER. USA: New Line Cinema.
Fever Pitch, 2005 [film]. Directed by Peter FARRELLY & Bobby FARRELLY. USA: 20th Century Fox.
Forrest Gump, 1994 [film]. Directed by Robert ZEMECKIS. USA: Paramount Pictures.
Four Weddings and a Funeral, 1994 [film]. Directed by Mike NEWELL. UK: Rank Film Distributors.
Freaks, 1932 [film]. Directed by Todd BROWNING. USA: Metro-Goldwyn-Mayer.
Greenberg, 2010 [film]. Directed by Noah BAUMBACH. USA: Focus Feathers.
Hall Pass, 2011 [film]. Directed by Peter FARRELLY & Bobby FARRELLY. Warner Bros. Pictures.
Happiness, 1998 [film]. Directed by Todd SOLONDZ. USA: Good Machine Releasing.
Hitchcock/Truffaut, 2015 [film]. Directed by Kent JONES. USA: Cohen Media Group.
How Stella Got Her Groove Back, 1998 [film]. Directed by Kevin Rodney SULLIVAN. USA; 20th Century Fox.
It's Complicated, 2009 [film]. Directed by Nancy MYERS. USA: Universal Pictures.
Jean de Florette, 1986 [film]. Directed by Claude BERRI. USA: Orion Pictures.
Kingpin, 1996 [film]. Directed by Peter FARRELLY & Bobby FARRELLY. USA: Metro-Goldwyn-Mayer.
La Famille Bellier, 2014 [film]. Directed by Eric LARTIGAU. France: Mars Distribution.
Mamma Mia!, 2008 [film]. Directed by Phyllica LLOYD. USA: Universal Pictures.
Margarita with a Straw, 2014 [film]. Directed by Shonali BOSE. USA: Wolfe Releasing.
Me Before You, 2016 [film]. Directed by Thea SHARROCK. USA: Warner Bros.
Me, Myself and Irene, 2000 [film]. Directed by Peter FARRELLY & Bobby FARRELLY. USA: 20th Century Fox.
Mondo Trasho, 1969 [film]. Directed by John WATERS. USA: Film-Makers' Cooperative.
Moonraker, 1979 [film]. Directed by Lewis GILBERT. UK: United Artists Corporation.
Movie 43, 2013 [film]. Directed by Steven Brill, Peter Farrelly, and 13 others. USA: Relativity Media.
National Lampoon's Animal House [film]. Directed by John LANDIS. USA: Universal Pictures
Nell's Eugenic Wedding, 1914 [film]. Directed by Edward DILLON. USA: Mutual Fillm.
Night of the Living Dead, 1968 [film]. Directed by George. A. ROMERO. USA: The Walter Reade Organization.
Osmosis Jones, 2001 [film]. Directed by Peter FARRELLY & Bobby FARRELLY/ Tom SITO & Piet KROON (animation). USA: Warner Bros. Pictures.
Out of Sight, 1998 [film]. Directed by Steven SODERBERGH. USA: Universal Pictures.
Outside Providence, 1999 [film]. Directed by Michael CORRENTE. USA: Miramax Films.

Pink Flamingos, 1972 [film]. Directed by John WATERS: USA: New Line Cinema.
Porky's, 1981 [film]. Directed by Bob CLARK. USA: 20th Century Fox.
Pretty Woman, 1990 [film]. Directed by Garry MARSHALL. USA: Buena Vista Pictures.
Rain Man, 1988 [film]. Directed by Barry LEVINSON. USA: MGM/UA Communications.
Rear Window, 1998 [film]. Directed by Jeff BLECKNER. USA: ABC.
Rio Bravo, 1959 [film]. Directed by Howard HAWKS. USA: Warner Bros.
Say It Isn't So, 2001 [film]. Directed by J.B. Rogers. USA: 20th Century Fox.
Shallow Hal, 2001 [film]. Directed by Peter FARRELLY & Bobby FARRELLY. USA: 20th Century Fox.
Sherlock, Jr, 1924 [film]. Directed by Buster KEATON & William GOODRICH (uncredited). USA: Metro-Goldwyn Pictures.
Shine, 1996 [film]. Directed by Scott HICKS. Australia: Ronin Films.
Silver Linings Playbook, 2012 [film]. Directed by David O. RUSSELL. USA: The Weinstein Company.
Snow White and the Seven Dwarfs, 1937 [film]. Directed by David HAND. USA: RKO Radio Pictures.
Something's Gotta Give, 2003 [film]. Directed by Nancy MEYERS. USA: Columbia Pictures.
Stronger, 2017 [film]. Directed by David Gordon GREEN. USA: Lionsgate.
Stuck on You, 2003 [film]. Directed by Peter FARRELLY & Bobby FARRELLY: 20th Century Fox.
Tangerine, 2015 [film]. Directed by Sean BAKER. USA: Duplass Brothers Productions.
The Big Sick, 2017 [film]. Directed by Michael SHOWALTER. USA: Lionsgate.
The Danish Girl, 2015 [film]. Directed by Tom HOOPER. USA: Focus Features.
The Heartbreak Kid, 2007 [film]. USA: Paramount Pictures.
The Idiots, 1998 [film]. Directed by Lars VON TRIER. Denmark: Scanbox Entertainment.
The Lobster, 2015 [film]. Directed by Yorgos LANTHIMOS. UK: Picturehouse Entertainment.
The Passion of Joan of Arc, 1928 [film]. Directed by Carl Theodor DREYER. France: Gaumont.
The Ringer, 2005 [film]. Directed by Barry BLAUSTEIN. USA: Fox Searchlight.
The Sea Inside, 2004 [film]. Directed by Alejandro AMENABAR. Spain: Sogepaq.
The Shape of Water, 2017 [film]. Directed by Guillermo DEL TORO. USA: Fox Searchlight Pictures.
The Spy Who Loved Me, 1977 [film]. Directed by Lewis GILBERT. UK: United Artists Corporation.
The Station Agent, 2003 [film]. Directed by Tom McCARTHY. USA: Miramax Films.
The Three Stooges, 2012 [film]. Directed by Peter FARRELLY & Bobby FARRELLY. USA: 20th Century Fox.
There's Something About Mary, 1998 [film]. Directed by Peter FARRELLY & Bobby FARRELLY. USA: 20th Century Fox.
Three Billboards outside Ebbing, Missouri, 2017 [film]. Directed by Martin McDONAGH. USA: Fox Searchlight Pictures.
Top Five, 2014 [film]. Directed by Chris ROCK. USA: Paramount Pictures.
Trainwreck, 2015 [film]. Directed by Judd APATOW. USA: Universal Pictures.

Tropic Thunder, 2008 [film]. Directed by Ben STILLER. USA: Paramount.
Un Chien Andalou, 1929 [film]. Directed by Luis BUNUEL. France: Les Grands Films Classiques.
Valentine's Day, 2010 [film]. Directed by Garry MARSHALL. USA: Warner Bros.
Willy Wonka, 1971 [film]. Directed by Mel STUART. USA: Paramount Pictures.
Wizard of Oz, 1939 [film]. Directed by Victor FLEMING. USA: Loew's, Inc..
Wonder, 2017 [film]. Directed by Stephen CHBOSKY. USA: Lionsgate.

Index

500 Days of Summer 66–67, 73

Abbott, Stacey 69
abjection 122, 141–143
ableism 8, 12, 23n5
actor employment: able bodied in disabled roles 126, 134, 141–142, 151–152; casting of disabled roles 7, 24n6, 24n14, 99n6, 99n7, 152; disabled actors, number of 152–153; impairment under-reporting 153; romantic leads, non-diverse 65–66, 70–71, 151
aesthetic nervousness 36, 37
ageism, romantic comedy 72, 74–75
Akass, Kim 123
Albrecht, Gary 50
Allan, Julie 33–36, 37, 50
Allan, Keith 28, 40
Allen, Woody 28
alternative comedy: class, comics and audiences 41–42, 43; Jerry Sadowitz's PC-baiting 45–46, 47–48; male dominated 41; popularity of 28
Altman, Rick 56
Anderson, Darla A. 159–160
anti-PC humour: broadcasting trends 38–40, 49n10; class, comics and audiences 42–43; gross-out and television comedy 119; Jerry Sadowitz's PC-baiting 45–46, 47–48; male dominated 52
Appadurai, Arjun 11
Appropriate Behaviour 66–67, 70
Aristotle 32, 40
Assayas, Olivier 14–15
audience experience: colour and lighting, viewer perceptions 91–94; cultural offence, Sadowitz's comedy 45–46, 47–48; disability awareness contrived 17; disability portrayals and discrimination associations 57–59, 60; disgust and comedy, gross-out film identifications 123–124, 125, 133; Farrelly Brothers' films, challenging gross-out prejudices 128–130, 131–132, 134, 135–137, 144–145; gross-out films and young male fans 121; *Me Before You*, targeting young females 95–96; reification of love and bodily difference, *The Lobster*'s challenge 106–108, 110–111, 116–117; rom-coms, emotional manipulation 63; rom-com's negative stereotyping 65–66, 86–87; social class and comedy 41–44; stalking, portrayals and responses 64–65; temporal and spatial strategies 14–15; 'tolerant subject' and diversity dilemmas 51–54
auteurism and romantic comedy 69, 76
auteur theory 7

Baby Driver 154
Bakhtin, Mikhail 25, 121–122
Barnes, Colin 19, 30
Baron Cohen, Sasha 39
Barrett, Gregory 19
Bauman, Jeff 80–81
Beckett, Samuel 36–37
Beck-Gernsheim, Elisabeth 66
Beckman, Frida 13
Beck, Ulrich 53, 66
Berger, Peter 107
Bergson, Henri 32, 33, 35
Big Sick, The 70, 72, 76, 97, 158
Bolt, Barbara 18, 36
Bordwell, David 10, 11, 12
Bowdre, Karen 71, 74, 111

Boyle, Susan 53
Brabazon, Tara 52
Breathe 151–152
Brooker, Alex 50–51
Brooks, Mel 28
Brown, Roy 'Chubby' 28, 42
Bunker, Chang and Eng 141
Burridge, Kate 28, 40
Byrne, Peter 127

Cadwallader, Jessica R. 69, 71
Cambridge Footlights 43
Campbell, Fiona Kumari 6, 23n5
Carlson, Margaret 30
'carnivalesque' concept 25, 121–122
Carpenter, Rick 56–57, 156, 157
Carroll, Noel 10, 11, 12
Chamarette, Jenny 13
Cheyne, Ria 55
chick culture 69, 95, 96, 100n24
Chivers, Sally 11, 29
Cieply, Michael 126
Clay, Andrew Dice 43
Coffin, Pierre 58
colour, filmmaker's influential use 91–94
comedy and humour: academic neglect and snobbery 25–27; anti-PC humour 38–40; comedy industry's elitism 46–47; cultural capital and taste hierarchies 27–28, 41; disability and oppression links 30–31; 'disability comedy' taboos 33–34, 35, 37, 38; disability, effect on agency and positioning 33–35, 50–51; diversity of associations 31–32; political correctness, reactions to 38–40, 49n11; 'popular culture' forms 25; punching up/down, perceptions of offence 41–42, 45–46, 47–48; role within disability portrayal 29–30; social class, comics and audiences 42–44; theories of 32–33
conjoined twins: portrayal in *Freaks* 141, 149n19; portrayal in *Stuck on You* 125, 128–129, 140–145; reported cases 140–141, 149n18
Coogan, Tom 33
Cooper, Sarah 106, 111–112, 115
Corker, Mairian 35–36, 37
Crenshaw, Kimberlé 98n3
'crip humour' 50
Critical and/or Disability Studies 1–3, 4–5, 21

cultural capitalism: comedy industry's elitism 46–47; comedy's status and consumption 27–28, 43–44; consumer's false charity 16–17; hierarchies of value, *Me Before You* 86–91

Darke, Paul 11, 16, 20, 29, 49n7, 122
Davidson, Jim 28, 43
Davis, Warwick 57–58, 59–60, 61–62n2
Deleuze, Gilles 18, 25, 83, 91, 116
Deleyto, Celestino 67–68
Del Toro, Guillermo 152
Dembina, Ivor 41
Derek 31, 49n4, 119, 126, 148n4
Dinklage, Peter 59, 62n3, 79
disability and media representation: disability politics and film theory 3–9; film study methodologies, use of 9–11; scholarly approach to analysis 1–3
Disability Arts community 35, 49n7
disability definition 23n1
disability humour: ambiguous impairments 119–120, 148n5; bodily depiction and disgust 122–124; disabled person's agency 50–51, 59; Farrelly Brothers, renegotiation of attitudes 125, 126, 128–130; non-disabled awkwardness, offence risks 54–55, 125–126, 144–145; pastiche, adoption risks 57–58, 79, 99n14, 126–127, 155; representational change, mixed success 59–61; satirical narrative 110–111, 112; 'tolerant subject' and diversity dilemmas 51–54
disability representation: aesthetic nervousness 36, 37; characters, definition debate 153–154, 160n1; comedy and cultural attitudes 20, 29–30; comedy and tragedy, cultural linkages 33–38; comedy, cultural agency and positioning 33–35, 50–51; cultural recognition, lack of 17–18; disability as 'metagenre' 156–157; disability content, subtlety and deliberate 154–156; disabled parenting 138–139, 149n17; disabled sexuality 138, 141; film industry themes and characters 156–157; hate crime and oppression 30–31; impairment and disability imagery critiques 15–18; interest convergence in films 79–80; men's negative stereotypes 66, 83–84; 'noble characters' in films 77–78;

psychoanalytic approaches 10, 12–13; ridicule for entertainment 30, 31; selfwork, cultural expectations 33–34, 37; stereotypes and archetypes 18–20; taste hierarchies, democratising challenges 28–29; temporal and spatial positioning 14–15; tragedy discourses 35–36
disabled writers/filmmakers discriminated 78–79, 80–81
disablism, concept 23–24n5
disablist comedians 28
disgust, cinematic: dead animals, use of 131 132; disgust-empathy 133; gross-out genre 123–124; sudden and anticipatory 132
Dogtooth 110
Dolski, Elizabeth A. 126–127
Downey, Sarah A. 147, 148
Dreger, Alice 141
Dumb and Dumber 123, 130–132
Dumb and Dumberer 146
Dumb and Dumber To 146–147
dwarfs 57–61, 138, 153

Edgar, Justin 78–79
Edwards, Claire 15
Eitzen, Dirk 123
Ellingson, Terry 77
embodiment and genre 14–15
Enns, Anthony W. 2–3, 4, 12, 21
Evans, Jessica 5–6
Extras 39

Faludi, Susan 39
Farrelly Brothers: disability, contested perspectives 120–121, 122, 123, 124, 158; disability, renegotiation of attitudes 125, 126, 127–130, 134–137, 148, 157; *Dumb and Dumber*, impairment portrayal and disgust 130–132; *Dumb and Dumber to*, criticisms of 146–147; *Kingpin* 133–134; *Me, Myself and Irene*, criticisms of 127–128; *Me, Myself and Irene*, stereotyping challenges 138–139; *Osmosis Jones* 139; *Outside Providence* 137; *The Ringer* 145–146; *Shallow Hal* 139–140; *Stuck On You*, disabled sexuality and abjectivity 140–145, 149n10; *Stuck On You*, reviewer reaction 128–130; *There's Something About Mary*, mimetic approach 134–137

Fenichel, Otto 6
film adaptions and disability portrayal 80–83
film genres: concept evolution 68–69; disability portrayals under-explored 55–57
film studies: disability politics and film theory 3–9; disability representation and analysis 1–3; film theory, criticism and advocacy 10; methodologies and disability studies 9–11
film theory: criticism and advocacy 10; phenomenological analysis 13–14; psychoanalytic approaches 10, 12 13
Follows, Stephen 72
Four Weddings and a Funeral 64, 71–72
Frank, Arthur 19
Freaks 141, 149n19
Freud, Sigmund 32, 35
Freund, Peter 15
Friedman, Sam 27–28, 41, 43–44, 46

Gardiner, Michael 151
Gavin, Jeff 20, 60, 61, 106, 156
Gehring, Wes D. 67
gender issues: ageism in rom-coms 72, 74–75; body and personality tropes 72–74; heteronormative monogamy in rom-com 67–68, 71; male gaze and body image 139–140; male gaze and sexism 73, 99n8; transgender, limited coverage 71; women's under-representation 156–157, 159
genrification 56–57, 156–157
Geraghty, Christine 81–82
Gervais, Ricky: anti-PC humour 39, 42, 119, 148n6; David Brent as 'tolerant subject' 51–54, 66; *Derek* 31, 49n4, 119, 148n4; disablist language 53–54; gross-out genre 119, 126; *I'm Spazticus* 39, 51, 54–55; *Life's Too Short*, criticisms of 57–58, 59–60, 61–62n2
Goodley, Dan 12, 23n5
Graeber, David 115–116
Green, Michelle 41
Grindon, Leger 63
gross-out genre: bodily depiction and disgust 121–124, 132, 133; comedic origins and traits 118–119; dead animals and disgust 131–132; disability and impairment themes 118–121; gross-out hybrid films 121;

romantic comedy hybrid 134–137; see also Farrelly Brothers
Guatarri, Félix 116

Haller, Beth 20, 29
Hall, Jeanne Lynn 112–113
Hall, Richard 46
Hall, Stuart 5–6
Hanitch, Julian 124, 132, 133
Happiness 121
Harris, Mark 108, 110
Harvey, D. 120
hate crime 30–31
Hawkins, Chelsea 7
Hawkins, Sally 152
Hills, Adam 50–51
Hilton, Daisy and Violet 141
Hitchcock/Truffaut documentary 14–15
Hoeksema, Thomas B. 1, 3, 4, 7–8, 10, 21
Hughes, Bill 34
Hunt, Paul 12
Hupperetz, Laura 102, 104, 107–108

Ilić, Vladana 115
illness narratives 19
impairment definition 23n1
Imrie, Rob 15
I'm Spazticus 39, 51, 54–55
Inahara, Minae 12
incongruity theories 32
'inspiration porn' 18, 19, 95
Irigary, Luce 128, 137
'ironic bigotry' 29
Irwin, William 25
Ivins, Molly 41

Jenkins, Eric S. 58
Jermyn, Deborah 69, 72, 74–75
Jones, Ruth S. 59

Kent, Deborah 15
Kettle, James 45
Kills on Wheels 154–156
King, Geoff: comedy as mode 31; gross-out genre 119, 121–122, 123; romance, status in films 67, 69; satire and parody 101–102
Kingpin 133–134
Klobas, Lauri E. 55, 57
Koller, Marvin 31, 32–33
Koutsourakis, Angelos 116
Kriegel, Leonard 15, 19

Lanthimos, Yorgos 102, 104, 106, 107, 116
Last Leg, The 38, 39, 50–51
Lauzen, Martha 159
LeBesco, Kathleen 131–132, 143–144, 147
Lee, Stewart 39–40, 44, 49n10
Life's Too Short 39, 57–58, 59–60, 61–62n2
Linton, Simi 8
Lippman, Julia R. 64–65, 98n2
Little Britain: ambiguous impairments 119–120, 148n5; anti-PC humour 38, 39, 148n6; gross-out genre 122, 123, 126; 'tolerant subject' 51
Littlewood, Jane 38–39, 41
Lloyd, Harold 131
Lobster, The: aestheticization of the violence 105–106; analysis focus 77; dark comedy elements 108–109; humour, romance and desire 112–115; impairment similarities as desirable 111–112; loneliness and narcissism themes 106–107, 108, 110; 'radical alterity' 115–116; reification of love and bodily difference 106–108, 109–110, 114–115, 116–117; rhizomatic storytelling 116; satire and parody, use of 101–102; storyline 102–105; unconventional romantic elements 104, 105, 109, 113
Lucas, Matt 39, 51, 148n5

male gaze 2, 73, 99n8
Mallet, Rebecca 18, 33, 51, 52, 53, 130
'Manic Pixie Dream Girl' 73–74
Manning, Bernard 28, 43
Manoharan, Krisho 59
Margarita with a Straw 77
Marine, Joe 92–94
Markotić, Nicole 11, 29
Marotta, Vince 52–53
Martin, Adrian 69, 76
McDonagh, Martin 80
McDonald, Jeffers 63–64, 65–66, 69
McRuer, Robert 52
Me Before You (book/film): analysis focus 76; aspirational female, target audience 95–96; assisted suicide, tailored narrative 84–85, 86, 94, 96–97; colour use and viewer perceptions 91–94; disability and impairment, cinematic perspectives 72, 83–85, 94, 95–97, 101, 158; disability barriers and

mise en scène deceptions 85–86; disabled person's agency undervalued 96, 96–98; failed masculinities 87–88, 95, 96; hierarchies of value and class 86–91, 96, 98; lighting for emotional effect 94; living with disability, curious inspiration 78; 'non-disabled gaze' narratives 78, 80; normality genre features 86; relationship shifts 90–91; rom-com troupes and imagining 82–83; sparring, rom-com troupe 88–89; 'tolerant subject position' 96; transposition over interpretation issues 81–82, 84, 96–97
Medhurst, Andy 26, 31, 34, 40, 42
Me, Myself and Irene 127–128, 138–139
Mendoza, Katherine 140
mental illness: challenging stereotypes 138–139; impairment portrayal and disgust 130–132
Miller, Jeremy 71
Mills, Brett 38
minions, animated 58–59
Mitchell, David 11, 29
Molloy (Beckett) 36–37
monologism 151
Monty Python 43
'moocher' concept 87
Moran, Carmen 31
Mortimer, Claire 69
Moyes, Jojo 78, 81, 84, 85
Mulvey, Laura 2, 12–13, 99n8
Mumford, Gwilym 120
Munnery, Simon 44–45
Murray, Jonathan 104, 117

National Alliance on the Mentally Ill 127
Neale, Steve 113
Nell's Eugenic Wedding 119
Nicolaou, Argyro 105–106
Nikulin, Dmitri 25, 26, 27, 30, 151
'noble characters' 77–78
non-disabled gaze: academic analysis 2, 3; factual film less appealing 80–81; film industry preference 78–80; 'male-gaze' (Mulvey) equivalent 2
Norden, Martin F. 12, 19, 83
Novic, Sara 152

Office, The: anti-PC humour 38, 39; David Brent as 'tolerant subject' 51–54; 'ironic bigotry' 29
O'Hara, Helen 7

Oscar awards: disabled character roles and nominations 17, 125, 126, 151–152; platform for diversity criticisms 5, 62n3, 160–161
Osmosis Jones 139

Palacio, R.J. 78
Palmer, Jerry 47, 53
Parks, Tim 37
Paterson, Kevin 34
people with restricted growth portrayals 57–61, 138, 153
Pickering, Mike 38–39, 41
Pink Flamingos 118
Plato 26–27, 32, 40
political correctness 28, 38–40
Porky's 118
Prose, Francine 114, 115
psychoanalysis and film theory 10, 12
public broadcasting and comedy, UK 38
Pullberg, Stanley 107
punching up and down 41–42
'pure cinema' 68, 99n5

Quayson, Ato 36–37, 49n8, 144

Rabin, Nathan 73–74, 99n9
race and ethnicity: black actors' characterisation 71, 98n3; challenging stereotypes 138; interest convergence in films 79–80; rape, cultural myths 98n3; romantic comedy's non-diversity 70–71, 74
Ragland, Ellie 113
Rand, Ayn 87
'Real' modalities (Žižek) 16
relief theory 32
Richardson, Niall 11
Ringer, The 145–146
Rivers, Joan 43
Robillard, Albert B. 34
romantic comedy genre: age and gender restrictions 72, 74–75; body and personality tropes 72–74; broadening the scope 68–69; class distinctions 71, 85–88; conservative ideologies dominate 66–68; contemporary films, analysis focus 76–78; definitions and traits 63–64, 69, 112–113; female perspectives undervalued 69–70; gender, sexuality and monogamy 71; impairment in peripheral portrayals 71–72, 75–76, 158; leading roles and discrimination 65–66, 70–71, 74, 98n4;

'Manic Pixie Dream Girl' 73–74, 82; 'meet cute' scenario 64, 66, 71, 83; romanticized pursuit, normalising of stalking 64–65; screwball comedy 63, 66, 67; sparring, rom-com troupe 88–89, 113; *see also Me Before You* (book/film)
Rosenbaum, Jonathan 116

Sadowitz, Jerry 45–46, 47
Sancho, Jane 134
Scannell, Paddy 53–54, 67, 95
screwball comedy 63, 66, 67
Seitz, Matt Zoller 77
Shakespeare, Thomas 2, 16, 38, 50
Shallow Hal 139–140
Shape of Water, The 152
Shiress, Ted 42
Siebers, Tobin 136, 153
Smit, Christopher R. 1, 2–3, 4, 7–8, 10, 12, 21
Smith, Stacy L. 153, 160n1
Snyder, Sharon 11, 29
social class, comics and audiences 42–44
social model of disability 4, 5–6, 8, 23n1
Solondz, Todd 119, 121
spectatorship 12
Spencer, Herbert 32
Spiegel, Charlie 152
stalking, portrayals and responses 64–65, 98n2
Startin, Simon 17
Station Agent, The 59, 77
stereotypes and archetypes: black actors' characterisation 70–71, 98n3; disability and impairment 18–20; disabled men's negative characterisations 66, 83–84, 98n4; heteronormative monogamy in rom-com 67–68, 71; 'Manic Pixie Dream Girl' 73–74, 82; 'noble characters' 77–78; people with restricted growth 57–61, 138, 153
Stevens, Christopher 31
Stiller, Ben 66, 126–127, 149n12
Streep, Meryl 74

Stronach, Ian 33–36, 37, 50
Stronger 80–81
Stuck on You 125, 128–130, 140–145, 149n10
subjectivity, psychoanalytic/phenomenological analysis 12–14
superiority theory 32, 33

Tan, Ed S. 106
Tarr, Béla 116
taste hierarchies 27–29, 41
Taylor, Stayci 69–70
There's Something About Mary 134–137
Three Billboards outside Ebbing, Missouri 59, 61, 62n3, 79–80, 99n14
'tolerant subject': comedic focus 51; continued presence 158–159; David Brent and society's diversity dilemmas 51–54; female lead, *Me Before You* (film) 96
tragedy, comedy and cultural linkages 33–38
Trier, Lars von 116, 144
Tropic Thunder 126–127

Van Alphen, Ernst 142–143
Vehmas, Simo 6
Visual Culture (Evans and Hall) 5–6
Vitale, Christopher 83

Walliams, David 39, 119–120
Walters, Tim 144
Wanshel, Elyse 152
Waters, John 118, 119, 120
Watson, Cate 26–27
Watson, Nick 6
Weinstein, Harvey 99n8
Wetherbee, Ben 8
White, Allon 26
Widdicombe, Josh 50–51
Williams, Linda 14, 15, 56, 123, 132
Willis, Louis-Paul 16
Wonder (book/film) 78, 80

Žižek, Slavoj 12, 13, 15–17, 113